1

P.O. 15365

D1520430

THE BEST SHORT PLAYS 1985

THE
BEST
SHORT
PLAYS 1985

edited and introduced by
RAMON DELGADO

Best Short Plays Series

Chilton Book Company
Radnor, Pennsylvania

for Ellen Kauffman

Copyright © 1985 by Ramon Delgado
All Rights Reserved
Published in Radnor, Pennsylvania 19089, by Chilton Book Company
Library of Congress Catalog Card No. 38–8006
ISBN 0–8019–7541–7
ISSN 0067–6284
Manufactured in the United States of America

1 2 3 4 5 6 7 8 9 0   4 3 2 1 0 9 8 7 6 5

Contents

INTRODUCTION

What an exciting year the 1983-84 theatre season (recently closed at the time of this writing) provided for enthusiasts of the short play! Three major international writers have had highly acclaimed professional productions of their short plays in New York. England's Harold Pinter offered *Other Places*, an evening of three one-act plays, at the Manhattan Theatre Club. France's Samuel Beckett had three short plays, *Ohio Impromptu, Catastrophe*, and *What Where*, directed by the late Alan Schneider, at the Harold Clurman Theatre. And Czechoslovakia's Vaclav Havel brought us *A Private View*, an evening of three one-act plays, at Joseph Papp's New York Shakespeare Festival. (The New York Shakespeare Festival also presented David Henry Hwang's *Sound of a Voice*, which is the first play in this volume.)

One Broadway offering, *Open Admissions* by Shirley Lauro (whose play *The Coal Diamond* appeared in the 1980 volume of *The Best Short Plays*), was an expansion of Ms. Lauro's earlier one-act of the same title. And the previous season's *Torch Song Trilogy*, a trio of related one-acts written by two-time Tony winner Harvey Fierstein, continued strongly on Broadway.

One-act plays were also performed at The American Place Theatre in the Young Playwrights Festival (hosted by the New York Shakespeare Festival), and other short plays were presented at innumerable Off-Broadway and Off-Off-Broadway theatres. Curt Dempster's Ensemble Studio Theatre (represented in this volume by the late James G. Richardson's *Eulogy*) continued its impressive Marathon Series of one-act plays, and Jon Jory's SHORTS Festival at the Actors Theatre of Louisville upheld its well-known quality with three plays in this year's collection (Ellen Byron's *Graceland*, Michael David Quinn's *Businessman's Lunch*, and Julie Beckett Crutcher's *Approaching Lavendar*).

As I reflect over my five years of editing this project, I rejoice with the playwrights who have seen additional productions of their work as a result of this publication. Once again, it may be noted that these pages have welcomed the talented first-play author as well as the seasoned professional. Undoubtedly, the selections in this anthology reflect not only the concerns of today's playwrights but also my penchant toward the poignant, the exquisite, and sometimes the outrageous and bizarre—and the thread that ties the selections together is always the special voice of the playwright that proclaims common humanity and unique individuality.

You may find that there have been more comedies and fewer absurdist pieces in the recent annual collections than there were under the previous editor—but this shift may be more a reflection of the times than of either editor's temperament.

One other—and quite significant—change over these five years is the increase in excellent scripts by women playwrights. This change is reflected in the current year's volume, with four of the ten plays penned by women. And though plays written by women tend to include more female than male characters, the issues and topics of the plays are no longer strictly "feminist issues" but rather human issues.

Another item worthy of note: the majority of writers who carve a successful niche for themselves as playwrights are also experienced in other areas of theatre. Many are actors or directors; some are theatre educators. It appears that knowledge of the playwright's craft comes, at least in part, through intimate knowledge of the living theatre. Also it is evident that these theatrically knowledgeable writers share the sentiment of the late director Alan Schneider, who said last year while directing an evening of one-act plays for the New York Shakespeare Festival, "I like one-acts. My grandmother told me, 'Diamonds don't come as big as bricks.' "

These five years would not have been possible without the enthusiastic support of those at Chilton who assist in the editorial process, especially Editorial Director Alan Turner and his able administrative assistant, Elsie Comninos, as well as the editors who have worked on this project over the years. Lastly, once again I applaud those playwrights and their representatives without whose patience, interest, and support this collection would not exist.

RAMON DELGADO
Montclair, New Jersey

David Henry Hwang

THE SOUND
OF A VOICE

David Henry Hwang

When David Henry Hwang's *Sound of a Voice* and *House of Sleeping Beauties* premiered in November 1983 under the collective title *Sound and Beauty* at Joseph Papp's New York Shakespeare Festival, John Beaufort of the *Christian Science Monitor* hailed the production: "A major theatrical event has taken place with the arrival of two plays by David Henry Hwang at the Public Theatre." Beaufort then describes the second half of the evening: "*The Sound of a Voice* unfolds with a compelling combination of strength and delicate nuance. In some respects, it is as strikingly formal as a Japanese print. As staged by actor-director [John] Lone, the unfoldment involves a subsurface intensity of feeling ready to erupt at any moment." Even the redoubtable John Simon, critic for *New York* magazine, was charmed by this fascinating encounter of a medieval, wandering Samurai with an enticing, solitary witch: "With *The Sound of a Voice,* the young playwright comes significantly closer to perfect pitch."

Mr. Hwang made his debut in the 1982 edition of this series with the highly acclaimed *Dance and the Railroad.* In its initial New York production at the Henry Street Settlement's New Federal Theatre in March 1981, the unusual play about Chinese railway construction workers during a strike in 1867 in the Sierra Nevada mountains was praised by Laurie Stone in the *Village Voice:* "David Henry Hwang . . . uses fantasy and poetry without coyness or inhibition, all the time dramatizing that there is no real freedom for these men—only novel forms of servitude. At 23, Hwang already knows how to take a bare stage and an hour and make something theatrical happen."

The playwright first came to public attention with his Obie-winning play *FOB* (which stands for "Fresh Off the Boat"), presented at the New York Shakespeare Festival in June 1980. The son of Chinese immigrants—his father arrived in the United States in the late 40s, his mother in 1952—Mr. Hwang, born in 1957, grew up in an upper-middle–class family in San Gabriel, a suburb of Los Angeles; yet Mr. Hwang identifies with the history of the Chinese in both this country and that of his grandparents, who used to tell him stories of their homeland.

Mr. Hwang entered Stanford University in the fall of 1975 and soon began writing plays. During his senior year in 1978, he wrote *FOB,* which was selected for the O'Neill Playwrights

Conference in Waterford, Connecticut. For a couple of years, Mr. Hwang taught writing at Menlo-Atherton High School in Menlo Park, California. Then he enrolled in the Yale School of Drama, where he first started work on *The Dance and the Railroad,* commissioned by the New Federal Theatre under a grant from the Ethnic Heritage Studies Division of the United States Department of Education.

Following *The Dance and the Railroad,* his play *Family Devotions* was produced at the New York Shakespeare Festival in the fall of 1981. *Family Devotions* shows three generations of Chinese-Americans in an affluent suburb of Los Angeles. Mr. Hwang explains, "It's about the myths that grow up around a family history and how legends of past family members affect the lives of the living." Frank Rich, writing for the *New York Times,* describes *Family Devotions* as a "sassy, contemporary American comedy with the gripping, mythological stylization of Oriental theater—ending up with a work that remains true to its specific roots even as it speaks to a far wider audience."

Mr. Hwang expresses concern about creating more opportunities for Asian-Americans in the United States theatre: "I write about Asian-Americans to claim our legitimate, but often neglected, place in the American experience. . . . One very important thing for me is to give Asian-American actors a chance to work and increase our visibility." Recently, Mr. Hwang expressed his reactions to writing *Sound and Beauty:* "These are the first plays I've written which don't deal with the idea of being a minority in America. They're still, I think, similar to the previous works in that they deal with Asian culture and are for Asian actors. But the themes are different. I'm starting to deal more with the idea of relationships."

In addition to the Obie, Mr. Hwang has received the Drama Desk nomination for Best Play for *The Dance and the Railroad* and *Family Devotions,* the CINE Golden Eagle award for the cable version of *The Dance and the Railroad,* and fellowships in playwriting from the Rockefeller Foundation, the National Endowment for the Arts, and the Guggenheim Foundation.

Mr. Hwang has shared his playwriting expertise as an instructor at the Basement Workshop in New York and the People's School of Dramatic Arts in San Francisco, and he has been an advisor for the Young Playwrights Festival for The Dramatists Guild. Mr. Hwang is on the selection committee of Plays-in-Process for the Theatre Communications Group. In addition, he has served on the Advisory Board and as Theatre Auditor for the National Endowment for the Arts.

His most recent play, *Rich Relations,* will have been performed by the time this collection comes off the press.

Characters:

MAN, *fifties, Japanese*
WOMAN (HANAKO), *forties or fifties, Japanese*

Place:

Woman's house, in a remote corner of a forest.

Scene One:

Evening. Woman warms tea for man. Man rubs himself, trying to get warm.

MAN: You are very kind to take me in.
WOMAN: This is a remote corner of the world. Guests are rare.
MAN: The tea—you pour it well.
WOMAN: No.
MAN: The sound it makes—in the cup—very soothing.
WOMAN: That is the tea's skill, not mine. (*She hands the cup to him*)
WOMAN: May I get you something else? Rice, perhaps?
MAN: No.
WOMAN: And some vegetables?
MAN: No, thank you.
WOMAN: Fish? (*Pause*) It is at least two days walk to the nearest village. I saw no horse. You must be very hungry. You would do a great honor to dine with me. Guests are rare.
MAN: Thank you.
(*Woman gets up, leaves. He gets up, walks to kitchen door, listens. The room is sparsely furnished, except for one shelf on which stands a vase of brightly colored flowers. The flowers stand out in sharp contrast to the starkness of the room. He crosses to the vase of flowers. He touches them. Quickly, he takes one of the flowers from the vase, hides it in his clothes. The Woman reenters. She carries a tray with food*)
WOMAN: Please. Eat. It will give me great pleasure.
MAN: This—this is magnificent.
WOMAN: Eat.

MAN: Thank you.
(*He motions for the Woman to join him*)
WOMAN: No, thank you.
MAN: This is wonderful. The best I've tasted.
WOMAN: You are reckless in your flattery, sir. But anything you say, I will enjoy hearing. It's not even the words. It's the sound of a voice, the way it moves through the air.
MAN: How long has it been since you last had a visitor?
(*Pause*)
WOMAN: I don't know.
MAN: Oh?
WOMAN: I lose track. Perhaps five months ago, perhaps ten years, perhaps yesterday. I don't consider time when there is no voice in the air. It's pointless. Time begins with the entrance of a visitor, and ends with his exit.
MAN: And in between? You don't keep track of the days? You can't help but notice—
WOMAN: Of course I notice.
MAN: Oh.
WOMAN: I notice, but I don't keep track. (*Pause*) May I bring out more?
MAN: More? No. No. This was wonderful.
WOMAN: I have more.
MAN: Really—the best I've had.
WOMAN: You must be tired. Did you sleep in the forest last night?
MAN: Yes.
WOMAN: Or did you not sleep at all?
MAN: I slept.
WOMAN: Where?
MAN: By a waterfall. The sound of the water put me to sleep. It rumbled like the sounds of a city. You see, I can't sleep in too much silence. It scares me. It makes me feel that I have no control over what is about to happen.
WOMAN: I feel the same way.
MAN: But you live here—alone?
WOMAN: Yes.
MAN: It's so quiet here. How can you sleep?
WOMAN: Tonight, I'll sleep. I'll lie down in the next room, and hear your breathing through the wall, and fall asleep shamelessly. There will be no silence.
MAN: You're very kind to let me stay here.
WOMAN: This is yours. (*She unrolls a mat*)

MAN: Did you make it yourself?

WOMAN: Yes. There is a place to wash outside.

MAN: Thank you.

WOMAN: Goodnight.

MAN: Goodnight. (*He starts to leave*)

WOMAN: May I know your name?

MAN: No. I mean, I would rather not say. If I gave you a name, it would only be made up. Why should I deceive you? You are too kind for that.

WOMAN: Then what should I call you? Perhaps—"Man Who Fears Silence?"

MAN: How about, "Man Who Fears Women?"

WOMAN: That name is much too common.

MAN: And you?

WOMAN: Hanako.

MAN: That's your name?

WOMAN: It's what you may call me.

MAN: Goodnight, Hanako. You are very kind.

WOMAN: You are very smart. Goodnight.

(*Man exits. She picks up the dishes and teapot, returns them off-stage to kitchen. She goes to the vase. She picks up the flowers, studies them. She carries them out of the room with her. Man reenters. He glimpses the spot where the vase used to sit. He listens at the various screens, then suddenly hears a sound. He prepares to draw his sword, then hears a shakuhatchi. He sits on the mat, looks at the flower, puts it away. Then he sits on guard with his sword ready at his side*)

Scene Two:

Dawn. Man is packing. Woman enters with food.

WOMAN: Good morning.

MAN: Good morning, Hanako.

WOMAN: You weren't planning to leave?

MAN: I have quite a distance to travel today.

WOMAN: Please. (*She offers him food*)

MAN: Thank you.

WOMAN: May I ask where you're traveling to?

MAN: It's far.

WOMAN: I know this region well.

MAN: Oh? Do you leave the house often?

WOMAN: I used to. I used to travel a great deal. I know the region from those days.

MAN: You probably wouldn't know the place I'm headed.

WOMAN: Why not?

MAN: It's new. A new village. It didn't exist in "those days."

(*Pause*)

WOMAN: I thought you said you wouldn't deceive me.

MAN: I didn't. You don't believe me, do you?

WOMAN: No.

MAN: Then I didn't deceive you, did I? I'm traveling. That much is true.

WOMAN: Are you in such a hurry?

MAN: Traveling is a matter of timing. Catching the light. (*Woman exits. Man finishes eating, puts down his bowl. Woman reenters with the vase of flowers*)

MAN: Where did you find those? They don't grow native around these parts, do they?

WOMAN: No, they've all been brought in by visitors. Such as yourself. They were left here. In my custody.

MAN: But—they look so fresh, so alive.

WOMAN: I take care of them. They remind me of the people and places outside this house.

MAN: May I touch them?

WOMAN: Certainly.

MAN: These have just blossomed.

WOMAN: No, they were in bloom yesterday. If you'd noticed them before, you would know that.

MAN: You must have received these very recently. I would guess—within five days.

WOMAN: I don't know. But I wouldn't trust your estimate. It's all in the amount of care you show to them. I create a world which is outside the realm of what you know.

MAN: What do you do?

WOMAN: I can't explain. Words are too inefficient. It takes hundreds of words to describe a single act of caring. With hundreds of acts, words become irrelevant. (*Pause*) But perhaps you can stay.

MAN: How long?

WOMAN: As long as you'd like.

MAN: Why?

WOMAN: To see how I care for them.

MAN: I *am* tired.
WOMAN: Rest.
MAN: The light?
WOMAN: It will return.

Scene Three:

Day. Man is carrying chopped wood. He is stripped to the waist. Woman enters.

WOMAN: You're very kind to do that for me.
MAN: I enjoy it, you know. Chopping wood. It's clean. No questions. You take your ax, you stand up the log, you aim—pow!—you either hit it or you don't. Success or failure.
WOMAN: You seem to have been very successful today.
MAN: Why shouldn't I be? It's a beautiful day. I can see to those hills. The trees are cool. The sun is gentle. Ideal. If a man can't be successful on a day like this, he might as well kick the dust up into his own face. (*Man notices woman staring at him. Man pats his belly, looks at her*) Protection from falls.
WOMAN: What? (*Man touches his belly, showing some fat*) Oh. Don't be silly. (*Man begins slapping the fat on his belly to a rhythm*)
MAN: Listen—I can make music—see? That wasn't always possible. But now—that I've developed this—whenever I need entertainment . . . (*He continues slapping*)
WOMAN: You shouldn't make fun of your body.
MAN: Why not? I saw you. You were staring.
WOMAN: I wasn't making fun. I was just—stop that!
(*He stops*)
MAN: Then why were you staring?
WOMAN: I was . . .
MAN: Laughing?
WOMAN: No.
MAN: Well?
WOMAN: I was—your body. It's . . . strong.
(*Pause*)
MAN: People say that. But they don't know. I've heard that age brings wisdom. That's a laugh. The years don't accumulate here. They accumulate here. (*He pats his stomach*) But today is a day to be happy, right? The woods. The sun. Blue. It's a happy day. I'm going to chop wood.

WOMAN: There's nothing left to chop. Look.
MAN: Oh. I guess . . . that's it.
WOMAN: Sit. Here.
MAN: But . . .
WOMAN: There's nothing left. Learn to love it.
MAN: Don't be ridiculous.
WOMAN: Touch it.
MAN: It's flabby.
WOMAN: It's strong.
MAN: It's weak.
WOMAN: And smooth.
MAN: Do you mind if I put on my shirt?
WOMAN: Of course not. Shall I get it for you?
MAN: No. No. Just sit there. (*Picks up his shirt. He pauses, studies his body*) You think it's cute, huh?
WOMAN: I think you should learn to love it.
(*Man pats his belly*)
MAN: (*To belly*) You're okay, sir. You hang onto my body like a great horseman.
WOMAN: Not like that.
MAN: (*Still to belly*) You're also faithful. You'll never leave me for another man.
WOMAN: No.
MAN: What do you want me to say?
(*Woman leans over to man. She touches his belly with her hand*)

Scene Four:

Night. Man is alone. Flowers are gone from stand. Mat is unrolled. Man lies on it, sleeping. Suddenly, he starts, awakened by the sound of the shakuhatchi. He sits up and grabs his sword, then relaxes as he recognizes the instrument. He crosses to a screen and listens, then returns to the mat and sits. He takes out the stolen flower. He stares into it.

Scene Five:

Day. Woman is cleaning while Man exercises. She is on her hands and knees, scrubbing the floor.

MAN: I heard your playing last night.

WOMAN: My playing?

MAN: Shakuhatchi.

WOMAN: Oh.

MAN: You played very softly. I had to strain to hear it. Next time don't be afraid. Play out. Fully. Clear. It must've been very beautiful, if only I could've heard it clearly. Why don't you play for me sometime?

WOMAN: I'm very shy about it.

MAN: Why?

WOMAN: I play for my own satisfaction. That's all. It's something I developed on my own. I don't know if it's at all acceptable by outside standards.

MAN: Play for me. I'll tell you.

WOMAN: No, I'm sure you're too knowledgeable in the arts.

MAN: Who? Me?

WOMAN: You being from the city and all.

MAN: I'm ignorant, believe me.

WOMAN: I'd play, and you'd probably bite your cheek.

MAN: Ask me a question about music. Any question. I'll answer incorrectly. I guarantee it.

WOMAN: (*Looking at the floor*) Look at this.

MAN: What?

WOMAN: A stain.

MAN: Where?

WOMAN: Here? See? I can't get it out.

MAN: Oh. I hadn't noticed it before.

WOMAN: I notice it every time I clean.

MAN: Here. Let me try.

WOMAN: Thank you.

MAN: Ugh. It's tough.

WOMAN: I know.

MAN: How did it get here?

WOMAN: It's been there as long as I've lived here.

MAN: I hardly stand a chance. (*Pause*) But I'll try. One—two—three—four! One—two—three—four! See, you set up . . . gotta set up . . . a rhythm—two—three—four. Used to practice with a rhythm. One—two—three—four. Yes, remember. Like battle . . . like fighting, one—two—three—four. One—two—three—four. (*The stain starts to fade away*) Look . . . there it goes . . . got the sides . . . the edges . . . fading away . . . fading quick . . . towards the center to

the heart . . . two—three—four. One—two—three—four—
dead!

WOMAN: Dead.

MAN: I got it! I got it! A little rhythm! All it took! Four!
Four!

WOMAN: Thank you.

MAN: I didn't think I could do it . . . but there—it's
gone—I did it!

WOMAN: Yes. You did.

MAN: And you—you were great.

WOMAN: No—I just watched.

MAN: We were a team! You and me!

WOMAN: I only provided encouragement.

MAN: You were great! You were!

(*Man grabs Woman. Pause*)

WOMAN: It's gone. Thank you. Would you like to hear me
play shakuhatchi?

MAN: Yes I would.

WOMAN: I don't usually play for visitors. It's so . . . I'm
not sure. I developed it—all by myself—in times when I was
alone. I heard nothing . . . The air began to be oppressive—
stale. So I learned to play shakuhatchi. I learned to make
sounds on it. I tried to make these sounds resemble the human voice. The shakuhatchi became my weapon. It kept me
from choking on many a silent evening.

MAN: I'm here. You can hear my voice.

WOMAN: Speak again.

MAN: I will.

Scene Six:

*Night. Man is sleeping. Suddenly, a start. He lifts his head up. He
listens. The shakuhatchi melody rises up once more. This time,
however, it becomes louder and more clear than before. He gets up.
He cannot tell from what direction the music is coming. It seems to
come from all directions at once, as omnipresent as the air. Slowly,
he moves toward the wall with the sliding panel through which the
woman enters and exits. He puts his ear against it, thinking the
music may be coming from there. Slowly, he slides the door open just
a crack, ever so carefully. He peeks through the crack. As he peeks
through, the upstage wall of the set becomes transparent, and
through the scrim, we are able to see what he sees. Woman is*

upstage of the scrim. She is carrying the vase of flowers in front of her as she moves slowly through the cubicles upstage of the scrim. She is also transformed. She is beautiful. She wears a brightly colored kimono. Man observes this scene for a long time. He then slides the door shut. The scrim returns to opaque. The music continues. He returns to his mat. He picks up the stolen flower. It is brown and wilted, dead. He looks at it, throws it down. The music slowly fades out.

Scene Seven:

Morning. Man is practicing sword maneuvers. He practices with the feel of a man whose spirit is willing but flesh is inept. He tries to execute deft movements but is dissatisfied with his efforts. Suddenly, he feels something buzzing around his neck—a mosquito. He slaps his neck, but misses it. He sees it flying near him. He swipes at it with his sword. He keeps missing. Finally, he thinks he's hit it. He runs over, kneels down to recover the fallen insect. He picks up the two halves of the mosquito on two different fingers. Woman enters the room. She looks as she normally does. She is carrying a vase of flowers, which she places on its shelf.

MAN: Look.
WOMAN: I'm sorry?
MAN: Look.
WOMAN: What?
(*He brings over the two halves of the mosquito to show her*)
MAN: See?
WOMAN: Oh.
MAN: I hit it—chop!
WOMAN: These are new forms of target practice?
MAN: Huh? Well—yes—in a way.
WOMAN: You seem to do well at it.
MAN: Thank you. For last night. I heard your shakuhat-chi. It was very loud, strong—good tone.
WOMAN: Did you enjoy it? I wanted you to enjoy it. If you wish, I'll play it for you every night.
MAN: Every night!
WOMAN: If you wish.
MAN: No—I don't—I don't want you to treat me like a baby.
WOMAN: What? I'm not.

MAN: Oh, yes. Like a baby who you must feed in the middle of the night or he cries. Waaah! Waaah!

WOMAN: Stop that!

MAN: You need your sleep.

WOMAN: I don't mind getting up for you. (*Pause*) I would enjoy playing for you. Every night. While you sleep. It will make me feel . . . like I'm shaping your dreams. I go through long stretches when there is no one in my dreams. It's terrible. During those times, I avoid my bed as much as possible. I paint. I weave. I play shakuhatchi. I sit on mats and rub powder into my face. Anything to keep from facing a bed with no dreams. It is like sleeping on ice.

MAN: What do you dream of now?

WOMAN: Last night—I dreamt of you. I don't remember what happened. But you were very funny. Not in a mocking way. I wasn't laughing at you. But you made me laugh. And you were very warm. I remember that. (*Pause*) What do you remember about last night?

MAN: Just your playing. That's all. I got up, listened to it, and went back to sleep. (*Gets up, resumes practicing with his sword*)

WOMAN: Another mosquito bothering you?

MAN: Just practicing. Ah! Weak! Too weak! I tell you, it wasn't always like this. I'm telling you, there were days when I could chop the fruit from a tree without ever taking my eyes off the ground. (*Continuing to practice with his sword*) You ever use one of these?

WOMAN: I've had to pick one up, yes.

MAN: Oh?

WOMAN: You forget . . . I live alone . . . out here . . . there is . . . not much to sustain me but what I manage to learn myself. It wasn't really a matter of choice.

MAN: I used to be very good, you know. Perhaps I can give you some pointers.

WOMAN: I'd really rather not.

MAN: C'mon—a woman like you—you're absolutely right. You need to know how to defend yourself.

WOMAN: As you wish.

MAN: Do you have something to practice with?

WOMAN: Yes. Excuse me. (*She exits. She reenters with two wooden sticks*) Will these do?

MAN: Fine. (*He takes one*) Nice. Now, show me what you can do.

WOMAN: I'm sorry?

MAN: Run up and hit me.

WOMAN: Please.

MAN: Go on—I'll block it.

WOMAN: I feel so . . . undignified.

MAN: Go on! (*She taps him playfully*) Not like that! C'mon!

WOMAN: I'll try to be gentle.

MAN: What?

WOMAN: I don't want to hurt you.

MAN: You won't. Hit me!

(*Woman charges at Man, quickly, deftly. She scores a hit*)

WOMAN: Did I hurt you?

MAN: No—let's try that again.

(*They square off again. Woman rushes forward. He blocks an apparent strike. She rushes in for another. She scores*)

WOMAN: Did I hurt you? I'm sorry.

MAN: No.

WOMAN: I hurt you.

MAN: Don't be ridiculous!

WOMAN: Do you wish to hit me?

MAN: No.

WOMAN: Do you want me to try again?

MAN: No. Just practice there—by yourself—let me see you run through some maneuvers.

WOMAN: Must I?

MAN: Yes! Go! (*Woman goes to an open area*) My greatest strength always was as a teacher.

(*Woman executes a series of movements. Her whole manner is transformed. Man watches with increasing amazement. Her movements end. She regains her submissive manner*)

WOMAN: I'm so embarrassed. My skills—they're so—inappropriate. I look like a man.

MAN: Where did you learn that?

WOMAN: There is much time to practice here.

MAN: But you—the techniques . . .

WOMAN: I don't know what's fashionable in the outside world. (*Pause*) Are you unhappy?

MAN: No.

WOMAN: Really?

MAN: I'm just . . . surprised.

WOMAN: You think it's unbecoming for a woman.

MAN: No, no. Not at all.

WOMAN: You want to leave.

MAN: No!

WOMAN: All visitors do. I know. I've met many. They say they'll stay. And they do. For a while. Until they see too much. Or they learn something new. There are boundaries outside of which visitors do not want to see me step. Only who knows what those boundaries are? Not I. They change with every visitor. You have to be careful not to cross them, but you never know where they are. And one day, inevitably, you step outside the lines. The visitor knows. You don't. You didn't know that you'd done anything different. You thought it was just another part of you. The visitor sneaks away. The next day, you learn that you had stepped outside his heart. I'm afraid you've seen too much.

MAN: There are stories.

WOMAN: What?

MAN: People talk.

WOMAN: Where? We're two days from the nearest village.

MAN: Word travels.

WOMAN: What are you talking about?

MAN: There are stories about you. I heard them. They say that your visitors never leave this house.

WOMAN: That's what you heard?

MAN: They say you imprison them.

WOMAN: Then you were a fool to come here.

MAN: Listen.

WOMAN: Me? Listen? You. Look! Where are these prisoners? Have you seen any?

MAN: They told me you were very beautiful.

WOMAN: Then they are blind as well as ignorant.

MAN: You are.

WOMAN: What?

MAN: Beautiful.

WOMAN: Stop that! My skin feels like seaweed.

MAN: I didn't realize it at first. I must confess. I didn't. But over these few days—your face has changed for me. The shape of it. The feel of it. The color. All changed. I look at you now and I am no longer sure you are the same woman who had poured tea for me just a week ago. And because of that I remember—how little I know about a face that changes in the night. (*Pause*) Have you heard those stories?

WOMAN: I don't listen to old wives tales.

MAN: But have you heard them?

WOMAN: Yes. I've heard them. From other visitors— young—hotblooded—or old—who came here because they were told great glory was to be had by killing the witch in the woods.

MAN: I was told that no man could spend time in this house without falling in love.

WOMAN: Oh? So why did you come? Did you wager gold that you could come out untouched? The outside world is so flattering to me. And you—are you like the rest? Passion passing through your heart so powerfully that you can't hold onto it?

MAN: No! I'm afraid!

WOMAN: Of what?

MAN: Sometimes—when I look into the flowers, I think I hear a voice—from inside—a voice beneath the petals. A human voice.

WOMAN: What does it say? "Let me out"?

MAN: No. Listen. It hums. It hums with the peacefulness of one who is completely imprisoned.

WOMAN: I understand that if you listen closely enough, you can hear the ocean.

MAN: No. Wait. Look at it. See the layers? Each petal—hiding the next. Try and see where they end . . . You can't. Follow them down, further down, around and as you come down—faster and faster—the breeze picks up. The breeze becomes a wail. And in that rush of air—you hear a voice.

(*Woman grabs flower from Man*)

WOMAN: So, you believe I water and prune my lovers? How can you be so foolish? (*She throws the flower to the ground*) Do you come only to leave again? To take a chunk of my heart, then leave with your booty on your belt, like a prize? You say that I imprison hearts in these flowers? Well, bits of my heart are trapped with travelers across this land. I can't even keep track. So kill me. If you came here to destroy a witch, kill me now. I can't stand to have it happen again.

(*Man begins to pull out sword—cannot use it*)

MAN: I won't leave you.

WOMAN: I believe you.

Scene Eight:

Day. Woman is modeling her kimono.

WOMAN: Do you like it?

MAN: Yes, it's beautiful.

WOMAN: I wanted to wear something special today.

MAN: It's beautiful. (*Man takes out his sword*) Excuse me. I must practice.

WOMAN: Shall I get you something?

MAN: No.

WOMAN: Some tea, maybe?

MAN: No, thank you. (*He resumes swordplay*)

WOMAN: Perhaps later today—perhaps we can go out—just around here. We can look for flowers.

MAN: All right.

WOMAN: We don't have to.

MAN: No. Let's.

WOMAN: I just thought if . . .

MAN: Fine. Where do you want to go?

WOMAN: There are very few recreational activities around here, I know.

MAN: All right. We'll go this afternoon.

(*Pause*)

WOMAN: Can I get you something?

MAN: What?

WOMAN: You might be . . .

MAN: I'm not hungry or thirsty or cold or hot.

WOMAN: Then what are you?

MAN: Practicing.

(*Man resumes practicing; woman exits. Man sits down. He examines his sword, thinks. He stands up. He places the sword on the ground with the tip pointed directly upward. He keeps it from falling by placing the tip under his chin. He experiments with different degrees of pressure. Woman reenters. She sees him in this precarious position*)

WOMAN: Don't do that!

MAN: What?

WOMAN: You can hurt yourself!

MAN: I was practicing!

WOMAN: You were playing!

MAN: I was practicing!

WOMAN: It's dangerous.

MAN: What do you take me for—a child?

WOMAN: Sometimes wise men do childish things.

MAN: I knew what I was doing!

WOMAN: It scares me.

MAN: Don't be ridiculous.

WOMAN: Don't! Don't do that!

MAN: Get back!

WOMAN: But . . .

MAN: Sssssh!

WOMAN: I wish . . .

MAN: Listen to me! The slightest shock, you know—the slightest shock—surprise—it might make me jerk or—something—and then . . . So you must be perfectly still and quiet.

WOMAN: But I . . .

MAN: Ssssh! (*Silence, then . . .*) I learned this exercise from a friend—I can't even remember his name—good swordsman—many years ago. He called it his meditation position. He said, like this, he could feel the line between this world and the others because he rested on it. If he saw something in another world that he liked better, all he would have to do is let his head drop, and he'd be there. Simple. No fuss. One day, they found him with the tip of his sword run clean out the back of his neck. He was smiling. I guess he saw something he liked. Or else he'd fallen asleep.

WOMAN: Stop that.

MAN: Stop what?

WOMAN: Tormenting me.

MAN: I'm not.

WOMAN: Take it away!

MAN: You don't have to watch, you know.

WOMAN: Do you want to die that way—an accident?

MAN: I was doing this before you came in.

WOMAN: If you do, all you need to do is tell me.

MAN: What?

WOMAN: I can walk right over. Lean on the back of your head.

MAN: Don't try to threaten . . .

WOMAN: Or jerk your sword up.

MAN: . . . or scare me. You can't threaten . . .

WOMAN: I'm not. But if that's what you want.

MAN: You wouldn't do it.

WOMAN: Oh?

MAN: Then I'd be gone. You wouldn't let me leave that easily.

WOMAN: Yes, I would.

MAN: You'd be alone.

WOMAN: No. I'd follow you. Forever. (*Pause*) Now, let's stop this nonsense.

MAN: No! I can do what I want! Don't come any closer!

WOMAN: Then release your sword.

MAN: Come any closer and I'll drop my head.

(*Woman slowly approaches man. She grabs the sword. She pulls it out from under his chin*)

WOMAN: There will be no more of this.
(*She exits with the sword. He starts to follow her, then stops. He touches under his chin. On his finger, he finds a drop of blood*)

Scene Nine:

Night. Man is leaving the house. He is just about out when he hears a shakuhatchi playing. Woman appears in the doorway to the outside.

WOMAN: It's time for you to go?
MAN: Yes. I'm sorry.
WOMAN: You're just going to sneak out? A thief in the night? A frightened child?
MAN: I care about you.
WOMAN: You express it strangely.
MAN: I leave in shame because it is proper. (*Pause*) I came seeking glory.
WOMAN: To kill me? You can say it. You'll be surprised at how little I blanch. As if you'd said, "I came for a bowl of rice," or "I came seeking love," or "I came to kill you."
MAN: Weakness. All weakness. Too weak to kill you. Too weak to kill myself. Too weak to do anything but sneak away in shame.
(*Woman brings out Man's sword*)
WOMAN: Were you even planning to leave without this? (*He takes sword*) Why not stay here?
MAN: I can't live with someone who's defeated me.
WOMAN: I never thought of defeating you. I only wanted to take care of you. To make you happy. Because that made me happy and I was no longer alone.
MAN: You defeated me.
WOMAN: Why do you think that way?
MAN: I came here with a purpose. The world was clear. You changed the shape of your face, the shape of my heart—rearranged everything—created a world where I could do nothing.
WOMAN: I only tried to care for you.
MAN: I guess that was all it took.
(*Pause*)
WOMAN: You still think I'm a witch. Just because old women gossip. You are so cruel. Once you arrived, there were

only two possibilities: I would die or you would leave. (*Pause*)
If you believe I'm a witch, then kill me. Rid the province of
one more evil.

MAN: I can't—

WOMAN: Why not? If you believe that about me, then it's
the right thing to do.

MAN: You know I can't.

WOMAN: Then stay.

MAN: Don't try to force me!

WOMAN: I won't force you to do anything. (*Pause*) All I
wanted was an escape—for both of us. The sound of a human
voice—the simplest thing to find, and the hardest to hold on
to. This house—my loneliness is etched into the walls. Kill
me, but don't leave. Even in death, my spirit would rest here
and be comforted by your presence.

MAN: Force me to stay.

WOMAN: I won't. (*Man starts to leave*) Beware.

MAN: Of what?

WOMAN: The ground on which you walk is weak. It could
give way at any moment. The crevice beneath is dark.

MAN: Are you talking about death? I'm ready to die.

WOMAN: Fear for what is worse than death.

MAN: What?

WOMAN: Falling. Falling through the darkness. Waiting to
hit the ground. Picking up speed. Waiting for the ground.
Falling faster. Falling alone. Waiting. Falling. Waiting. Falling.

(*Woman goes out through the door to her room. Man reenters from
the outside. He looks for her in the main room. He goes to the mat,
sees the shakuhatchi. He puts down his sword, takes off his bundle
and coat. He goes inside. He comes out. He goes to the mat, picks
up the shakuhatchi, clutches it to him. He moves everything else off
the mat, sits, and puts the shakuhatchi to his mouth. He begins to
blow into it. He tries to make sounds. He continues trying through
the end of the play.*

*The upstage scrim lights up. Upstage, we see the woman. She is
hanging from a rope suspended from the roof. She has hung herself. Around her swirl the thousands of petals from the flowers.
They fill the upstage scrim area like a blizzard of color.*

Man continues to attempt to play. Lights fade to black)

The End

Ellen Byron

GRACELAND

Ellen Byron

Ellen Byron's first play, *Graceland,* a bold character study of two contrasting Elvis Presley fans, premiered at the Philadelphia Festival Theatre for New Plays in April 1983 to critical acclaim. The roving critic for station WFLN reports, "*Graceland* may at first impress you as a satirical send-up of southern American attitudes and beliefs, but it will surprise you in the end by cutting below its slick surface to a climax of unexpected compassion." And Cherry Hill *Courier-Post* reviewer Robert Baxter writes, "Byron makes her debut as a playwright . . . and proves herself to be adept at creating characters at once poignant and comic."

Graceland was then produced in the Actors Theatre of Louisville's 1983 SHORTS Festival. Companion piece *Asleep on the Wind* has been published together with *Graceland* in an acting edition for the amateur theatre. *Graceland* was first presented as a staged reading at Manhattan's Ensemble Studio Theatre, where Ms. Byron's plays *Return of the Vestals, But will Zabars Deliver after the Apocalypse?,* and *The Quando Si Sposa Fund* received staged readings and workshop productions. *The Quando Si Sposa Fund* was also presented as part of the WPA Theatre series *Works in Progress.* In 1984, *Graceland* won the Women's Community Theatre Award.

The versatile Ms. Byron is an actress as well as a playwright, and she has appeared in a variety of stage productions ranging from regional theatre to Off-Off-Broadway. Improvisational comedy is her specialty, and she has worked with several improvisation groups throughout the country. She is one of a handful of New York actors trained in the Canadian improvisational technique known as TheaterSports, and she has participated in challenge matches throughout the New York metropolitan area. She has also performed in television, film, and commercials.

In addition to her playwriting and acting accomplishments, Ms. Byron has worked as an administrator at the Manhattan Theatre Club, the Theatre Communications Group, and The Dramatists Guild.

Born and raised in the New York City area, Ms. Byron earned a magna cum laude degree in theatre from the Newcomb College of Tulane University. She also spent a year and a half at State University of New York at Binghamton studying the Lessac technique. Currently a member of the New York group, the Writers Bloc, Ms. Byron teaches playwriting workshops to young students in the New York metropolitan area under the auspices of the Young Playwrights Festival.

Characters:

BEV DAVIES, *forty-two*
ROOTIE MALLERT, *twenty-two*
VOICE OF RADIO ANNOUNCER

Place:

The yard in front of Graceland, Elvis Presley's mansion.

Time:

Five A.M., June 4, 1982. Three days before the opening of Grace-land to the public.

At Curtain:

As the lights begin dimming, we hear the sound of a car pulling up and the sound of a car radio being played. We hear the tail end of an Elvis song such as "I Can't Help Falling in Love with You."

RADIO ANNOUNCER: Boy, that is some song, huh? Hello, Memphis, you're listening to WKTY, the heart of the Memphis sound, on this beautiful night of June 4, 1982, and we're just three days away from the historic opening of Elvis Presley's magnificent mansion, Graceland. *And* we're right in the middle of our week-long KTY Salutes Elvis Festival. Now I'm gonna play another song, and the first person to call and tell me what movie he sung it in wins a ten-dollar gift certificate from Harry Cully's Elvis Lives Memento Shop. Here we go—
  (Plays beginning of a song such as "Teddy Bear," which quickly fades. Bev Davies enters, humming snatches of the same song. Bev is from Wilmington, Delaware, a strong-willed and opinionated woman but also very generous and open. She is wearing a matching polyester pants and vest set and a heavily curled wig à la Dolly Parton. She is totally dedicated to Elvis Presley and expects nothing less from those around her. She has at least a twenty-pound weight problem, not helped by her love of junk food. She carries a cooler, large bag, beach chair, and pop-up tent. She sets down everything but the tent, which she begins to assemble. It comes together rapidly.

Absorbed in her efforts, she doesn't notice the entrance of Rootie Mallert, whose gaze is held by the vision of the mansion out front. Rootie comes from a tiny town outside Lafayette, Louisiana, Cajun country. She is frail and extremely thin, with an almost childlike body. From a distance, she could pass for thirteen. She is uneducated and extremely simple, naive, and unworldly. She could almost be mistaken for being somewhat slow witted, but she isn't. Her lack of education and experience have made her very innocent and trusting. Having grown up surrounded by men, she is unsure of how to act with women but wants very much to be liked. Rootie is wearing tattered shorts, a faded shell-neck T-shirt, and clunky sandals. She carries a pillow and a brown paper bag.

As Rootie rests herself on the pillow, Bev notices Rootie and sets up her chair in an authoritative manner. Rootie takes a makeup purse out of her brown paper bag and begins checking herself intently. This is a nervous habit that she repeats several times during the play. She is suddenly aware of Bev through the compact mirror and looks over. There is a moment of silence)

ROOTIE: Hey.

BEV: Hello.

(There is another awkward pause. Finally:)

ROOTIE: Nice chair.

BEV: Thank you. I was here first.

ROOTIE: Pardon?

BEV: I said I was here first. I was. *I* was here first.

ROOTIE: Oh. *(Pause)* I think I was.

BEV: Excuse me?

ROOTIE: I'm sorry ma'am, I hope you don't mind, but I think I was here first, I really do.

BEV: *(Stares at Rootie then turns and stares straight ahead. With finality)* I was here first.

ROOTIE: I put my pillow down before you put your chair down.

BEV: What?!

ROOTIE: Well, I heard you put your chair down in the grass, and my pillow was already down by then.

BEV: That's crazy, that is just crazy. How the hell could you hear that? Grass doesn't make noise.

ROOTIE: A chair is louder than a pillow.

BEV: What the hell does that mean? A pin is louder than a feather, but that doesn't mean you could hear it fall in the grass.

ROOTIE: I put my pillow down first.

BEV: But my tent was already up.

ROOTIE: But I sat down before you, that's what counts.

BEV: No it doesn't . . .

ROOTIE: Yes it does . . .

BEV: No it doesn't . . .

ROOTIE: Yes it does . . .

BEV: No it doesn't.

ROOTIE: Yes it *does*.

(*A stalemate*)

BEV: What are you doing here anyway? Why don't you just chase after one of those teenage idol types and leave this to the people who really care?

ROOTIE: I care.

BEV: You care?

ROOTIE: I care.

BEV: What could you possibly know?

(*Rootie just looks at her for a moment, then faces front and begins speaking. As she speaks, her face develops a radiant, almost mystical glow*)

ROOTIE: He was born on January 8, 1935, at 12:02 P.M. His identical twin, Jessie Garon, was stillborn and buried the next day. He attended Lawlor Elementary School and got his first guitar on his eleventh birthday. It cost $12.75, and his mama bought it for him at the Tupelo Hardware Store. He made his first record on Monday, July 5th at Sun Studio, and his whole life changed when his mama died on August 14, 1958.

(*Bev is silent for a moment. Then rapid-fire*)

BEV: What she die of?

ROOTIE: (*Equally fast*) Heart attack complicated by hepatitis.

BEV: What was the first song he ever recorded?

ROOTIE: "My Happiness," in 1953.

BEV: What's his father's name?

ROOTIE: Vernon.

BEV: When was his father born?

ROOTIE: April 4, 1916.

BEV: (*Pause*) I was still here first.

(*Pause*)

ROOTIE: Who wrote "Heartbreak Hotel"?

BEV: Hoyt Axton's mother.

ROOTIE: Who was his favorite actress to work with?

BEV: Shelley Fabares.

ROOTIE: When did he make his first screen test?

BEV: April 15, 1956, and he read from some play called *The Rainmaker*.

ROOTIE: What's his favorite cigarette?

BEV: Lucky Strike.

ROOTIE: (*Pause*) Elvis didn't smoke.

BEV: Of course he didn't smoke. Lord, I knew that, you just threw me off with all that other stuff. It's early. I don't think good early.

ROOTIE: *I* was here first.

BEV: Now one damn minute. I was the first person to enter the Meditation Garden and Gravesite when it opened and I was the first person to go into his museum when it opened and I was the first person to touch his statue when they unveiled it and now that they are finally going to open his home, the most sacred place of all, I am goddamned well going to be the first person to set foot through those doors.

ROOTIE: I have to be. I'm sorry, ma'am, but I have to be.

BEV: What the hell do you mean, you *have* to be?

ROOTIE: I have to get to him.

BEV: Get to him? Are you crazy? He's dead.

ROOTIE: I know that. But I'm gonna make him come back. If you love somebody enough, you can. I was watching this movie yesterday and it was called *Brigadoon,* and Gene Kelly made a whole village come back just because he loved the girl so much.

BEV: What are you talking about?

ROOTIE: If I got in there first, and was just by myself for five minutes, I could talk to him . . .

BEV: Hold on one minute. First of all, you will never get in there alone, they got guards on the laundry shelves for chrissake, and second: *I was here first.*

ROOTIE: Yeah, but if you're first, don't they give you a prize or something? I could ask for my prize to be just five minutes alone in there. My cousin was the first customer when they opened a new K-Mart in her town and they gave her all sorts of stuff.

BEV: Oh come on, does this look like a K-Mart to you? (*She waves toward the house. Rootie is silent*)

ROOTIE: I have to go in first.

BEV: Who the hell do you think you are? I have dedicated my life to this man, to preserving his memory, to showing the world there is only one true singer and that's Elvis. I turned my whole basement into a memorial room to him. Threw out my kids' ping pong table and set up my whole collection. I got records, pictures, even a scarf he used to wipe the sweat from his face in Vegas, '72. I have got every liquor bottle that was ever made as an Elvis statue. Even TV shows have interviewed me. I have loved him with the purest and truest love possible since I was fifteen, and if you think I'm just gonna hand that over to some stupid kid, all I have to say to you is no, repeat NO, goddamn, repeat GODDAMN, way.

ROOTIE: But I have to be in there first or it won't work.

BEV: What do you mean? What won't work? Are you talking about magic or some—oh my God, you're one of those crazy cult people. I'm getting the guards.

ROOTIE: Please, I don't know nothing about that stuff . . .

BEV: I am getting you thrown off these grounds.

ROOTIE: Okay, okay, fine. You go ahead and get 'em, but you can't prove nothing. Besides, then they'll probably chase both of us away.

(Bev hesitates for a moment. Rootie grabs her pillow and throws it down directly in front of Bev's chair, then sits with resolute determination. Bev turns around, sees her, and grabs her chair, placing it squarely in front of Rootie. Rootie grabs her pillow and throws it in front of Bev's chair. Bev grabs her chair and puts it in front of Rootie, who picks it up from the back and places it behind her. As she is doing this, Bev grabs Rootie's pillow, heaves it behind her chair, and throws herself into the seat. Rootie grabs the pillow and they face off for a moment. Then Rootie walks around her, heading toward the mansion. Bev scoots forward in her chair, and Rootie stops. Rootie goes to take another step, and Bev goes to scoot again. A standoff. Rootie decides to try another approach. She slowly lowers herself to the ground, on an even level with Bev's chair)

ROOTIE: That's a beautiful suit.

BEV: What?

ROOTIE: I always wanted a suit like that.

BEV: What the hell are you talking about?

ROOTIE: Well, they never come in my size.

BEV: Why not? What size do you wear?

ROOTIE: (Very nonchalant as she adjusts her pillow so that it is slightly ahead of Bev's chair) Oh, I guess about a three.

(Bev stands up)

BEV: A three? Well, that just ain't healthy. How can you be a real woman and wear a scrawny size like a three? (As she sits, she pulls her chair ahead)

ROOTIE: My Weebo always said that if a woman ain't got a shelf, then she should at least be as thin as a sideways door.

BEV: Your who-bo?

ROOTIE: Weebo. That's my husband. Since he was best friends with my brother Beau, Weebo was like little Beau. See?

BEV: Sure Wee-bo. Well, I guess that's about the name I'd expect from a man who thinks women should look like sideways doors—what the hell am I doing *talking* like this?! (*She pulls her chair forward*)

ROOTIE: Ma'am? Excuse me, ma'am?

BEV: What?!

ROOTIE: I'll tell you why I got to go in there first.

BEV: Shoot.

ROOTIE: Well—the day it opens is Beau's birthday.

BEV: Weebo?

ROOTIE: No, Beau, my brother.

BEV: Oh, that explains everything. You want to get in there first so you can ask Elvis's ghost to wish your brother a Happy Birthday. Look, I'll make a deal with you. I'll give you a dollar and you can go buy him a card, ok? (*She gets her bag and begins searching through it*)

ROOTIE: I can't, I can't send it to him.

BEV: What's the matter, can't spell his address?

ROOTIE: He's dead.

BEV: Oh. I—oh. Well, my God, why the hell didn't you say so? That's a terrible thing to do, letting me go on like that.

ROOTIE: I'm sorry.

BEV: I accept your apology.

ROOTIE: He died in the war.

BEV: Korean?

ROOTIE: No, Vietnam.

BEV: Oh.

ROOTIE: He was a Marine. They're the toughest.

BEV: I know it. My husband was a Marine, too.

ROOTIE: No, you're kidding. Ain't that something? Here we are, two total strangers, and we're both related to Marines.

BEV: Small world.

ROOTIE: The funny thing is—I don't mean ha-ha funny, I mean funny, funny—well, there are people, you just can't see them going on past a certain point. It's like with Beau. I could never think what he'd be doing later on. I don't think he knew either, and that's why he joined up.

BEV: I know what you mean. I had this best friend in high school, Francene. We were like sisters, just so close. But Francie was wild, drove like a maniac, went all the way with boys, drank like a truck driver. Killed in a car crash senior year. Guess I kind of expected it all along.

ROOTIE: I talk to him sometimes. Least I try to. Elvis was his favorite person in the whole world. I bet they're probably best friends by now.

BEV: Well if that's so, I bet Francie's friends with him, too. We were crazy for him together.

ROOTIE: Maybe they're dating up there.

BEV: Who?

ROOTIE: Elvis and Francene.

BEV: That's the craziest thing I ever heard. Dating in Heaven?! (*Half to herself*) I'll kill her.

ROOTIE: Well, who knows? Ain't nobody I ever heard of who could tell you firsthand what goes on up there. For all we know, maybe they got Friday night beer blasts and drive-in movies.

BEV: (*Laughing in spite of herself*) Stop.

ROOTIE: No, I know that can't be. Because if Heaven is in the clouds, all those cars would come crashing through.

BEV: I can't believe you. You're like one of those kids they find in the woods after ten years. Haven't you ever heard of gravity?

ROOTIE: What?

, BEV: Gravity. That's what keeps things in the sky from falling on your head, like planes and cars. Wait—now I still don't see what all this has to do with you going in there first.

(*Bev moves her chair again. Rootie moves with her, eager to explain*)

ROOTIE: See, I got something I need Beau to help with. And Elvis was the most important person in Beau's life, he walked like him, dressed like him, he even tried to talk like him. So since Beau's birthday is also the very first day Elvis's house is open, I figured that if I were the first person inside, everything would all come together, and I'd get a sign from the Heavens, and Weebo would see me on TV and be real sorry about what he done, and everything would be all taken care of.

BEV: Honey, I'm gonna tell you something, and I hope you'll understand and not take it too personal. This is *nutty* talk. Now why don't you just run along . . .

ROOTIE: I don't care, I gotta do something. Beau's the only one who ever talked to me, and I know Elvis would help, he's such a good person.

BEV: Honey, they are both dead, may they rest in peace.

ROOTIE: I know, but there are some things more powerful than death even. Like Brigadoon.

BEV: Your mama ever tell you about fairy tales?

ROOTIE: I don't remember, she died when I was little. (*Wanting to change the subject*) What's your name? Mine is Rootie. Rootie Mallert. (*She sticks her hand out, and disconcerted, Bev shakes it*)

BEV: Huh? Oh, Bev. Bev Davies.

ROOTIE: Bev. That's a nice name.

BEV: I hate it. It's a fat name. Even feels fat. (*She puffs out her cheeks as she says it*) Bev. No wonder I got such a weight problem. When you got a fat name, the deck's already stacked against you. Now, Rootie. That's a skinny name. And look at you—see what I mean.

ROOTIE: (*She says it experimentally*) Rooo-tie. You're right. It does feel skinny.

BEV: See?

ROOTIE: Bev, now do you believe me, about Beau and being here, and all?

BEV: Well, I am just so confused I don't know what to think. How do I know you're not just making all of this up? You win my sorry feelings and then when I get good and sappy, you zip in right ahead of me.

(*Rootie runs to get a frayed picture out of her bag*)

ROOTIE: Look—there's Beau, and that's Weebo right next to him. They were best buddies. I never even figured he saw me, but I guess after Beau, I was the next best thing.

BEV: Nice-looking boys. Who are all the others?

ROOTIE: That's Billy, Barney, Baxter, and Brad. And that's my dad.

BEV: Where are they now?

ROOTIE: Well, Billy and Barney died in a car wreck right after Beau, then Baxter—no wait, I'm sorry, that ain't right. First Brad went off to California, then Baxter got thrown in jail for stabbing that guy in a bar, then Billy and Barney got killed, and Daddy died of a heart attack. I keep getting it all mixed up. But look, doesn't Beau look just like Elvis? And Weebo always dressed like Beau, so he looks like Elvis, too. A little.

BEV: You ain't seen nothing yet. (*Bev pulls out two pictures from her bag*) Take a look at these pictures. What can you see?

ROOTIE: One's Elvis. Who's the other one?

BEV: What do you mean, who's the other one, they both look exactly alike. That's my husband, Tyler.

ROOTIE: He's blond.

BEV: I know. Elvis was blond when he started.

ROOTIE: ELVIS?? Oh, Bev, Elvis wasn't blond, he had real, real dark hair.

BEV: Oh, no he didn't. When Elvis first started he had light hair, just like Ty's. The Colonel made him dye it. *That's* a little-known fact.

ROOTIE: Really?

BEV: Yes ma'am. So in a way, Ty looks more like Elvis than Elvis did.

ROOTIE: But Ty's got two chins.

BEV: So? What does that matter? Look at those faces—they could practically be identical twins.

ROOTIE: Even their eyes are different colors . . .

BEV: (*Highly insulted, she whips the pictures out of Rootie's hand*) Well, what the hell would you know anyway?

(*Bev sits down and pulls out a* Reader's Digest. *Rootie makes a move toward her then moves her pillow sideways. Thinking that Bev is unaware, she sneaks her pillow ahead slightly. Without looking up from her magazine, Bev snaps at her*)

BEV: *Don't* you move that rag another inch. Look honey, people have tried to sneak ahead of me every goddamn time and no one's made it yet. I didn't come all the way from Delaware three days early just to get a tan, so watch it.

ROOTIE: I was just trying to get comfortable.

BEV: Hah.

(*Bev turns back to the magazine and adjusts herself in the chair. Uncomfortable, she pulls a pillow out of her bag. It is a needlepoint depicting Elvis's face situated over a map of the world. She starts to place it behind her back*)

ROOTIE: (*Gasping*) Oh, Bev . . .

BEV: What?

ROOTIE: That's just about the most beautiful thing I ever seen. Where'd you get it?

BEV: I made it.

ROOTIE: *Made* it?

BEV: Yes. By hand.

ROOTIE: I cannot believe it. Weebo says that the only things a woman should make are dinner, the beds, and out.

BEV: Sounds like a Weebo remark.

(*Bev goes back to her magazine. Rootie nervously takes out compact, checks makeup, and dabs checks, trying to think of a new tack*)

ROOTIE: Bev—would you like a hard-boiled egg? I got one left. Would you like it?

BEV: No, I hate 'em.

ROOTIE: Oh.

BEV: Besides, I got everything I need right here. (*Bev opens her cooler and takes out a box of Mallomars. She begins eating one*)

ROOTIE: Oooooo, Mallomars—I ain't had a Mallomar since I was a baby almost. Weebo never lets me eat good stuff. Says it'll make me fat. I used to be real bad-looking. Weebo said I put the "ug" in ugly and that a woman could be pretty and dumb or smart and ugly, but dumb *and* ugly just don't work. So he's been fixing me up. And he said I should always hold my mouth open a little, like in the magazines. Weebo thinks that is a very sexy thing to do. (*She puts down the makeup she's been applying and illustrates this for Bev*)

BEV: Looks to me like sinus trouble. This Weebo fella gonna pick you up later?

ROOTIE: No. Why?

BEV: I'm thinking there're a few things I'd like to say to him. (*She grudgingly offers Rootie a Mallomar*)

ROOTIE: Oh, no thank you. He'll probably be out bowling or something. He's always out with the boys, playing or drinking. Or whatever they do.

BEV: Playing and drinking, huh? Oh hon, have I seen that before. I am gonna give you a little warning, honey. That man is sending you a sign.

ROOTIE: A sign?

BEV: Trust me, Rootie, I know what I'm talking about.

ROOTIE: I'm sorry, I don't think I understand.

BEV: Tyler and I almost hit the rocks.

ROOTIE: Why, what happened? What did you do?

BEV: Elvis, Lord bless him, saved us.

ROOTIE: You mean you knew him, you actually knew him?!

BEV: No, no, of course not. See, Tyler first started liking me because I am a very good listener. Ty was a big baseball star back in high school, and I tell you, those were the best years of his life. He has lots of stories about it. When we first started dating, I would listen to him for hours, and Ty would love every second of it. Well, we got married, and everything was fine, except Ty has what you might call a limited amount of those stories. After a while, he began repeating himself— over and over—and I began getting kind of bored. I guess he noticed because suddenly he was out with the boys all the time, or on the road, and we were just . . .

ROOTIE: That's it, that's just like Weebo, I never . . .

BEV: I am *not* finished. Anyway, as I was saying, we began drifting off from each other. I didn't know what the hell to do. Then one night Ty came home right after I'd seen Elvis in *Viva Las Vegas* on TV and I was all dreamy-like. Ty begun telling me all about this game he had played, and I pretended to listen, but really I was thinking about how cute Elvis was in that movie, and how romantic. I got this real happy look on my face and Ty went nuts. So I figured it out. Whenever he told me his stories, I'd daydream about Elvis. And Ty would say, "Bev, honey, I've met some beautiful women, some real clever ones, too, and you ain't one of them, but you can listen like nobody's business." And it's been wonderful ever since. Even the s——, the you-know-what, got better. That's why I had to come here today. I had to show my love and gratitude to the most important man in my life—Elvis.

ROOTIE: That's the smartest way of keeping a man I ever heard.

BEV: Thank you.

ROOTIE: Bev—is Tyler the only man you ever been with?

BEV: Of course he is, he's the only man I ever married, isn't he?

ROOTIE: Well—sometimes marriage ain't marriage, if you know what I mean.

BEV: I do. You have to forget about those woman itches, don't pay them any mind when they act up. You got to find ways to keep yourself busy. Ty's sometimes gone three or four weeks out of every month, but I just put on my records, dust all my statues, and plan the official layout of my memorial room. Takes a lot of effort to honor a person's memory. You want to do it just right.

ROOTIE: You got any kids, Bev?

BEV: Two boys.

ROOTIE: That's nice.

BEV: Sometimes.

ROOTIE: Weebo don't want kids. Says once you have 'em, you're never alone again.

BEV: What the hell does marriage have to do with being alone?

ROOTIE: Got me. I don't know a whole lot about it. Just fifteen when I got married.

BEV: Yes, well—when it comes to men and their women, marriage is the law, no matter what they are or are not doing to you. You remember that.

(*Bev turns back to magazine but just flips it, not able to concentrate*)

ROOTIE: Bev, maybe we should draw straws or play tic-tac-toe or something.

BEV: What?

ROOTIE: Well, the person who wins would go in first.

BEV: That's ridiculous.

ROOTIE: It's fair.

BEV: It's silly.

ROOTIE: It'd be a real easy way to decide.

BEV: If I win, you leave, right?

ROOTIE: Right. And if I win . . .

(*Bev cuts her off*)

BEV: Well, if we have to be democratic, I guess it's the thing to do. (*She gets a pad and pencil from her bag*) Here. I'll draw the board.

ROOTIE: Okay.

BEV: By the way, I think it is only fair to warn you that I'm real good at games.

ROOTIE: Thank you for telling me. You can go first.

BEV: Fine. Let's see. (*Examines board*) I chose O's.

(*Bev makes her mark with a flourish. The game begins*)

ROOTIE: Sure you don't want an egg?

BEV: Positive. Got anything else?

ROOTIE: I stole a couple of bags of chips off Weebo's truck before—Weebo drives a Frito-Lay delivery truck. It's his job.

BEV: No, you're kidding?

ROOTIE: Un uh, why?

BEV: Didn't I tell you? Ty's a driver too, that's why he's on the road so much.

ROOTIE: I cannot believe this. Both our husbands drive trucks, both of us have Marine relatives, and we both lost loved ones in car wrecks.

BEV: This world gets smaller and smaller, I tell you.

(*Rootie makes a mark then jumps up in excitement*)

ROOTIE: I won, I won—I can't believe it! I never won anything before.

BEV: It has to be two out of three. That's how all these games are played.

ROOTIE: Oh. Okay. (*Bev begins to draw board. Sound of car. Rootie looks up toward house*) Bev—look at that car. (*Bev is involved with picking her first move and doesn't pay much attention*)

BEV: What about it? Not the first car come by here.

ROOTIE: But it stopped. And a man got out. It's a real fancy one, too.

BEV: (*Gets up and stands next to Rootie*) Is it ever.

ROOTIE: He's at the gate. They parked.

BEV: Whoa—hold on one minute. I'll be goddamned if anyone's gonna sneak in front of us.

ROOTIE: (*Beginning to get hysterical*) But what can we do?

BEV: We could scream and scare them away.

ROOTIE: Then the guards might chase us off.

BEV: Well, we gotta do something.

ROOTIE: I can't . . . think, Bev, my mind's all empty.

BEV: Okay, hon, don't panic. I've got an idea.

ROOTIE: What?

BEV: I'll pretend I'm the housekeeper and tell them no one's allowed to wait on the grounds.

(*She starts off. Rootie stops her*)

ROOTIE: What should I do?

BEV: You guard the stuff.

(*Bev goes off. Rootie gathers stuff around her, like in an Indian circle, nervously humming a song like "I'm All Shook Up." There is the sound of a car leaving. Bev reenters*)

ROOTIE: What happened?

BEV: They *fell* for it! I think this calls for Mallomar toast. (*She goes to cooler and gets out two Mallomars*)

ROOTIE: That is so smart, Bev, I never would have thought of that.

BEV: I know. (*Hands a Mallomar to Rootie, very pleased with herself*) Here. (*Holds it out in a toast*) To Elvis.

ROOTIE: To Elvis.

(*They eat. Rootie hasn't eaten anything like this in years. She savors every bite*)

BEV: They'll be back, though.

ROOTIE: I know. Others'll start coming soon, too.

BEV: But we're here now.

ROOTIE: Yup. We're here now.

(*Bev begins to get pad, then changes mind. Starts rearranging the stuff*)

BEV: Phew. That was a scare. I think I need to relax a minute.

ROOTIE: I know what you mean. I'm sweating like crazy. (*She takes out compact and begins reapplying her makeup again*)

BEV: Don't you worry. I would have given them some fight, let me tell you.

ROOTIE: I bet you would have.

BEV: Hey. You should take it easy with that stuff, honey. You're starting to look like the wrong side of a lady, if you know what I mean.

ROOTIE: (*Continuing to apply it*) I gotta wear it. If my makeup comes off, it's the same old "ug-in-ugly" Rootie. It's like I'm always wearing one of those Halloween masks, Bev. Once you take it off, you ain't the princess no more.

BEV: Rootie, honey, it's really not everything. I swear, sometimes in those early mornings when Ty's about to leave, I look so awful I think he's gonna run out screaming and never come back. But he always does. Hell, it's 5:30 in the morning, who's gonna see you? Take some off.

ROOTIE: Never. It'd be worse than taking off my clothes.

BEV: Be brave, honey, no one's around.

ROOTIE: I said NO. I *can't.* What if he came, what if Elvis actually did come, and Beau came, all that I've been wishing and praying for, and here I was with all my makeup off??

BEV: Say no more. I understand.

ROOTIE: Wish I was like you, Bev. You're natural pretty. Beau used to say that you could always tell a natural pretty woman 'cause she had bones. Good face bones.

BEV: I'm telling you, honey, it's not all so natural. I gotta fix myself up real careful, too.

ROOTIE: I think your hair must be the prettiest I ever seen.

BEV: You really think so? I decided for the opening I'd do something kinda fancy, lots of curls and stuff. (*Bev pulls wig off and hands it to Rootie. Her own hair is bobby-pinned up*) Here. Wanna try it on?

ROOTIE: Huh? (*Bev offers it to her*) Sure you don't mind?

BEV: Wouldn't offer, would I?

ROOTIE: Guess not. Well . . . okay. Thank you. (*Rootie tries on the wig. It's a little like she's wearing a Ziegfeld headdress*) How do I look?

BEV: Gorgeous.

ROOTIE: Gosh . . . I feel so different.

(*She begins to move very cautiously then starts to really enjoy the sensation. Getting into the spirit of the elaborate hairdo, she begins*

*to pretend she is a country rock singer, slowly singing a hot Elvis
tune, having more and more fun as she goes.*

*Catching the spirit, Bev breaks in with another Elvis song, this
one a dancey, catchy melody.*

*Totally caught up in it, Rootie excitedly interrupts Bev with a
new selection. Bev joins in and the two begin to jitterbug as they
sing with great gusto.*

*Then Rootie begins a popular rock and roll number that both
Bill Hailey and Elvis Presley sang. Bev picks up the tune and sings
along. The women sing and dance themselves into a frenzied and
joyous peak. Then Bev suddenly stops. Rootie keeps singing)*

BEV: Wai—— wai—— wait one second! Elvis didn't sing
that.

ROOTIE: (*Stops dead*) Huh?

BEV: That wasn't an Elvis song, that was someone else.

ROOTIE: I know he sung it, it's Beau's most favorite record, he was always playing it . . .

(*She begins singing the song again. Bev interrupts her*)

BEV: Wait, honey, I'm telling you, it's someone else, damn,
it'll come to me in a minute.

ROOTIE: Bev . . .

BEV: Ah! Bill Hailey and the Comets, that's who, Bill
Hailey. Not Elvis.

ROOTIE: He *did*.

BEV: Now dear, I should know . . .

ROOTIE: He did. He recorded it in September 1956, it had
"Lawdy Miss Clawdy" on the other side, and it got all the way
to number 12. (*Pause*) I guess you just forgot.

BEV: What?

ROOTIE: It's okay you forgettin', Bev. Shoot, I forget
things that happened last week.

BEV: You're making it up . . .

ROOTIE: No, I'm not, I swear . . .

BEV: Yes, you are, you're trying to catch me again.

ROOTIE: I am not! He even sung it on TV, February 11,
1956.

BEV: Look, just because I shared my Mallomars and a little
small talk with you, don't start thinking I'm gonna let you
waltz in there ahead of me.

ROOTIE: Bev, I'm sorry, I just know all of this 'cause of
Beau . . .

BEV: You probably memorized it just before you left

home, sat up late with a book or something. Well, I will tell you one thing, I don't care what you "know," because the fact is that I was here before you, fair and square, and you damn well better remember that.

(*Rootie looks at Bev then begins running toward mansion. Bev grabs her*)

BEV: Wait a goddamn minute—where the hell do you think you're going?

ROOTIE: I gotta get in there first . . .

BEV: Hey, what the hell are you trying to pull?

ROOTIE: Bev, I told you, I have to reach 'em, I have—

BEV: I have had it up to *here* with all this nonsense. I've been listening to you rattle on and on with your wild stories, dumb games, and stupid husband, and it doesn't mean anything, *anything*. I'm sick of them. No one ever stopped me before and I'll be goddamned if a crazy runt like you is gonna get in my way this time, do you hear me?!

(*She has heaved all Rootie's possessions at her as she speaks*)

ROOTIE: Weebo tried . . .

BEV: I don't want to hear another word about that son of a bitch.

ROOTIE: He takes care of me, Bev . . .

BEV: Oh yeah, then why are you traveling around with nothing but a paper bag and some hard-boiled eggs?

ROOTIE: I like these eggs now. I didn't at first, but now I do.

(*Bev totally loses patience as Rootie tries to dodge past her. Grabs Rootie and starts shaking her*)

BEV: WHAT THE HELL ARE YOU TALKING ABOUT?!

ROOTIE: Stop, please . . . (*Bev lets go. Rootie takes a breath. Removes wig and clutches it in her hand with other possessions*) Well—where we live in Luziana is a real small town kind of near the Gulf. We're Cajun folks. Beau's real name was Beaufils. Know what that means?

BEV: No.

ROOTIE: Beautiful son. Beaufils.

BEV: So?

ROOTIE: Well, everybody's been there a while, so we all pretty much know each other. The guy's are all good buddies and do stuff together . . .

BEV: Like playing and drinking.

ROOTIE: Right. Anyway, about a month ago, right down the street from us, some guys who work on one of the oil rigs off the Gulf took a house. And one of the guys was named Drew. And the funny thing about Drew was that he looked so much like Beau. I know I wasn't just seeing things, because Weebo noticed too, and they got real close. They'd go hunt or fish the bayou, and we'd have dinner, all three of us. It was real nice. (*She stops*)

BEV: What'd they do, Rootie?

ROOTIE: Well, Weebo had to make a run up to Shreveport for a week, but Drew kept coming around. We'd go for walks, or just sit and talk sometimes. Then I noticed something real strange—Beau used to kind of turn his head sideways like this (*Shows Bev*) when he asked you a question. One day Drew was asking me something and he did the exact same thing, turned his head just that way. Gave me prickles on my arm. That's when I decided I would share my most special place with him. See, I got this special place that Beau used to take me to. I never been there with anyone else, even Weebo. But I had to be 100 percent sure I could share it with Drew, so I said, "Drew, who is your absolute most favorite hero who ever was?"

BEV: And when he said Elvis, you knew.

ROOTIE: Like in a vision or something. So last night I got all dressed up, and at midnight, I took Drew there. About a mile from us is this dirt road. And if you follow it, you come to two long lines of the most beautiful trees you ever seen, with a big wide alley between them. And you follow this alley for a ways, thinking you'll come to something real neat at the end. But all there is is a field. It's where a plantation was about a hundred years ago, but it burnt down and now all that's left is the alley of trees. When I was little, Beau used to take me there late at night, put me on his shoulders, and run down the alley. And sometimes we'd dance in all the quiet and dark, just Beau and me. When Drew and me got there, all the stars were out and it was just like I was little again. Everything was so beautiful. But then I saw that there were these people down on the field having a picnic or something. I didn't want to go, but Drew pulled my arm and said to come on. Then I saw who it was. It was Weebo and all his friends.

BEV: But how did they know where it was?

ROOTIE: Drew told them. See, Weebo told Drew I had this

place I always went off to by myself and he was just dying to know where it was. Drew bet him fifty dollars that he could find out all about it. Weebo was so mad at me. Kept yelling that I cost him fifty bucks and I was just another stupid tramp.

BEV: Poor thing.

ROOTIE: It wasn't just that. They'd all been drinking a while, I guess, and Weebo was real drunk. He grabbed me hard and yelled to all the other guys, "You wanna see what Drew could've ended up with?" Then he poured beer onto a napkin, grabbed my face, and began scrubbing off all my makeup. He just kept scrubbing and pouring, and my face got all red and scratchy, my hair got all wet, my clothes were just fulla beer. Then he stood me right in the middle of everyone and said, "Now, Rootie, you gotta walk all the way home through the center of town just the way you are. I want to be sure everyone can see the real Rootie Mallert for once." So I walked home all fulla beer, then I washed myself, took my kitchen money, and left. I had to. I couldn't face anyone again after what they seen. And my special place was gone, it was like it burnt down all over again.

BEV: How much money have you got?

ROOTIE: I got about thirty dollars. And my favorite pillow. See, Bev, where I come from, everyone's always putting together special things so they can touch God, charms and stuff. So I figured if I came here right at this special time, everything might come together, like Beau's birthday, and the house opening, and maybe I could touch . . . (*Rootie trails off. Pause*)

BEV: I have got a very wonderful treat here. Look. (*She pulls a pack of strawberry-marshmallow covered Sno-balls out of her cooler*) These are my absolute favorite ever. Here.

ROOTIE: Ooo. I love Sno-balls. Thanks, Bev.

(*They eat in silence for a moment*)

BEV: Beautiful place, isn't it?

ROOTIE: Most beautiful I ever seen. I feel like I should kneel or something.

BEV: You should only kneel for God, honey.

ROOTIE: Well, I'm not for certain God's there, but I know Elvis is.

BEV: When he died, I came right here. Drove straight through from my house in Wilmington without any stop but for gas. I swear, I thought my heart would crack open. I sent a $100 wreath to the grave. Ty said I wouldn't even send him a wreath like that.

ROOTIE: Was he hurt?

BEV: No, Ty's very practical. He says it's better that I should chase after a dead man than a live one.

ROOTIE: Bev, do you think Beau'll hate me now? 'Cause I lost the special place?

BEV: 'Course not, baby. (*Pause*) Rootie—I'm sorry I jumped on you before.

ROOTIE: Oh—that's okay, Bev.

(*Rootie hugs her pillow to her chest and begins to nod off. Bev notices*)

BEV: You tired, Roo?

ROOTIE: Guess so.

BEV: You're gonna get one fierce crick if you fall asleep like that. (*Motions to tent*) Why don't you take a rest in there?

ROOTIE: What about you, Bev?

BEV: Too stuffy for me. And here. (*She hands Rootie her Elvis needlepoint*) Bet that'll give you nice dreams.

ROOTIE: Oh Bev, it's so beautiful. I'm afraid I might get hair dirt on it or something.

BEV: That's just silly. But wait, better give me the wig. (*Bev takes wig, then goes into her bag and pulls out a wig stand. She carefully arranges the wig on the stand*) There. Now you can wear it when you take the very first step into the mansion.

ROOTIE: Bev . . .

BEV: Come on, rest. Sun's almost up.

(*Rootie starts into tent, then stops*)

ROOTIE: Now I feel kinda bad. You loved him for so long—

BEV: (*Gives Rootie a little push*) Just go. Sleep.

ROOTIE: Okay. (*She starts to go, then turns around and impulsively hands Bev her beat-up pillow*) Here. This is real comfortable. It was Beau's, and he used to push it and mash it until it got all flat and mushy the way he wanted.

BEV: Thank you, Rootie. (*She looks at her, then gives her a big hug, which is returned by Rootie*) Tell Beau and Elvis I send all my love.

ROOTIE: I will.

(*She goes into tent. Bev sits silently for a moment. Then she reaches into her bag and pulls out a liquor bottle in the shape of Elvis playing the guitar in a hot pink suit. Bev pops open the bottle, pours a shot into a Dixie cup, closes the bottle, and raises drink in a toast)*

BEV: This one's for you, Ty baby, whatever highway you're on right now. God bless you.

(She takes a drink, then puts away the bottle. Looks first at the house then at the tent. She picks up her cooler and places it in front of the tent, then places her wig on top of the cooler. As she does this, she begins to sing quietly. This time she sings Elvis's most tender love ballad.

Still singing, she folds up her chair and picks up her bag.

Then, looking straight at the house as if to bid her idol a final farewell, she sings the final two lines of the song.

She pauses for a moment, then slowly exits without looking back)

The End

Joel Ensana

THE SACRED
DANCE OF
YELLOW THUNDER

Joel Ensana

Joel Ensana returns to *The Best Short Plays* with the publication of *The Sacred Dance of Yellow Thunder*. Published here for the first time, the play is based on an actual conflict in a Gordon, Nebraska, American Legion Hall between veteran members and a local native American Indian. With poignant insight, the playwright links the conflict between the whites and the Indian to parallel abuses during the previous century. Mr. Ensana dedicates this play to the Indians at Camp Yellow Thunder, Black Hills, who are attempting to establish a traditional Sioux Indian village, and thanks especially Iron Teeth, a Cheyenne-Sioux woman, and Luther Standing Bear, a Lakota and a member of the Teton or Western Sioux.

Mr. Ensana's earlier appearance in this series was in the 1969 edition with *Please, No Flowers*, a touching, bittersweet comedy that won several major awards and has since proved popular in high-school and college productions. In 1965, *Please, No Flowers* was a prize winner in the Des Moines Drama Workshop's play contest, and later that year it achieved first prize in the national contest sponsored by the YM/YWHA Arts Council of Philadelphia (with playwright Edward Albee as the final adjudicator). In 1967, the play took top honors in the Norman Corwin One-Act Play Contest, with a subsequent production supervised by Mr. Corwin at San Diego State College. In 1969, the play was produced by the highly regarded American Conservatory Theatre (ACT) at the Forum Theatre, San Francisco.

Other plays by Mr. Ensana have appeared on television, in colleges throughout the country, at the Quaigh Theatre and the Joseph Jefferson theatre in New York, and at the Group Repertory Theater in Los Angeles.

A graduate of San Francisco State College with a B.A. in creative writing and an M.A. in drama, the author received a Sam S. Shubert Fellowship in Playwriting and had a production of his work staged at the college.

Mr. Ensana, who now makes his home in California, was born in New Brunswick, New Jersey.

As this volume goes to press, Mr. Ensana reports that *The Sacred Dance of Yellow Thunder* is among the finalists in the Maxwell Anderson Playwriting Contest, sponsored by Mrs. Anderson and the Stamford Community Arts Council.

Characters:

RAYMOND YELLOW THUNDER, *a fifty-one-year-old American Indian*

RHONDA, *an attractive girl in her twenties*

JOE, *a veteran of World War II, in his fifties but attempting to look and act younger*

CHARLIE, *a veteran of the Korean War, in his early forties*

HARRY, *a veteran of World War I, in his late seventies or early eighties*

VOICE OF AN OLD INDIAN WOMAN

VOICE OF AN OLD INDIAN MAN

Time:

February 1972.

Place:

The American Legion Hall in a small town in Nebraska. At stage rear are a library-type table and chairs. Displayed behind the table are American and State-of-Nebraska flags. At stage left are a small bar, several stools, and a juke box. Photos of past American Legion leaders are displayed on the wall.

Scene:

Lights up on stage left but not on entire set. Raymond Yellow Thunder is standing in a doorway next to the entrance of the American Legion Hall. Smoking a cigarette and trying to keep out of the freezing wind, he looks off into the distance and hears the voice of an old Indian woman.

VOICE OF INDIAN WOMAN: The entrance to the Black Hills was through a narrow passage known as Buffalo Gap. The wild animals came in through this gap for protection from the icy blasts of winter and so did the Sioux. There were springs of clear water and plenty of wood. Nature seemed to hold us in her arms. And there we were satisfied to live in our tipis all through the rough weather. . . .

(*Joe and Rhonda enter, hurrying past Raymond. They see him but pay no attention because they are anxious to get in out of the cold. They enter the hall*)

VOICE OF INDIAN MAN: In our country it grew very cold. The snow would freeze very hard after it fell. After the snow had frozen hard, we would start to play the *hu-ta-na-cu-te* game. On clear days we played this game dressed in breech-cloth and moccasins only. In those days, we did not have the white man's shirt and stockings, but we did not feel the cold, as the game was very exciting and the exercise kept us warm. I was born in the Black Hills—ninety-five years ago. The time of my birth was in the moon when the berries are ripe. My father was a Cheyenne, my mother was a Sioux . . .

(*Lights out on Raymond and lights up on the interior of the hall where Harry is seated at the table and Charlie is dragging up a case of beer from behind the bar. They are both wearing Legionnaire hats. Rhonda and Joe remove their coats, Joe helping Rhonda*)

RHONDA: (*She looks about the hall*) I don't believe this. Where's the band? No balloons—just those two old flags. Hey, I thought you said this was to be a dance party.

JOE: We're going to have music, but we gotta have the business meeting first.

RHONDA: Oh, no, a jukebox . . . (*She goes to the jukebox*) I came out on a freezing night like this—to dance to records. (*She looks at the titles of the records*) Not one rock number—not one shit-kicking country-western.

CHARLIE: Hey, Joe, you think I can get some help down here?

JOE: There's an Indian outside, maybe he can give you a hand.

(*Charlie enters carrying a box of liquor bottles*)

CHARLIE: Yeah, think I'll just try that. Basement needs a good cleaning, too.

JOE: Hell, Charlie, he'll probably do it for nothing. Just to get his ass in out of the cold. It's freezing out there.

(*Charlie exits*)

RHONDA: And that's all this big old barn is good for—it's not for partying, that's for sure. And certainly not with that old geezer being in charge. Well, I mean, my mother says he has the first penny he ever made.

JOE: Rhonda, will you please shut the hell up. You know, if it weren't for that "old geezer" you just might not be here. Yeah, you might have been born a German.

RHONDA: You horse's ass. My grandfather told me all about "good old Harry Dunwell." He never saw a German except on the newsreel because he never left the country. Army supplies. And that's how he started his hardware business. Stole the government blind. Well, can I at least have a drink while you're over there—talking big business?

JOE: All right, all right . . .

RHONDA: And Joey, the jukebox. I promise I'll keep it low. (*Charlie returns with Raymond*)

CHARLIE: You're right. It's getting colder. This here's Yellow Thunder.

(*Joe and Rhonda look at each other and laugh*)

JOE: Sounds like a big fart after a dinner of burritos and beans.

RHONDA: Or like something after a nuclear bomb.

CHARLIE: Come on, Yellow Thunder—booze is down in the basement—you can bring up as many as you can.

RHONDA: Save your strength—they just need one. Nobody's here as usual—big American Legion dance—social event of the year.

JOE: Goddamn! You know, this is the last time I'm bringing you . . .

RHONDA: You can say that again. Next time I date someone old enough to be my father, it's Vegas or nothing.

(*Joe hands her a drink*)

JOE: Here, now please keep quiet, will you—and you know, maybe next month I will take you to Vegas.

RHONDA: And the jukebox, remember—I don't believe the numbers—another time, another place . . .

(*Joe plugs the cord of the jukebox in—Rhonda presses some of the buttons. A record such as one by Glenn Miller is heard. Charlie returns from the basement*)

CHARLIE: Nice guy. He's Sioux. Well, I'll have a quick drink and then we can start the meeting.

(*Lights out on the hall. Lights up on Raymond Yellow Thunder in basement, merely spotlighted as he is moving a crate but hearing the Indian Voice*)

VOICE OF INDIAN MAN: My father had led his men many times in battle and when I was born he gave me the name of

Ota Kte or Plenty Kill because he had killed many enemies.
But in those days it was considered a disgrace, not an honor,
for a Sioux to kill a white man. Killing a pale-face was not
looked upon as a brave act. We were taught that the white
man was much weaker than ourselves . . .

(*Lights out on Raymond. Lights up on the table where the three
men are now seated, holding their meeting*)

HARRY: That Indian, is he a friend of yours?

CHARLIE: Nah, just helping out—we can pay him out of
the kitty.

HARRY: I thought maybe he was a new member.

JOE: We're not that desperate. Not yet, anyway.

CHARLIE: I thought we were. Christ, nobody's showing up.
You know, I can remember guys with their wives—party
would get wild—and I'd wind up with someone's nice, plump,
love-starved wife.

HARRY: And we lost another member last week. Gus Far-
ney. First World War navy man. That Gus knew the best
jokes. We'll have to send flowers.

CHARLIE: I'll make a note of it.

JOE: Never came to the meetings. I never met the guy.

HARRY: Before your time. Sickly—got influenza in 1917.
Well, have you been doing any recruiting?

JOE: Yeah, and I thought sure I had one. A Viet vet—
truck driver—nice guy. I told him about all the benefits. Said
he didn't want to hear about that war or any other. Said he
just wanted to forget the whole fucking thing.

HARRY: I would, too, if I were him. First war this country
didn't win. Bunch of gutless cowards. I told you to forget
about those guys. Spoiled brats. I heard they even had gook
room-boys. Best equipment, too.

CHARLIE: Their heads all soft anyway. I heard they were
all high on one thing or another.

JOE: Look, we gotta get some new blood.

HARRY: Fewer members make it more exclusive. We still
have enough members for a parade.

JOE: Yeah, but not for a dance.

CHARLIE: They'll come around, you'll see. Man's gotta get
away from his wife sometime. Legion Hall—only place you
can really be yourself—unless you're out hunting.

HARRY: Speaking of wives, could you tell yours to lower
the jukebox.

JOE: She's not my wife, Harry. My wife ran off a few years

back. She's my date—and young ones—they like their music loud—very loud. (*He leaves the table*)

HARRY: Don't know why he'd bring her anyway. We never brought our wives or our girlfriends. Had more fun that way. Could say whatever we damned pleased—tell the dirtiest jokes. One of the reasons for joining the Legion—just being out with the boys.

CHARLIE: We're having a dance tonight, Harry, remember. Thought that might bring in some new members, but the weather's against us.

HARRY: Only thing that'll bring in new members is a nice big war. One that we win. Something patriotic. Hell, I remember in the first war we had posters, I mean, these great posters, and the music—none of that shit she's playing—songs with words everyone could sing and words that moved you—to cry, to shout—not just to move your ass to. Yeah, we knew how to give a war in those days. I mean, Americans—we were Americans then.

CHARLIE: You know, I always said, you got Ed Sullivan to thank for it all—oh, yeah, bringing over the Beatles . . . it started it all—dope, long hair.

(*Joe has walked over to Rhonda at the jukebox. Rhonda is moving to the music*)

JOE: I told you—keep it low. We're talking business. And watch the drinks.

RHONDA: You have to get something for your dues. You know, Joey, I am so goddamn tired of this dull, boring life. I wish my daddy had never moved back here. I loved it out there in California. And as for you—you are one boring person. Dismal. I mean, this town—this club—it's getting you nowhere. Joe, you know what, I'm dropping you. Oh, yeah, once this party is over—I am dropping you.

JOE: Now, Rhonda, I'm sorry. It's the weather. Look, just a few more minutes and we'll be dancing our asses off. Shoot, we'll be having a ball soon.

RHONDA: If it wasn't so cold out, I'd have left soon as I saw no one else was coming. You know, I find you men boring. I mean—boring!

JOE: Here . . . (*He quickly mixes her a drink*) Have another one. We'll be through soon. Just gotta read last month's minutes.

RHONDA: Big deal—like it mattered. I remember the last parade. Six people showed up—and all of them were relatives. Everyone else was out of town.

JOE: Now, that's not true. Don't you remember that whole bus load of protesters.

RHONDA: I don't count them . . . on second thought they turned out to be more fun. I almost left town with them—would have if they hadn't been arrested.

JOE: Here you go . . . (*He hands her a drink*) Now why are you watching that Indian so much?

RHONDA: Because he's moving—only live thing in the place.

JOE: Has he been trying to make you?

RHONDA: Joe, please, your meeting. I'm in a dancing mood—and not Indian style. Although, right now, I might even do that—at least I'd be warm.

JOE: Rhonda, if I catch him eyeing you . . .

RHONDA: That's all I need—from one loser to another . . . and just what would you do—wave your old flag at him—show him your medals . . .

CHARLIE: (*Calling over*) Hey, Joe—Harry can't stay all night.

JOE: I'm coming. (*He hurries over to the table*) Sorry about that.

HARRY: Isn't she a little young for you? A man gets your age—hard to keep up with a girl like that.

JOE: It's not easy, I'll tell you. She just wants to go, go, go, but she sure makes me feel good. A hundred years young . . . yeah, I need that girl—yup, right now I really need that girl.

HARRY: Maybe I should get me one.

CHARLIE: Now, come on—sooner we get this meeting over with sooner we can start the party.

(*Lights dim on the men at the table as they discuss financial matters and lower on Rhonda, now seated at the bar and watching Raymond Yellow Thunder. Lights bright on Raymond as he pauses a moment before opening a crate*)

VOICE OF INDIAN WOMAN: My grandmother was a medicine woman. She told me lots of things about how to care for myself. She said that if I should be bitten by a rattlesnake I must not get excited and run as that would heat up my blood. She told me a cedar tree is the safest place when lightning is flashing. Once in a while an old Sioux man talks as if he himself had killed Custer, but most of the old men say that none of the Indians in the fight recognized any one soldier there. I have heard different old men say: "All white men look the same to me." At our tribal gatherings at Pine Ridge we played old-time Indian games. In one game four people stood in a row and sang four different songs. One had a war-song, another a death-song . . .

(The Indian Voice is interrupted by Rhonda calling to Raymond. Lights now brighter on Rhonda and Raymond)

RHONDA: Hey, you—Yellow Cloud.

RAYMOND: It's Yellow Thunder.

RHONDA: I like Yellow Cloud better. Lightning and thunder scare me. Do you dance?

RAYMOND: Yeah, but not rock and roll . . . the fox-trot, a two-step rhumba.

RHONDA: I mean Indian dances. You know, like dancing around a fire, beating your tom-tom.

RAYMOND: When I was a kid, but it's been so long I've forgotten.

RHONDA: You know, my father took us to Disneyland once . . . when we lived in California, and they had all these Indians dancing. It was beautiful . . . looking down, looking up . . . *(She mimics an Indian)* their feathers shaking . . . and bells, bells on their boots. I like this number . . . great for dancing.

RAYMOND: Not for me, beats all wrong.

RHONDA: I can teach you. I taught Joe, and at his age it wasn't easy. Come on. It's freezing in here and they'll take hours, you know, once they get started—talking about the wars they were in. Well, I mean, how many times can you relive the happiest days of your life.

RAYMOND: Over and over again. Look, I still have some more boxes to bring up. Hey, I was cold out there.

RHONDA: Just one. I know you've got it in you. Those Indians at Disneyland—I never saw dancers move like that. Like a spirit was really in them.

RAYMOND: But were they really Indians or professional dancers from Hollywood . . . or those robots made in Japan?

RHONDA: They were real. And believe me, Walt Disney would never lie to children—my father maybe, the Pope, the president, but never Walt Disney.

RAYMOND: Probably from a different tribe.

RHONDA: Playing it safe. Look, I don't blame you. It's freezing out there, but this whole town plays it safe . . . like Joey, and it's . . . boring.

RAYMOND: I'm not a member and I catch colds easy.

RHONDA: Neither am I. In fact, come morning, I'll never

be seeing that old warrior again. Good for a laugh now and then and free dinners at Velmas on the highway. But, I mean, I know every move he made during the war. Every buddy he ever had. You know, I'd still love to see you dance—Disneyland, happiest days of my life.

RAYMOND: Just like those old soldiers, uhn . . .

RHONDA: All right, I admit it. You see, we were all together then, and somehow, Disneyland, I guess it's catching. Even my folks joined in the fun. Now my daddy's gone. Oh, yeah, right after he brought us back to this hole he took off. What about you?

RAYMOND: They never really took place, not for me. The stories the old folks told about the good old days, but they all took place before my time.

(*As the lights dim very slowly an Indian Voice is heard*)

VOICE OF INDIAN MAN: Early the next morning I was called to climb to the top of the tipi and remove the little sticks that held it together. Soon we were moving toward the south. We boys climbed on our ponies and rode alongside the moving caravan, chasing everything in sight. We made three camps before we arrived where it was thought the buffalo would be . . .

(*Lights out. Lights up on the men at the table*)

JOE: I don't understand how they could have lost. Hell, they were in Vietnam fighting for democracy.

CHARLIE: So were we in Korea, and look what they've got.

HARRY: You don't regret it, do you, Charlie?

CHARLIE: I was over there for two years. My cousin—now he played it smart—got out of going by entering college. But, hell no, I don't regret it. I met a lot of nice guys over there. Look, my country calls, I go. Besides, it was the only time I ever did get out of Nebraska.

JOE: Next war's going to be the one that really ends all wars. The one that will get rid of those Commies once and for all.

HARRY: I'm only sorry I won't be here to see it. Well, I mean, man can only live so long. Hell, there used to be sixty men at this very table from the first war. Now there's only me and Eddie Luce, and he's in the old soldiers' home. You know, I can remember one parade on a Fourth of July—a veteran of the Civil War leading the parade. He was in a wheelchair, but he was still there, waving that flag.

JOE: And this year, Harry, you're it—parade marshal.

HARRY: And no one to watch. Well, you remember last year. Each year the turnout gets smaller. All the young people—either moving out west or too busy enjoying the day off. I hardly sell any poppies anymore.

JOE: It'll be changing, you'll see . . . soon as we get the right man in the White House.

HARRY: One good slogan . . . a gimmick. Hell, Viet vets, they're men, just like you and me . . . put the fear of God in their hearts soon as they accumulate enough money, get a house . . . a good slogan like "for God and country."

JOE: "The right to bear arms."

CHARLIE: Or something for nothing . . . like a year's free membership and all the beer you can drink for a month.

JOE: Or a girl like my little Rhonda, popping naked out of a cannon. Hey, you see what I see?

CHARLIE: He's just talking to her while he's working.

JOE: And that's how trouble always starts . . . someone just talking. Hell, let's get this meeting over with. I propose this meeting be adjourned. And then on with the party.

CHARLIE: I second the motion.

HARRY: (*He pounds a gavel*) Meeting adjourned. I'll have the usual, Charlie.

CHARLIE: One boilermaker coming up. Hey, Harry, I've got a good one for you. You see, there were these two nigger kids—sitting in front of a whorehouse . . .

(*Lights out on the table. Lights up on the bar as the three men join Rhonda and Raymond. They are all drinking now, except Raymond, and are beginning to feel the drinks*)

JOE: It's sure quiet here. You people plotting something?

RHONDA: Yes, a war.

CHARLIE: Did you finish bringing up those cases?

RAYMOND: Almost.

RHONDA: We were just talking . . . about dancing.

JOE: As long as you're just talking about it. (*He draws her close*) Anybody else come in?

RHONDA: Are you kidding? And it isn't just the weather. It's the atmosphere. I'm bored, Joe. I mean it.

JOE: I never met someone who got bored so easy. Well, what the hell can I do about it? Look, people just aren't patriots anymore.

CHARLIE: I think those Viet vets are ashamed to show their faces.

RHONDA: There's no shame in losing.

CHARLIE: Is that right, Yellow Road?

JOE: Yeah, talk about losers.

RHONDA: They shouldn't have been in Vietnam to begin with.

HARRY: What do you know? Here, have another drink. Or is it only pot you young girls have now? Why if it weren't for men like us the enemy would have taken over years ago. Girls like you being raped . . . work camps.

CHARLIE: I'm glad we're not getting any new members. Yeah, let's keep it exclusive—only good Americans.

RHONDA: And only winners are good Americans, right, Charlie? Joe, can we have some music? It's like a morgue in here.

HARRY: Maybe this place needs a woman's touch. I remember when we used to have parties and whole familes would show up. Maybe if we had a theme . . . like July Fourth . . . or an Hawaiian one.

RHONDA: He's right. You do need a gimmick . . . and some new music. Young guys want music from their time in life.

JOE: An Indian theme. Yeah, what about an Indian theme?

CHARLIE: That sounds good. And Yellow Sky could help out. Hey, Yellow Sky, forget the boxes. What about it? We can get the pickup with the loudspeaker and drive around town announcing our dance.

RHONDA: With costumes . . . right, babe? You know, in Disneyland, they have these people walking around dressed up like Dumbo and Mickey Mouse.

JOE: The vets could wear their old uniforms. Yeah, I still have mine. I have this bomber jacket—even my old fatigues.

RHONDA: Do they still fit?

(*She pats his beer belly. Joe and Charlie look at Raymond*)

RAYMOND: Hey, don't look at me. It's freezing out there. I was the only one on the streets.

CHARLIE: We'll turn the loudspeaker way up, give out free booze.

HARRY: No free booze. We'll just get all the wrong people. They said the army in Vietnam was seventy percent black.

RHONDA: That's better than no people, right, Joe? And think of all the money you can make—a door fee. Why, then, Harry, you can have all those spectacular fireworks the next Fourth of July.

JOE: I don't know, you start giving away drinks . . .

RHONDA: Joey, I'm bored. Look, you go with me, you'll have to quit. I mean, no party, no Rhonda. You know, I was just saying to Yellow Bird. I liked it out West. You know, I might just move to Anaheim. It never freezes there. Someone my own age . . . surfing . . . hitchhiking on Sunset Boulevard.

JOE: Come on, we'll get the truck . . . bring back some people. Fill up the place. Like old times, Harry. When you were young—before everyone started dying off, started turning pinko. Yellow Feather, come on, and we'll give you a bottle of the best . . . Jim Beam.

RAYMOND: I still have some more boxes to move.

CHARLIE: The hell with the boxes. We need that red ass of yours.

RHONDA: But dressed like that he doesn't look like an Indian. The ones at Disneyland wore these loincloths.

RAYMOND: Not me, I catch colds easy.

HARRY: I knew some Indians—winter, summer . . . always hunting, practically naked. Just a few rags.

JOE: Come on, chief. Besides the cold air, it'll get that ass of yours dancing.

RHONDA: And I'm sure he can dance. Rain dances, sacred dances, dances to the gods.

CHARLIE: Maybe he'll do a dance . . . to make it as warm in Nebraska as it is in Californiay.

JOE: (Speaking to Rhonda) And then you might never leave, right, babe?

RHONDA: Minute to minute . . . I live from minute to minute.

HARRY: All the young people do these days. Hell, we offer those Viet vets the best funeral benefits, death insurance, and they don't care about those things—living just for today, and all of it . . . pleasure, just pleasure.

(Raymond has slowly walked away and is picking up his backpack and jacket. Joe and Charlie notice that he is planning to leave. They surround him)

RAYMOND: Look, I told you, I catch colds easy. I'm not going.

(Joe reaches behind the bar and brings out a handgun)

JOE: The hell you're not.

RAYMOND: You palefaces and your guns. Uhn, where would you be without them?

(*Charlie and Joe grab him then strip him down to his shorts. Rhonda is excited by the sudden activity. They drag him out, Rhonda following*)

RHONDA: (*Singsong manner*) Yellow Fish is a party-pooper, a party-pooper. Well, I mean, just a few dances. I'll hold the flashlight on you.

JOE: That'll keep you warm. Now just start dancing.

(*Raymond, Joe, Charlie, and Rhonda exit*)

HARRY: Boys will be boys. I remember some of the old days . . . some of the tricks we pulled. I remember one convention up in Chicago . . . (*He laughs*) I'll never forget that night . . .

(*Lights dim out. The sound of a strong, cold wind and of drunken laughter is heard, the starting up of a truck, then of a voice speaking over a loudspeaker*)

CHARLIE: Come one, come all! It's Indian night at the American Legion. Two dollars admission for all the beer you want plus a sacred dance performed by Chief Yellow Sands . . . veterans free.

RHONDA: (*Offstage*): I knew he could do it.

CHARLIE: (*Offstage*): You'd dance too—with a gun pointed at you and weather like this.

(*Lights up on interior of hall. There is a strong spot center stage, dim lights stage left on Raymond, Rhonda, Charlie, Joe, and Harry*)

RAYMOND: Look, man, I'm freezing. . . .

JOE: Give him a drink, Harry.

HARRY: (*Using the theatre audience as their own*) I've never seen so many people come out in weather like this.

RHONDA: Anything to escape being bored to death.

CHARLIE: I hope the beer doesn't run out.

JOE: Come on, Yellow Sun, start dancing.

RAYMOND: I told you, I don't know any Indian dances.

RHONDA: Oh, yes, he does. The M.C. at Disneyland said they hand it down from father to son . . . sacred dances.

RAYMOND: If you didn't have that gun, white man . . .

HARRY: I turned the music on.

(*They hear a big-band number*)

RAYMOND: Glenn Miller? Ignorant . . . you are so ignorant.

RHONDA: He's right. Shut it off . . . better nothing than that.

HARRY: Well, you better hurry up. Beer's almost all gone.

RHONDA: The music . . . it's in their soul. I wish I had it.

JOE: Didn't I tell you, honey . . . I promised you a party.

CHARLIE: Goddamn you, Injun, start dancing.

JOE: Hell, yes. You've seen Western movies, haven't you? Charles Bronson, Tonto.

(*Harry steps into the spotlight and speaks to the crowd*)

HARRY: Now, folks, especially you mothers and wives, I want you to tell your sons and husbands, the ones that are veterans, this here's a special offer—first year's membership is free. And now, like we promised you—a sacred dance by that greatest of Indian warriors—Yellow . . . Yellow . . .

RAYMOND: Thunder! My name is Raymond Yellow Thunder. And I'm freezing. Why don't you turn the heat up—cheap bastards.

HARRY: Chief Yellow Thunder!

(*Joe changes the light to a bright orange as Yellow Thunder steps into the spot*)

RHONDA: A special light. Oh, Joe, it's just beautiful.

JOE: It's the one we use for our swearing-in ceremony.

(*There is complete silence as Raymond takes a deep breath. The Voice of the old Indian man is heard*)

VOICE OF INDIAN MAN: I told them I did not expect ever to be as great a man as my father had been. Then the chiefs began to sing a brave song and all got up to dance. Now that I was one of them, I had to dance with them. That was the first time in my life that I had the honor of dancing with the old chiefs.

(*Raymond begins to dance, slowly at first*)

RHONDA: Oh, Joe, it's perfect. Just like when I was a kid.

JOE: Hell, Indians for you, Dagos for me. I remember we were entering this town in Sicily and these young girls, tiny little things, do anything for something to eat . . .

HARRY: I never saw an Indian dance like that. Course, they all have different dances. Depends on the tribe, I guess.

CHARLIE: What's it mean? All that mumbo jumbo.

RHONDA: I think this is the one to the sun-god. I remember the man saying it had to do with things growing—the corn and the trees, the rivers full of fish.

(*Raymond is now dancing faster. The Old Indian Man's voice is heard*)

VOICE OF INDIAN MAN: It was about the middle of the summer of 1879 that I saw the last great Sun Dance of the Sioux near Rosebud Agency. A man would go to the Medicine Man and say, "I will sacrifice my body to the Wakan Tanka, or Big Holy, for the one who is sick." Or if the buffalo were beginning to get scarce, someone would sacrifice himself so that the tribe might have something to eat. These men were to dance for three or four days without food or water. The braves started dancing as soon as the sun started to rise. Some of their relatives cried, others sang to praise the brave.

RHONDA: I've never seen dance steps like that.

CHARLIE: Looks to me like he's just trying to get warm. Hell, I move that way while shaving on cold mornings.

RHONDA: You've got no sense of poetry. And the audience—it's so quiet—like they're having a religious experience.

(*Raymond's shorts have fallen off*)

JOE: (*Laughs*) That's cause he just lost his loincloth.

(*Raymond is now kneeling*)

RHONDA: It's beautiful, but you know, Joe, come to think of it, I liked the ride on the Matterhorn much better.

JOE: Yeah, well, you stick with me and maybe I'll take you to Europe. Yeah, I'd like to see the places I fought in . . . those old battlefields.

HARRY: Those noises he's making . . . I've been hearing it a lot these past few years, and I hate it.

VOICE OF INDIAN MAN: There was silence while one old man handled the pipe. Lighting it, he pointed it toward the blue sky, then to the east, north, south, and west, then lastly to Mother Earth. I was also expected to give away something on this great occasion.

(*Raymond suddenly stiffens, leaps, then falls*)

VOICE OF INDIAN MAN: After the dance was over the tribes moved away, but afterward if we ever returned to the sacred spot where the pole was yet standing, we stood for a long time in reverence because it was a sacred place to us.

(*Raymond is no longer breathing. He has had a cerebral hemorrhage*)

RHONDA: The dance didn't end like that. That's a downer. Walt Disney always made sure everything ended on an upbeat.

JOE: Well, not all dances are alike.

CHARLIE: Danced himself right into a trance, I bet. (*He runs out and checks Raymond*) Yellow Star—hey, Mellow Yellow—whooee. (*He runs to Joe*) Man's dead, Joe . . . dead.

HARRY: Turn on that jukebox fast.

(*Joe presses a button on the jukebox. A song like* "American Patrol" *by Glenn Miller plays. Harry steps into the spot as Charlie drags Raymond's body off*)

HARRY: That's it, folks. You—just saw the most sacred dance ever. Now, remember, we need new blood to keep the Legion going. You guys show us your honorable discharges, and we'll give you a year's free membership, and remember, something's always doing at the Legion. We're always planning bigger . . . and better things.

(*Lights out*)

The End

Michael David Quinn

BUSINESSMAN'S LUNCH

Michael David Quinn

Michael David Quinn's satire on the corporate world, *Businessman's Lunch,* was featured in the Actors Theatre of Louisville's 1983 SHORTS Festival. Mel Gussow of the *New York Times* finds the play to his liking: "Brightening the atmosphere was Michael David Quinn's *Businessman's Lunch,* which cleverly skewered corporate stereotypes, including a self-satisfied food faddist . . . " The play was teamed with a companion piece, *The Sweet Life,* for the Yale Repertory Theatre's Winterfest IV. *The Sweet Life* examines the lives of blue-collar workers at the same firm as the executives in *Businessman's Lunch.*

The playwright was born in New York of Scottish-Irish, German-Jewish parentage. Mr. Quinn received a B.A. and an M.A. in theatre studies from the State University of New York at Binghamton, and an M.F.A. in playwriting from the Yale School of Drama. Mr. Quinn's other works include *Last Laughing Man,* a study of an antifascist comedian trying to ply his trade in Nazi Germany, which premiered at the Playwrights Premiere Theatre; *The Enemies of Johnny Granger,* the story of an actor and a playwright and the moral choices they make during the McCarthy era, first produced by the Columbia School of the Arts.

Mr. Quinn dedicates this play: "Yeah, it's still for Marcia."

Characters:

JOHN, *an executive for Stars and Stripes Caramels, Inc., in his early thirties, the prototypical single male, into health, meditation, and profound speculation about utterly superficial matters—ambitious*

NICK, *an executive for Stars and Stripes Caramels, Inc., in his early fifties, overweight, with a hairline that has receded to the back of his neck, somewhere between gregarious and obnoxious—ambitious*

FRANK, *an executive for Stars and Stripes Caramels, Inc., in his midfifties, in excellent shape; could have stepped out of a Steve Canyon cartoon—ambitious*

THE WAITRESS, *blonde and harried*

BENTLEY, *a sheep in sheep's clothing*

Scene:

Lights up on a booth at Harrigan's Hideaway, a restaurant done up in wood paneling, brass fixtures, overly plush upholstery, and a scattering of movie posters and Picasso prints—an attempt at sophistication that simply draws attention to its own failure. We hear the murmur of background conversation and perhaps music from a jukebox in good repair. These sounds will persist through the play, with the jukebox playing a standard mix of current soft rock hits and overplayed pop standards. We absorb these surroundings for a moment or two, and then we hear a burst of boisterous male laughter stage right. The three businessmen, John, Nick, and Frank, enter in midconversation.

JOHN: See, it all comes down to a question of image—what are people's associations when they hear the words "Stars and Stripes Caramels"? I was honest with the man, 'cause, you know, that's my whole approach. I like to keep those channels of communication clear. So I told White, I said to him, "Alex, I'm going to be right up front about this. Your candy has an image problem."

NICK: (*Cutting in*) Yeah, just a sec, John— (*Indicating booth*) How's this?

FRANK: (*Sliding into the booth*) Perfect.

JOHN: (*Noting with distaste the flotsam of the previous meal*) Wait, can't we wait till they clear a place off?

FRANK: You have to learn to think strategy, John. We sit here, this'll be the first table they clear off and we'll get served faster. And I plan on being back at my desk at . . . (*Consulting his watch*) 1400 hours. So . . .

(*John shrugs and slides into the booth*)

NICK: (*To John*) So you were telling White—

JOHN: Right, I was telling him, "Look, business in America today is a battle of images. And the image I think we have to go with is the Stars and Stripes Caramel as a luxury item—an affirmation that they have made it, they have broken free from the pack, they are *survivors,* and a Stars and Stripes Caramel is part of their reward. Something they *owe* themselves. You see what I'm saying?

NICK: Yeah, but—

JOHN: What I'm saying is that we have to reposition our candy, connect it to that young, savvy, upscale life-style that all our market reports show is where the consumer's head is at these days. No more of these four-color glossy spreads with a kid in knickers and "The Best in Taste Since 1929" written across his beanie. I mean, the real money out there is in the wallets of people who never *heard* of the Great Depression. You want to go after the *young* money, the—

(*The waitress rushes on and begins clearing off the table. She is wearing an utterly demeaning uniform*)

THE WAITRESS: I'm sorry, gentlemen, I'll be with you in a moment. (*She rushes off. John and Nick look at Frank*)

FRANK: (*Smiles an "I-told-you-so" smile*) No, no, you know what's ruining this company? *Dieting.* That's why we can't move these candies. Everybody and his brother is on a diet. Even my wife, my two girls. We're down in New York a few weeks back to see this show on Broadway, you know, that thing with the orphans and the dog? So I take 'em to this fantastic restaurant right nearby—wine bottles in the ceiling, plastic toothpicks, the whole bit—and you know what they order, every damn one of them? Cottage cheese! I say to them, "What are you trying to do, ruin me?" And my wife's a good-looking woman. Dieting . . . that's what's sending this company down the tubes . . . .

THE WAITRESS: (*By now, she has cleared off the table. She returns, her enforced cheerfulness not quite disguising the fact that this is turning into a difficult day*) Good afternoon, gentlemen. Welcome to Harrigan's Hideaway. (*They nod and murmur greetings*) Would anyone care for a cocktail before lunch?

JOHN: Uh, yeah, I would like a seltzer, please, with a twist of lemon. Seltzer, *not* club soda.

FRANK: And you can make mine a Manhattan.

NICK: A beer.

THE WAITRESS: Any partic——

NICK: What's on tap?

THE WAITRESS: Budwei——

NICK: Yeah, bring me some of that.

THE WAITRESS: Fine. (*She exits, the men watching her retreat*)

NICK: Mmmm . . . *she's* OK, huh?

FRANK: Not bad . . . she's new here, isn't she?

NICK: No, no, I seen her before.

FRANK: Yeah?

NICK: Hey, I'm not so good on names, but I never forget an ass.

JOHN: So . . . some meeting this morning, huh?

(*The others nod solemnly*)

NICK: Unbelievable . . .

JOHN: You could just feel the negativity in the room, you know what I'm saying?

NICK: Unbelievable . . .

JOHN: I'm just saying it was . . .

NICK: Unbelievable . . .

JOHN: . . . incredible.

NICK: White was fucking *pissed*.

FRANK: Sure, sure he was . . . Bentley showing up with a presentation like that. Wasting everybody's time. The man doesn't do the job. He just doesn't do the job.

NICK: Uh huh . . .

FRANK: I'll tell you, I don't know what the hell he's doing in the operation in the first place. Half the time all he wants to talk about is his comic book collection. Here we are with the biggest inventory we've had in ten years, and all Bentley's got on his mind is Spiderman.

JOHN: No question, we're looking at a serious case of unfocused energy here.

FRANK: I mean, don't misunderstand, I *like* Bentley. I think he's an all-right guy.

NICK: Hey, sure.

JOHN: No argument.

FRANK: But I'm sorry, that just does *not* change the facts. The man does not perform. And here, we're right up there on the frontlines, each man depending on his buddy to hold up his end. 'Cause when you get into a firefight, you don't want to be worrying about your flank or your rear . . . you know, it takes just one bad man to foul up a good platoon . . . and if I can say so guys, I think we are one hell of a platoon. A *hell* of a platoon.

NICK: Well, you know what I think of *you* guys.

JOHN: I hear you Frank, I really do. Marketing is a collaborative process, a group experience. Each element contributing to the whole. That's why you have got to compartmentalize your life—this part here is your job, this part here is your family, this part here is . . . is whatever. And you can't compartmentalize unless you are *centered*. Now right there, that's always been Bentley's problem. Bentley is not centered. You can tell it right off, just looking at him.

NICK: You can?

JOHN: Oh yes, definitely.

NICK: Well . . . I still say he's OK. But that's me, you know, I'm your easy-going, everyday kinda guy. I always say when you really get to know somebody deep down, everybody got something good about them. Now Bentley, one thing you got to give Bentley, he knows how to have a good time . . . like at Christmas, remember him at the Christmas party?

FRANK: He was plastered.

NICK: So? That's a good time . . . (*To John*) Hey, what about this girl Bentley's seeing? Who is she?

JOHN: I hear it's somebody with the company, maybe. Delores in Accounting saw him being picked up last month by some girl, after work—and this girl was driving a company car.

FRANK: So Bentley's hitting the private stock, huh?

NICK: That's dumb. You don't go pissing in your own pond, that's what I say.

JOHN: Well, what did I tell you? Bentley just does *not* compartmentalize.

NICK: Hey, no shit.

FRANK: Whoever she is, for his sake, she better own a couple of oil wells. The way I figure, it won't be long now before Bentley gets his discharge papers.

NICK: Think so?

FRANK: Figure it out yourself. It's been an open secret for months that White is looking to cashier one of his second looies, get this unit back into fighting trim. Now it sure isn't gonna be one of us. Who does that leave? Masteroff, the man White's always calling like his "second son," who just got his third raise of the year, or Bentley, who should have been dropped ages ago. You tell me.

NICK: Gee, you put it like *that,* you can see—

FRANK: Oh, listen, I've seen this one coming a mile off. *Two* miles. Bentley never really was a real Stars and Stripes Caramels man. He's never understood what it is that *makes* this company, what's got us where we are today.

JOHN: What's that, Frank?

(Frank's answer is postponed with the return of the waitress, bearing a platter of drinks)

NICK: OK!

THE WAITRESS: *(Placing each drink in front of its owner)* Here we are, gentlemen . . . seltzer and a twist . . . Manhattan . . . and a Bud.

NICK: What's this?

THE WAITRESS: You—you wanted a Bud, right?

NICK: Yeah, but . . . but they usually come in these frosted mugs. What happened to the frosted mugs, sweetheart?

THE WAITRESS: Uh . . . this is my first day . . .

NICK: Well, without the frosted mugs, I might as well get a bottle, right? What do you say, can you do that for me? A Bud in a bottle?

THE WAITRESS: *(A pause. With sudden spriteliness)* OK . . . have you all decided what you'll be ordering?

JOHN: I'll have the raisin/asparagus quiche, please. With the perpetual salad bar.

FRANK: And . . . I'll have the barbequed sirloin tips. I think.

THE WAITRESS: Steak fries or mashed potato?

FRANK: Oh, a baked potato, please.

THE WAITRESS: Broccoli, peas, or zucchini?

FRANK: Broccoli.

NICK: *(Laughing)* Jesus Christ, Frank, you and broccoli—I mean it's getting ridiculous. Everytime, broccoli, broccoli!

FRANK: Oh yeah, I guess I'm a broccoli man from way back. *(The men laugh)*

THE WAITRESS: *(Writing)* . . . broccoli . . .

NICK: *(Scanning the menu)* And you can make mine a . . . a roast beef sandwich on . . . rye bread . . . no, on a roll. On a hard roll. With the salad bar too.

THE WAITRESS: Lettuce and tomato on that roast beef?

NICK: Yeah . . .

THE WAITRESS: Mayonnaise?

NICK: Uh . . . I tell you, you got any specials today?

THE WAITRESS: (*Stops writing*) You mean instead of the roast beef?

NICK: Yeah.

THE WAITRESS: (*With remarkable composure, she races down the list*) We have . . . baked chicken, Harrigan style, that's a baked boneless chicken stuffed with ham and cheese, served with the vegetable of the day, shrimp a la Harrigan, that's jumbo shrimp cooked in a tomato broth served over rice, the Harrigan salad, that's a curried chicken salad served with cold vegetables and chutney, and the Harrigan plate of the day, which today is London broil in mushroom sauce with the vegetable of the day. And the soup of the day is New England clam chowder.

NICK: That's the white kind?

THE WAITRESS: Yes . . . and all the specials come with the perpetual salad bar.

NICK: Uh . . . I tell you, I think I'll stick with the roast beef sandwich.

THE WAITRESS: (*The smile broader than ever*) Fine. (*She makes a note of it and then gathers the menus*) You can help yourself to our salad bar any time you like.

NICK: Good, I'm so hungry, I could eat a fucking horse. (*He places his hand on top of the waitress's hand*) Thanks honey . . . you know, I hope you don't mind me saying so, but when you turn around and sashay away from us here, it's the high point of our day.

THE WAITRESS: (*Coolly*) Mine too. (*She removes her hand, a bit sharply, and exits*)

NICK: (*Genuinely hurt*) How do you like that, huh? You're nice to the girl, you try to be a little friendly, and what do you get? . . . Unbelievable . . .

FRANK: It's like that all over these days . . .

NICK: Yeah, it's these women's liberals . . . like that Marge in Payroll.

JOHN: Yeah, it's a shame, it's ruining the whole human dimension of the work space . . . I mean, you're developing a project with one of your girls, you have this common goal together, it'd be almost unnatural if you didn't start relating on some kind of human level . . . but everybody is so judgmental, you know what I'm saying?

NICK: (*Shrugging*) Hey, it's a fucking crazy world and there's nothing you can do about it . . . (*He rises*) Think I'll take a crack at the salad bar . . . Frank? (*Frank recedes into the upholstery as much as is possible as Nick climbs over him*) Thanks. (*Having struggled to the floor, Nick smoothes his suit and chuckles heartily*) Broccoli. (*He exits, laughing. The others watch*)

JOHN: (*Shakes his head*) That Nick . . .

FRANK: (*Smiling*) Yeah . . . yeah, I *like* him, I do.

JOHN: Nick?

FRANK: Yeah. A real, reliable foot soldier, Nick . . . not a big man on strategy, when you get right down to it . . .

JOHN: No, not really—

FRANK: . . . but the kind of guy who takes his orders and executes the assignment . . . no fuss, no bother, just a real "can do" sort of guy.

JOHN: I know what you mean, Frank . . . Yeah, I really feel I can relate to Nick . . . he's got a—a sort of old-fashioned style of interfacing, but you know, I can relate to that too . . . I mean, he'd be lost out in the field, but he's a good infrastructure man.

FRANK: Still—I worry about Nick sometimes. I . . . worry.

JOHN: What about?

FRANK: This drinking thing of his, he's . . . the man is treading a thin line. A very thin line.

JOHN: I—I always knew he was a serious drinker, but—

FRANK: Serious? *Critical,* I'd call it. Look, it's better he hears it from his allies than somebody else hearing it from his enemies, right? Right?

JOHN: (*Indicating agreement at the same time that he's drinking*) Nnnnn . . .

FRANK: What?

JOHN: I said "Nnnnn."

FRANK: Oh . . . anyway, he's a good guy . . . all in all.

JOHN: Oh, yeah . . .

FRANK: I—I don't mean to make a big thing about it, I mean, make it bigger than it is . . .

JOHN: Oh no . . . still, you know, that's why I ordered this . . . (*Lifting his glass*) No alcohol, no sodium . . . you gotta be *clear,* that's what I'm working on . . . nothing in my body, nothing in my mind—outside of clearness, I mean . . .

FRANK: Well . . . compared to Bentley, he's a teetotaler.

NICK'S VOICE: Who is?

(*Nick returns with a plate buried in salad fixings*)

FRANK: Oh . . . you name it.

NICK: Hey, no shit . . . Frank?

FRANK: Oh, sure. (*Frank slides into the booth to make room for Nick. As a result, they must trade drinks and table settings as Nick takes Frank's former seat*) Thanks . . . boy, you know, I was up there just now, serving myself, and, I don't know, I just couldn't help thinking about all the countries in the world where they don't got salad bars . . . it really makes you appreciate life in America, it really does . . . (*He scans the table and frowns*) The food not here yet?

(*There is a sudden electronic beeping. It comes from a watch worn by Frank. He turns it off*)

FRANK: (*Rising*) I'll be right back . . . John?

JOHN: Oh, excuse me. (*Now it is John who leans back as Frank climbs over him to reach the restaurant floor*)

NICK: What's the problem?

FRANK: (*As he works his way over John*) No problem . . . Just have to call the office, remind Peggy she has to start Xeroxing those reports . . . (*Starting to leave*) Gotta stay on top of things, right? Be prepared . . . (*He exits*)

NICK: (*Shakes his head*) Jeez . . .

JOHN: What?

NICK: That Frank, huh?

JOHN: Yeah . . .

NICK: Really got his nose up the grindstone.

JOHN: He's no Bentley.

NICK: All right, but c'mon, there's gotta be something in the middle. I mean, I *like* Frank, I like him a hell of a lot.

JOHN: He's direct. Very direct.

NICK: Always pushing like that, always with the, the schedules and the plans—

JOHN: Well, I guess that's part of his military background.

NICK: What military background?

JOHN: Well . . . the—the army and—

NICK: John, I hate to tell you, but the guy never served a day in his life.

JOHN: No? But—

NICK: Not a *day*. He wanted to. But they wouldn't take him. Something about his feet.

JOHN: (*Taking this in*) Wow . . .

NICK: Yeah—don't let him know I told you that, by the way, he don't like it getting around.

JOHN: You can trust me, Nick . . . and you know how I feel about trust.

NICK: Hey, that's why I tell you these things . . . No, Frank is . . . well, he's Frank, you know? You can work with him, and that's the important thing . . .

JOHN: That's for sure—

NICK: It's just . . . you got to keep your people happy.

JOHN: Uh huh.

NICK: Yeah, that's it in a nutshell. When your people are happy, *you're* happy. You can't run 'em into the ground, you can't ride 'em like he does . . .

(*The waitress appears with a bottle of Bud*)

NICK: They work better if they don't know they're on a leash, and they *won't* know if you don't pull on it.

(*The waitress exits*)

JOHN: Yeah, what I feel about Frank, I just feel he's too . . . linear.

NICK: Uh . . . is that bad?

JOHN: Oh, yeah . . . see, we've got to make that all-important leap from goal orientation to process orientation . . . like the Buddhists. You see what I'm saying?

NICK: Uh—

JOHN: —I'm saying if a Buddhist looked at Stars and Stripes Caramels, he wouldn't just see the end result, the sale. He'd see the whole interaction of forces leading up to the sale. He'd see that the important thing is the *experience* of the sale, rather than the sale itself.

NICK: I—I don't think they look at it that way in Marketing.

JOHN: I tell you, Nick, I really think the Western executive has a lot to learn from the East.

NICK: Well . . . they sure know how to make cars.

(*Frank returns*)

JOHN: You got to Peggy?

FRANK: Oh, sure. She always knows to stand-by when I'm at lunch. (*John slides further into the bench. Frank takes his seat and they exchange drinks and plates, etc.*) But you know, I was in the middle of my instructions, and it happened again—we got cut off.

NICK: This happen a lot?

FRANK: Yeah . . . but only when I'm calling from lunch, for some reason . . . I gotta get someone to check out that phone . . . (*He shrugs and continues eating*)

NICK: (*Laughs suddenly*) Hey, you hear about White's daughter?

JOHN: What?

NICK: She—she's getting married! Can you believe it? (*He laughs again*)

FRANK: So?

NICK: So from what *I* hear, this girl is supposed to have a face that'd take you out of action quicker than a vasectomy. I mean, imagine White in a dress, huh? They say he's been trying to unload her for years. Look's like he finally found a taker.

FRANK: Who's the guy?

NICK: Don't know. But whoever he is, he's just *got* to be screwing the money.

JOHN: Well, at least he's clear on his priorities.

NICK: Hey, no shit. Christ, White must be worth . . . what?

FRANK: A lot.

NICK: At least. (*John rises*) Hey, you going to the salad bar?

JOHN: Yeah, I'm . . . I'm getting hungry.

NICK: Uh huh, that waitress . . . How about bringing me back some of . . . of this macaroni thing here? (*He points to a point on his plate*)

JOHN: Sure.

NICK: Thanks . . . save myself a trip, you know?

JOHN: No problem. (*He climbs over Nick and exits*)

NICK: (*Calling*) Thank you, John . . . And none of that sprout shit! (*Laughing*) He's an all-right kid, that John.

FRANK: Oh yeah, a good find.

NICK: Uh huh.

FRANK: Just what Stars and Stripes needs, too . . . fresh troops.

NICK: Yeah . . . I mean, he got his funny side, too . . . but hey, who don't? That's what I say.

FRANK: . . . funny side . . .

NICK: Yeah, he's one of these, you know, one of these vegenarians.

FRANK: Oh?

NICK: Yeah, won't even—we were at a bar once, he

wouldn't even split a Slim Jim with me . . . (*Laughing*) But he's OK, he's OK.

FRANK: Well . . . you know, Nick . . .

NICK: What?

FRANK: A good businessman is a *hunter* . . . hunting opportunities, hunting weaknesses in his prey . . . and a hunter eats *meat*.

NICK: Well . . .

FRANK: Figure it out yourself, Nick. Your Jap soldier ate rice. Your GI ate beef.

NICK: (*Recalling*) Is that what that was? . . . Well, I still say John's . . . OK.

FRANK: Oh, I couldn't agree more.

NICK: White seems to like him . . . he's getting a new cubicle, know that?

FRANK: (*Struggling to conceal his shock*) What?

NICK: Yeah . . . he's gonna be right across from the coffee and doughnuts, the lucky son-of-a-bitch.

FRANK: That's near White's office.

NICK: Yeah . . .

FRANK: I . . . I was here ten years before they gave me a new cubicle. (*A sudden thought*) It doesn't have a window, does it?

NICK: Oh, c'mon, Frank—they wouldn't give Jesus Christ a cubicle with a window . . . 'course if the kid keeps going like he's going, maybe one of these days . . . Funny, too, I mean, he was kinda wild back in his school days, back in college.

FRANK: Yeah?

NICK: 's what he tells me.

FRANK: Like what?

NICK: Oh, nothing much . . . like he was wrapped up in this anti-war marching and . . . that sort of thing.

FRANK: *Anti*-war.

NICK: But look, the way I look at it, we've all done things we been ashamed of later.

FRANK: Oh sure . . .

NICK: I mean, we all got our skeletons in the backyard.

FRANK: No, no, I agree . . . anti-war, huh?

NICK: Yup.

FRANK: Boy, these kids today, they think they got it all worked out, huh? If they mouthed off in Cuba the way they mouth off here, they'd be locked up by lunchtime. You'd think they'd have enough respect for freedom of speech in this country to keep their mouths shut.

NICK: Well . . . I wouldn't get too worked up about it, Frank, he's—he's a good guy, mostly.

FRANK: Oh yeah, sure . . . it just gets to me, Nick. I think of all the great, talented commanders struck down by disloyalty.

NICK: Yeah?

FRANK: Sure, didn't you ever see *The Caine Mutiny?*

(John returns to the table with two plates, one of which he places in front of Nick)

JOHN: Here you go, Nick.

NICK: Thanks.

JOHN: Frank? . . .

FRANK: Oh . . .

(Frank slides into the booth. John takes his place. They exchange glasses and cutlery, etc. All the while, Frank stares intently at John, who scowls at his salad)

JOHN: They were all out of croutons. It's funny, all morning, I just had this premonition they'd be out of croutons.

(The waitress appears bearing the entrees)

THE WAITRESS: Here we are . . . thank you for waiting . . . let's see, that's sirloin tips . . . *(She places the order in front of Frank)* . . . roast beef sandwich . . . *(She places the order in front of Nick)* . . . and the quiche. *(She places the order in front of John)* Will that be all?

NICK: Uh . . . how about another Bud over here?

THE WAITRESS: A Bud.

NICK: In a bottle.

THE WAITRESS: Anyone else? . . . Fine then.

(She exits. The men pick up their utensils and assault the main courses)

FRANK: *(Up-ends a catsup bottle and robustly whacks its rump, as if disciplining an unruly child)* So . . .

JOHN: Yes?

FRANK: *(Whacks catsup bottle)* Heard you're moving to a new cubicle . . .

JOHN: Uh, yes, I'm moving about twenty feet down the hall.

FRANK: Uh huh . . . *(Whack, whack on catsup bottle)*

JOHN: Yeah, the one I have now is too near the Xerox machine . . . those fumes, you know, those chemicals they use—on a busy day, they really back up into my cubicle. For hours. I'm sure that's not good. So White's gonna switch me with one of the girls.

FRANK: Just like that . . . (*Whacks the catsup bottle*)

JOHN: Well, it took a little politicking, of course . . .

FRANK: Uh huh . . . (*Whack, whack on the catsup bottle*)

NICK: Hey, how'd White go for these new ads, this campaign of yours? You didn't say—

JOHN: Well, Nick, you know how it is—a new concept, you always get negative feedback. At first. But I really feel this is going to grow on him, I really do. And you know, I *always* go with my feelings. (*Opening his briefcase, warming to his subject*) Now right from the start, we said to ourselves, "Look, let's be daring, let's be adventurous about this." And why not? Isn't it time for a little risk taking at Stars and Stripes Caramels?

FRANK: Affirmative.

NICK: Yeah, go for it.

JOHN: (*Withdrawing a large manila envelope from his briefcase*) Just what *we* thought. You want an approach that will really impact on those demographics, an approach that's unique, maybe even ground-breaking—but in a familiar sort of way, 'cause still, you want to associate with the positive life experiences of the consumer. Now with those ground rules, we did a couple of weeks of really intense brainstorming—and sure enough, we got our approach.

NICK: What?

JOHN: Sex. (*He takes an ad mock-up out of the envelope. The image of a provocatively dressed woman is clearly discernible to the audience. He hands the ad to Nick*) What do you think? I've got problems with the graphics, but I think the subliminal message comes through anyway.

NICK: (*Reading*) "Are YOU man enough to CHEW?" (*He nods approvingly and passes it to Frank*)

JOHN: We're very excited about the whole thing. We think it conveys a real urbane, sophisticated image people generally don't associate with taffy. We're doing another right now with a real beef-cake kind of guy, maybe with cowboy boots, and the copy'll read—

FRANK: "Are you *woman* enough to chew?"

JOHN: You got it. Or we might go for a sexy-looking couple under the words, "It takes two to chew." I mean, we are just beginning to generate the possibilities of this. You know what I'm saying? I'm saying—

NICK: Hey! Hey guys!

JOHN: (*A bit annoyed at the interruption*) What?

NICK: Over by the cashier . . . look who's digging into the after-dinner mints.

FRANK: (*Smiling derisively*) Oh yeah . . . it's Bentley . . . Christ, how many can the man swallow?

NICK: Looks like the whole damn dish, damn near . . .

JOHN: Unreal . . . the whole place can see him.

NICK: Yeah . . . and it isn't even after dinner yet.

JOHN: Wow . . .

NICK: Unbelievable . . .

JOHN: You know what all that added sugar does to your system?

FRANK: (*Staring at John sharply*) Now that's a funny thing for a man in the candy business to say.

JOHN: (*Waving his hand dismissively*) I just promote the product, Frank. What people do with it after that I leave up to them.

NICK: (*Disgustedly*) Oh terrific, he's coming over here now.

FRANK: Look . . . what the hell, guys . . . I mean, one of these days, Masteroff and us, we'll be sitting through one of White's meetings, and who knows, maybe we'll even miss Bentley a little. I mean, you gotta admit, the guy's been a real character, huh?

NICK: Hey, no shit . . .

(*Bentley appears, dressed neatly in a lime green three-piece suit—in fact, too neatly, somehow suggesting a freshly scrubbed ten-year-old on his way to parochial school. This is accentuated by his soft, babyish features and his child-like inability to keep his gaze fixed on any part of the room for more than a few seconds at a time. As far as he knows, the whole world likes him*)

BENTLEY: Hi, everybody! (*He extends his hand, which the others assume they are expected to shake. Hence, they likewise extend their hands*) You want a mint? (*The mints are held in Bentley's outstretched hand. The other men awkwardly withdraw their hands*)

FRANK: Uh . . . I think I'll pass on that, Bentley.

NICK: Yeah, I prefer them out of the bowl, myself.

BENTLEY: Me too—Oh boy, lookit! (*Abruptly takes a seat in the booth as something on the table catches his attention*)

JOHN: (*As he is involuntarily shoved*) Hey, will you—?

BENTLEY: This is neat! (*The other men have no idea what Bentley is referring to until he reaches into the small cup containing packets of sugar*) They got presidents' faces on the sugars . . . boy, George Washington sure was funny looking, wasn't he?

FRANK: Bentley—

BENTLEY: George Washington had teeth made out of wood, did you know that?

FRANK: Bentley, didn't you come with anybody?

BENTLEY: (*Completely missing the point of the question*) Yeah, she's over there, see? Right under the "Ask About Our Famous Cheeseburgers" sign.

NICK: Oh, yeah . . . (*Laughing*) Yeah, looks like she's asked more than once. See her guys? (*He makes a barking noise, and Frank and John laugh. Bentley, apparently engrossed in sugar packets, doesn't react*) "President Gerald Rudolph Ford" . . . Remember that issue of *Action Comics* where Superman saves President Ford from a runaway ski-lift in Aspen?

NICK: Gee Bentley, I think I missed that one.

BENTLEY: Oh, it was neat. See, Lex Luthor had invented this death beam that—

JOHN: So Bentley, is that your girlfriend over there?

BENTLEY: Yup . . . we're getting married in June . . . You know, *our* sugars only got state birds on them.

FRANK: *Married?*

BENTLEY: Uh huh.

FRANK: Oh, Bentley, you don't want to do that.

BENTLEY: I don't?

FRANK: Take it from me, there are a hundred reasons for staying single.

NICK: Yeah—and one of them is sitting under the "Ask About Our Famous Cheeseburgers" sign. (*The men laugh once more*)

JOHN: Why you been hiding her?

NICK: *Why* he's been hiding her? I'd like to know *how* he's been hiding her. (*The men laugh yet again*)

BENTLEY: Well, Candy didn't want people knowing about it too soon, 'cause of her being White's daughter and everything. (*The three men turn in her direction simultaneously*)

FRANK: *That's* White's daughter?

BENTLEY: Yeah, that's what I said. That's Candy White.

JOHN: *That's* the girl you been—I mean, you and she are—

BENTLEY: Uh huh. (*Now the three businessmen laugh without restraint*)

NICK: Well congratulations, Bentley. She sure is as pretty as everybody says. (*Laughter*)

FRANK: So I guess you were right, John. Bentley's girl *is* somebody with the company. (*Further laughter*)

JOHN: Yeah, Bentley—I guess *your* job is safe.

(*Another round of laughter as they simultaneously raise their cutlery—and one-by-one fall silent and somber as it dawns upon each man that yes indeed, Bentley's job is safe. They stare ahead, numb. The waitress breezes on with Nick's bottle of beer*)

THE WAITRESS: Here you go. (*She places the beer in front of Nick*) Another round for anyone else? (*Frank, Nick, and John do not answer but silently ponder their fate. The waitress turns to Bentley*) How about you, sir? Will you be wanting anything?

BENTLEY: (*Rising*) No, no, I better be getting back to Candy. I been with you guys long enough, huh?

NICK: (*Snapping to attention*) No, no, wait, Bentley, you—you can't leave without a drink. Right?

JOHN: (*Picking up the cue*) Oh, that's right, Nick, I can take care of the next round.

BENTLEY: I don't know, I think I got to—

FRANK: Sit *down*, Bentley . . . (*He grabs Bentley by the jacket sleeve and virtually drags him into the booth*) Now. What'll it be?

BENTLEY: Well, if you really wanna . . . I guess a sloe gin fizz, maybe.

(*Frank, Nick, and John speak simultaneously and with great energy*)

FRANK: A sloe gin fizz for the gentleman, miss.

NICK: (*Overlapping*) Hey honey, a sloe gin fizz over here, OK?

JOHN: (*Overlapping*) Excuse me, miss, I'd like to order a sloe gin fizz.

BENTLEY: Oh, one'll be enough for me, thanks.

THE WAITRESS: (*Writing*) One sloe gin fizz . . . that'll be just a minute.

(*She exits. A pause*)

FRANK: So, Bentley . . . marriage, huh? That's terrific. Just terrific. Yeah, the thing about marriage is it's such a perfect command structure. You got one branch to defend the fort, another to go out on sorties and capture material . . . you know what I mean?

BENTLEY: No.

JOHN: Yeah, that's right, Bentley, it's . . . it's like a twoness becoming a oneness . . . and when you have kids, it's like a threeness or a fourness into a oneness . . . you know, I bet if *my* wife had seen things like that, we'd still be married.

NICK: Yeah, marriage . . . it's a great thing, Bentley . . . knowing that when you come home at night and you're tired and you're hungry, there's someone ready to unfreeze your frozen dinners for you . . . no more eating canned food over the sink, you know? Now you can sit down and eat it at the table like decent people.

BENTLEY: Yeah, it's gonna be real keen . . . You know where we're gonna get married? You know where?

NICK: Uh . . . maybe you could give us a little hint there, Bentley.

BENTLEY: Adventure City!

JOHN: You mean . . . you don't mean the amusement park?

BENTLEY: Uh huh . . . We got it all planned out, see . . . me and Candy already picked out the bumper cars we want, and the priest'll have *his* own little bumper car and the guests too . . . and then right after the ceremony, the band'll start playing this song that Candy picked out special, "Someone to Watch Over Me," and Candy and I'll have our first bump as man and wife.

JOHN: Isn't that a little . . . unusual?

BENTLEY: Yeah, well, she really likes George Gershwin, so I didn't say anything.

JOHN: Well, uh . . . that's good. I mean, nontraditional wedding ceremonies are really breaking a lot of ground that's—that's really crying out to be broken. Really.

BENTLEY: Uh huh . . . and you know where we're going for the honeymoon? You'll never guess.

NICK: I don't know . . . Disney World?

BENTLEY: (*Crestfallen*) How'd you guess?

NICK: It just came to me.

BENTLEY: Anyway, we're staying just long enough to catch all the really good rides and still make it back to New York for the comic book convention.

FRANK: Well, there you go—planning ahead, that's what it's all about, Bentley. That's why you and me and White get along so well. 'Cause we're strategy men all the way, right from the start.

NICK: (*A straight forward question*) Oh, you and White get along, Frank?

(*In a swift and steady cross, the waitress enters stage left, deposits Bentley's drink, and exits stage right. By the time Bentley mumbles "Thank you," she is gone*)

FRANK: (*With more than a trace of annoyance*) I'm not talking

about penny ante shit like who's got which cubicle where . . .
esprit de corps, Nick. That's what the French call it.

BENTLEY: (*Engrossed in his sloe gin fizz*) Oh boy, I think they
gave me *two* cherries by accident.

JOHN: Well, I guess nobody here has the kind of interpersonal relationship with White that Bentley has, huh, Bentley?

BENTLEY: (*Indicating assent with his mouth wrapped about a
straw*) Mmmmm *hmmmm*.

JOHN: I mean, you must have a pretty good idea of what
he looks for in an executive . . .

BENTLEY: Mmmmm *hmmmm*.

JOHN: Fresh ideas, new approaches, you know what I'm
saying?

BENTLEY: Mmmmm *hmmmm* . . .

JOHN: I'm saying that—

FRANK: We *know* what you're saying, John. But how about
experience, huh? That counts for something. White needs
men who know how to work under fire, not raw recruits. Isn't
that right, Bentley?

BENTLEY: Mmmm.

JOHN: Yeah, but he needs that *young* input, too, that *youthful, young*—

FRANK: What he *doesn't* need is people taking two-hour cat
naps around here.

JOHN: (*An edge*) I *told* you, Frank, it wasn't napping, it was
meditating.

FRANK: (*Innocence personified*) Did I mention any names?
Did I mention a single name?

JOHN: Anyway, I think Mr. White would be more upset
about people who waste money, don't you, Bentley?

BENTLEY: Mmmmm.

NICK: Who you mean, John?

JOHN: Look, I don't want to bring personalities into this
. . . but you know about the cups, the styrofoam cups next to
the coffee?

NICK: What about 'em?

JOHN: Well, I'm just saying how White freaks out about it,
how he's always telling us to hang onto the first cup of the day
cause the company's going broke buying so many cups like we
been doing. But believe it or not, we still got people running
through those cups like they're for free, I mean four, five,
half a dozen a morning at least—

FRANK: Aw come on . . .

JOHN: And Nick, those things aren't even biodegradable,

Nick! I mean here we all are on Spaceship Earth, the only planet we got, and some insensitive son of a bitch is choking us to death on his goddamn styrofoam!

FRANK: Nickel and dime! This is very nickel and dime!

JOHN: Oh yeah? And how about using company phones for personal calls? How about a certain long-distance conversation to a kid in a certain military academy?

FRANK: How about a certain fist in a certain face?

NICK: Guys, *guys* . . . maybe we're getting worked up over nothing here. Maybe it's just a rumor after all, all this talk about firing . . . What about you, Bentley, you hear any of these stories about someone getting the sack?

BENTLEY: (*Nodding as he continues to draw on the straw*) Mmmmm *hmmmm*.

NICK: Well *you'd* be the one to know if White was really planning on it, right?

BENTLEY: Mmmmm *hmmmm*.

NICK: (*Slightly exasperated*) Well *is* he?

BENTLEY: Mmmmm *hmmmm*.

NICK: (*A pause as Nick's line of argument deflates*) Oh . . .

JOHN: (*Suddenly desperate*) Who is it, for Christ's sake?

(*The alarm on Frank's watch goes off*)

JOHN: (*Loses all composure*) Will you tell that watch to shut up?

FRANK: (*Defending a loved one*) Don't you say anything bad about this watch. There's nothing wrong with this watch.

JOHN: You don't wear that thing . . . it wears *you*. I swear, Frank, you are a typical example of American psychic dependency on technology.

FRANK: (*Coldly*) Something you don't like about America, John? (*He rises*)

NICK: More Xeroxing for Peg?

FRANK: No . . . (*He shuts off the alarm*) Collating. (*He climbs over Nick, laughing—a bit unconvincingly*) Don't do anything important . . . while I'm gone.

(*He exits, with a quick, backward glance. Bentley reaches the bottom of his drink and fills the stage with the sound of sucking on the dregs*)

NICK: Like that, huh, Bentley?

BENTLEY: That was delicious. I'd like another.

NICK: Why, sure, sure . . . whatever you like . . . (*Looking for the waitress*) . . . soon as that waitress hauls her ass over here.

JOHN: You know Nick, I think you may be transferring.

NICK: Where? Cleveland? Terre Haute? Who—who told you?

JOHN: (*Grateful for the chance to retreat into jargon*) No, no, I mean . . . I think you may be transferring your . . . your anxiety about . . . you know . . . transferring that to your anger at the waitress.

NICK: Uh huh . . . you know, John, sometimes you talk like television . . . I mean, it's *your* fucking future we might be talking about here.

JOHN: *My* future?

NICK: Hey, we got Bentley backing it up now—somebody's gonna be the guest of honor at a farewell lunch one of these days.

JOHN: (*Alarm rising once again*) Nick, they—they wouldn't do that to me, I got an MBA from—

NICK: Oh yeah, right . . . of course, Blumenstein had one of those too . . .

JOHN: Blumenstein?

NICK: Sure, you remember—the guy you replaced.

(*John pales perceptibly. The waitress returns*)

THE WAITRESS: Yes?

NICK: Oh, nice of you to drop by, *honey* . . . another of these . . . what the hell is that again, Bentley?

BENTLEY: A sloe gin fizz—

NICK: Yeah, another of those for my buddy here. And I'll have a Bud . . .

THE WAITRESS AND NICK: . . . In a bottle.

THE WAITRESS: (*She nods and writes down the order*) Anyone else? . . . Very well . . . (*She exits*)

BENTLEY: You guys are really great.

JOHN: Sure, sure Bentley. We like you. You're our friend. And you should always know who your friends are, you know . . . speak up for 'em when they need it.

BENTLEY: Oh, you can count on me, Frank.

JOHN: (*Appalled*) *Frank?* Frank's the one on the phone. I'm John. *John!*

BENTLEY: Oh. OK.

JOHN: (*Rises*) Excuse me, Nick.

NICK: What's the problem?

JOHN: I just have this *real* need for a couple of—of mantras. Would you please . . . ?

(*Nick makes room and John climbs over him. He reaches the restau-*

rant floor and exits, but not before we see him withdraw a vial from his pocket that contains an impressive quantity of Valium capsules)

NICK: So . . . how long you been going with Candy?

BENTLEY: About half a year.

NICK: Uh huh . . . right around the time you got hired by Mr. White?

BENTLEY: Yup . . . at first, you know, I was really scared 'cause I never had a job this big before . . .

NICK: Hey, no kidding.

BENTLEY: Yeah . . . but then one day, I just had a good long talk with myself. I looked right into the mirror while I was shaving and I said, "OK, Bobbie . . . what would the Batman do if he were in your place?"

NICK: Yeah, I bet he'd use that X-ray vision of his to look into the briefcase of the other guy . . .

BENTLEY: (*The voice of expertise*) That's Superman you're thinking of. Batman doesn't have any super powers.

NICK: Oh.

BENTLEY: And Superman wouldn't do anything that unethical.

NICK: Hey, you got a point there, Bentley, I got to admit.

BENTLEY: Anyway . . . things have been a lot better since then . . . only sometimes, I think maybe . . . maybe Mr. White isn't too happy with me.

NICK: (*A ridiculous idea*) Naw.

BENTLEY: No, really . . . I think he thinks I think too much about the comic books.

NICK: Tell him it's an investment. I hear some of those things are worth hundreds of bucks.

BENTLEY: Yeah, but I wouldn't sell them . . . You sell them, you can't read them anymore.

NICK: That's true . . . Well, you just stick with me, Bentley. I'll see you—(*Bentley laughs for the first time*) What's so funny?

BENTLEY: (*He points at Nick's plate*) You got beets.

NICK: So?

BENTLEY: (*Laughing again*) You eat beets at *home*. You don't eat beets out.

NICK: It's from the salad bar . . . Hey, I'm going back there for another round. Why don't you come with me, pick something out?

BENTLEY: Won't we get in trouble?

NICK: Not if they don't find out. (*As they rise and exit*) You just come with me, I'll fix you up real good . . .

(*They are gone. A pause. The waitress does another rapid cross in which she leaves a Bud and a sloe gin fizz on the table. A pause. Frank returns*)

FRANK: That took longer than I— (*He sees the empty table*) Oh, shit.

(*John returns from the other direction*)

JOHN: I tell you, one or two mantras, and I'm as fit as a . . . (*John also sees the empty table*) Where'd Nick and Bentley go to?

FRANK: Don't *you* know?

JOHN: No.

FRANK: You mean you left Nick alone with Bentley?

JOHN: I was just taking a . . . a relaxing walk . . .

FRANK: The only relaxing walk *you* ever took was one with a drug store at the end of it. Christ, don't you know *anything* about strategy?

JOHN: Frank, I'm really getting bummed out by this strategy crap of yours . . . who the hell do you think you are, anyway, the General Patton of taffy?

(*Offstage, we hear Nick's raucous laugh*)

FRANK: (*Spins about*) There they are! The salad bar at two o'clock!

JOHN: (*Looking along with Frank*) Oh for Christ's sake.

(*Again, we hear Nick's laugh*)

JOHN: (*A pause*) You know . . . I think I'm going to be sick.

FRANK: *Very* smart . . . the oldest tactic in the book . . . divide and conquer.

JOHN: Well—well, we can talk to Bentley, too. Right? Nothing stopping us.

FRANK: Not a thing, John . . . anyway, Bentley's got a lot on the ball, you know. I bet he can see through Nick.

JOHN: Sure, he'll know hypocrisy when he sees it.

FRANK: Quite a lot on that ball . . .

JOHN: Sure, he knows who his friends are.

(*Nick laughs offstage*)

JOHN: Oh God . . .

FRANK: What?

JOHN: They're laughing, they're laughing together!

FRANK: Oh, *he's* laughing, but I don't think you can say *Bentley's* laughing.

JOHN: What do *you* call it?

FRANK: Chuckling, maybe . . . yeah, definitely more of a chuckle.

JOHN: OK, a chuckle. So what?

FRANK: Well, a chuckle can mean a lot of things, John.

JOHN: Yeah, and that one means we better start updating our resumes.

FRANK: Snap out of it, mister! Look, the man is a dinosaur. He can wheel and deal all he likes, but the future belongs to the men who belong to the future. Men like you and me . . . and Bentley. Men who know what the world of today is all about . . . machines gossiping with other machines . . . powdered breakfast . . . electric hearts . . . digital grandfather clocks . . . even war, John, it's all computers and satellites and laser beams.

JOHN: Right now, I'd settle for a fucking crowbar and two minutes alone with that fat-assed ass-kisser.

FRANK: John . . .

JOHN: Nothing like a crowbar to really fuck up your karma, you know?

FRANK: Strategy, John.

JOHN: To hell with strategy, Frank. I'm talking skull fractures.

FRANK: Look, there are certain people in the company who don't exactly think the world of Nick . . . for every ass he's kicked, there's a bunch of toes he's stepped on . . . and the things they tell me . . . I mean, you might not believe it, John, coming out of business school where they're long on theory but short on hand-to-hand combat . . . but there are guys—and I'm sorry, but Nick is one of them—who will do or say just about anything to get just a little ahead of the other guy . . . anything, no matter how sneaky or backstabbing . . .

JOHN: Gosh.

FRANK: Yeah . . . we don't have to be sitting ducks for it, though . . . look, you remember how Nick was bragging once, right here in this restaurant, about all the expense account money he never turned in?

JOHN: Uh . . . no, no, I don't remember that.

FRANK: You were there. I know you were.

JOHN: (Shrugging) I'm—I'm sorry, I just don't—

FRANK: That's too bad. If I could have somebody to back me up when I go to White, it could make all the difference . . . but—

JOHN: Hold it! Hold it . . . yeah, right here, wasn't it? . . . Sure, I remember it now, it was—

(*More offstage laughter*)

FRANK: Here they come! Watch it . . .

(*Another laugh*)

JOHN: That smug little—

FRANK: Save it, kid. We'll get our turn.

(*Nick and Bentley return, Bentley with about half the salad bar loaded on two plates*)

FRANK: Well, you two seem to be enjoying yourselves.

BENTLEY: (*As everybody takes a seat in the booth*) Yeah, Nick and I were making plans for a big party—oh, wow, look! (*He attacks the sloe gin fizz*)

JOHN: So . . . just talking about a party, were you?

NICK: Yeah, you know . . . a bachelor's party for Bentley here . . . the works; booze, entertainment, maybe a girl jumping out of a cake.

BENTLEY: (*Between sips*) Won't that be bad for the cake?

NICK: We're inviting the whole second floor . . . Jackson, Masteroff, Glick—

BENTLEY: No, not Masteroff . . .

NICK: Why not? He's one of the bunch.

BENTLEY: Not anymore. Mr. White just fired him.

(*Suddenly, there is absolute silence, but for the noisy slurping of Bentley. The other men slowly turn and look at him*)

JOHN: (*Softly*) Fired? Masteroff?

BENTLEY: Yup. Mr. White told me so. Just this morning.

(*Bentley continues drinking. Nick, John, and Frank have just received their phone calls from the governor*)

JOHN: Wow . . .

NICK: Hey, no shit . . .

JOHN: I thought—I thought Masteroff was like a son . . .

FRANK: I guess he's been disowned.

JOHN: Jesus . . . how old is Masteroff?

NICK: A lot older than when he came in this morning, I can tell you. (*He laughs*)

FRANK: So that's who White's letting go . . . well . . . a little housecleaning. Every company does it now and then. You got to be a little cold about it sometimes, but it makes things easier for the rest. In the long run.

JOHN: Sure . . .

(*The waitress reappears*)

THE WAITRESS: Everything OK, gentlemen?

BENTLEY: (*Again slurps up the dregs of his drink and holds out his glass*) Can I have another, please?

NICK: Uh, Bentley, shouldn't you be getting back to Candy?

BENTLEY: (*Suddenly active*) Holy smokes, I almost forgot. (*He struggles over the others to the restaurant floor*) I'll see you guys back at work, OK? (*They mumble their good-byes*) Bye. (*He exits*)

NICK: (*Shaking his head*) What an asshole.

THE WAITRESS: Perhaps some coffee and dessert?

(*A final shriek from Frank's watch*)

FRANK: I . . . don't think so. Time to head back for me. What do you say, guys?

NICK: Yeah, just the check.

(*John nods*)

THE WAITRESS: Very well . . . (*She exits*)

FRANK: So . . . what did I say, huh? We are one *hell* of a platoon!

NICK: Hey, I got to give you that, Frank.

JOHN: Yeah . . . too bad, though. About Masteroff.

NICK: Yeah . . . look, why don't we all take him out to lunch Friday. Kind of a bon voyage, you know?

(*The waitress returns with the check*)

THE WAITRESS: Thank you very much for coming to Harrigan's Hideaway. Have a good day. (*She exits as the men murmur their farewells*)

FRANK: Let's see . . . I think it's my turn, huh? (*He takes the check—and reaches into his pocket for a small notebook and pencil*) OK . . . we'll say that you are . . . Mr. Kennedy and Mr. Washington . . . and we discussed . . . new markets for Stars and Stripes . . . (*He writes it down in his notebook*) . . . and the receipt . . . (*Tearing off the bottom of the check*) There. (*He counts out some money*) What do we give her for a tip?

NICK: (*A short, cruel laugh*) Stiff her.

JOHN: Aw, Nick.

NICK: Hey. She stank. The service was slow, she was never around . . . and tell you the truth, I just didn't like her whole attitude. Not a bit.

FRANK: But Nick, nothing?

NICK: Listen, I'm not running Employee Relations for my health. You got to know how to handle these people. Now you got your carrot and you got your stick. And I say, give this one the stick.

FRANK: All right, ten percent.

NICK: Well . . . oh, OK. (*Shaking his head*) I'm such a softie, you know. Such a pushover.

FRANK: (*He counts out the tip. They rise from the table. As they exit, Frank waxes philosophically*) You know, guys . . . in a way, it all makes sense, this business with Masteroff . . . He was a good man. But he wasn't a Stars and Strips Caramels man . . . I just never got the feeling that he really knew the—the secret ingredient in this company. What it is that makes us what we are . . .

NICK: What is it, Frank?

FRANK: Teamwork.

NICK: (*Absently picks up one of the sugar packets Bentley scattered across the table*) "Pierce" . . . who the fuck is Pierce?

(*He shrugs, tosses the packet on the table, and exits with the others. A pause. The waitress returns to clear the table*)

THE WAITRESS: (*She counts the money carefully. She looks in the direction of the departed businessmen*) Cheap bastards.

(*Blackout*)

The End

Murray Schisgal

CLOSET
MADNESS

Murray Schisgal

Murray Schisgal—whose delightful character comedy, *A Need for Brussels Sprouts,* appeared in *The Best Short Plays 1983* (and was produced on Broadway in 1982, paired with *A Need for Less Expertise* under the title *Twice Around the Park*)—scores again in *The Best Short Plays* with the provocative *Closet Madness.* This new comedy bounces another variation off the sex-role identity problems raised by the screenplay *Tootsie,* which Mr. Schisgal coauthored. (*Tootsie* was one of the most honored films of 1982, receiving the Los Angeles Film Critics Award, the New York Film Critics Award, the Award of the National Society of Film Critics, and the Writers Guild of America Award. It was nominated for an Oscar by the Academy of Motion Picture Arts and Sciences and for an award by the British Academy of Film and Television Arts.)

The whimsical events in the plays of Murray Schisgal are glittering reflections of his varied background. Before his writing supported him, he supported it with such odd jobs as setting pins in a bowling alley, playing the saxophone and clarinet in a small band, pushing a hand truck in Manhattan's garment district, and hanging dresses in Klein's Department Store. Mr. Schisgal was a high-school dropout; he later earned his diploma in the U.S. Navy, where he became radio-man, third class. Mr. Schisgal attended the Brooklyn Conservatory of Music and Long Island University, received a law degree from Brooklyn Law School and a B.A. from the New School for Social Research, taught English at the James Fenimore Cooper Junior High School in East Harlem, and wrote sixty short stories and three and a half novels—all before the age of thirty-five.

The first productions of Mr. Schisgal's plays suggest the luck of the enchanted. Having written five one-act plays while employed as a teacher, he confidently quit the security of educating American youth and took off for Spain to continue his playwriting. On his way, he left the five short plays with The British Drama League in London, which immediately offered to produce *The Typists* and *The Tiger*—this was in 1960, three years before the plays were presented in New York. When the plays opened in New York, they received both the Vernon Rice Award and the Outer Critics Circle Award. Mr. Schisgal's first commercial success, *Luv,* was also first produced in London in 1963, a year before the play opened at the Booth Theatre in New York with Eli Wallach,

Anne Jackson, and Alan Arkin, directed by Mike Nichols. *Love*, a musical adaptation of the book by Jeffrey Sweet (author of *Porch* in *The Best Short Plays 1976* and *Stops Along the Way* in *The Best Short Plays 1981*), premiered in New York in April 1984.

A steady flow of plays has bubbled forth from Mr. Schisgal's artesian well. Among these are a collection of one-acts, *Fragments, Windows, and Other Plays* (published in 1965); *Jimmy Shine* (published in 1968); *Ducks and Lovers* (published in 1972); *The Chinese and Dr. Fish* (published in 1973); *All American Millionaire* (published in 1974); *All Over Town* (published in 1975); *The Pushcart Peddlers* (in *The Best Short Plays 1981*); and *The New Yorkers* (produced Off-Off-Broadway in 1984).

Mr. Schisgal dedicates *Closet Madness*: "To my progenitors, Irene and Abe, who made this evening possible."

Characters:

SAM KOGAN
BILLY WESKER

Place:

The Hotel Ritz in Boston: the sitting room of a suite, with the entrance door in the left wall and the bedroom door in the right wall. French curtained windows opening to a terrace are in the rear wall.

In the sitting room are a sofa, end tables, a coffee table, armchairs, an oval bar, a writing table, a chest of drawers with a wall mirror above it, two suitcases lying on aluminum stands and overflowing with new clothes, some still in the bags they were purchased in, and an open closet with new jackets and pants hanging in it.

Time:

Afternoon.

At Curtain:

Sam Kogan is seated on edge of armchair, hunched over a pocket mirror on his lap, plucking his eyebrows. It is the first time he's done so, and every now and then he squeals in pain. He wears only a pair of white boxer shorts, shoes, and socks. He is shaven but looks nonetheless as if he's just come off a binge.

The phone rings. Sam jumps to his feet, startled, forgetting for the moment where he is. He grabs the phone.

SAM: *(Into phone)* Yes? *(A beat)* Tell him to come up. Thanks.

(He puts phone down, moves to the bar, where he pours himself a glass of Perrier water from a quart bottle. He drinks.

Now in double-quick time, he puts on plaid pants and a white undershirt, spilling clothes onto the floor. He then puts on a double-breasted suit jacket and impulsively adds a straw fedora. He glances at his reflection in the mirror, angles fedora, grins, grim-

aces, etc., then finally changes his mind and switches fedora for a beret.

The doorbuzzer rings. In a panic, he opens jacket and sprays cologne into his armpits. Then he buttons jacket, takes one last look at the mirror, and hurries to door and opens it.

Billy Wesker, dressed in cords, turtleneck, and hacking jacket, wearing black horn-rimmed eyeglasses, enters, stops to stare at his old friend, his eyes filled with admiration and affection)

BILLY: Sam. *(Sam closes door, turns to Billy)* Let me look at you. Let me . . . Sam, you look horrible.

SAM: You don't like the hat?

BILLY: I'm not talking about the hat. I'm talking about how you look. When's the last time you saw your doctor?

SAM: Recently.

BILLY: And?

SAM: *(Throws beret aside)* I'm fine, Billy. I am. I was on a binge, but . . . No more. I'm getting myself together. *(Drinks Perrier)* I stopped boozing and smoking, I jog every day, I'm eating fish and chicken, no meats, raw vegetables, fruit, I'm taking vitamins C, A, E, B, Zinc, dolomite, selnium, and garlic. I eat a clove of garlic a day.

BILLY: And you feel better?

SAM: No. Not really. Not physically, that is. Not yet. Mentally, though, I feel much better.

BILLY: *(Holds Sam's shoulders; stares at him)* I want you to take care of yourself. You mean a lot to me. *(A beat)* I love you, Sam.

SAM: I know you do. And I really appreciate your saying so. Do you like the shirt I'm wearing?

BILLY: The undershirt?

SAM: Yes.

BILLY: Not with that jacket.

SAM: I'll change it. *(He takes off jacket and undershirt; puts on checkered shirt)*

BILLY: *(Sits in armchair)* Mentally, you should be feeling wonderful. You have another hit. Your ninth Broadway play, isn't it?

SAM: My seventh. And it's not a hit. It'll run a hundred and fifty performances, tops.

BILLY: I don't believe it. You received fantastic reviews. I'm planning to see it next weekend.

SAM: The theatre isn't what it used to be, Billy. Fantastic reviews aren't enough anymore. Nowadays you have to write a media event, a spectacle that's more talked about at cocktail parties than seriously thought about. What do you think of this shirt?

BILLY: It's better but . . .

SAM: But what?

BILLY: It doesn't match the pants.

SAM: I'll change them. (*He scrounges through suitcases, tearing open packages and bags on floor; finds brown leather pants and puts them on*)

BILLY: Since when have you become so interested in what you wear?

SAM: Since I started changing my life.

BILLY: You weren't happy with the life you had?

SAM: I thought everybody knew that.

BILLY: I didn't. I always envied how you lived. Or at least how I imagined it.

SAM: Imagine three divorces, two kids you never see, furnished apartments, long Sundays, and cold hamburgers and . . . Let's drop it. Did you know that when you brush your teeth you should also brush your tongue?

BILLY: Your tongue?

SAM: And your palate. I read it recently.

BILLY: Were you always unhappy with the life you had?

SAM: Pretty much. (*Turns to show very tight leather pants on him*) What about these pants?

BILLY: Are they leather?

SAM: You don't like leather?

BILLY: Not on you.

SAM: I'll change them (*Takes pair of khaki pants from closet; changes*)

BILLY: It's hard for me to believe you haven't been enjoying yourself. You're the only member of the Hinsdale Avenue Literary Club who gained international recognition and . . .

SAM: Billy, I'm fine. You don't have to . . .

BILLY: Let me finish. Please. Lately, I've been thinking a lot about the years we spent growing up together in East New York. It seems to me that we were an exceptionally close and happy bunch of guys.

SAM: I guess we were.

BILLY: Me, you, Robby, Seymour, Harold, Freddy Rutner . . . But of all of us, Sam, you were the only one who realized his potential, who went on to fulfill his dream of becoming a professional writer.

SAM: Professor of American History at B.U. is no small potatoes.

BILLY: It is small potatoes. It's very small potatoes compared to your achievements. Last year when your screenplay was nominated for an Academy Award, I ran through the streets like an idiot screaming: "I grew up with Sam Kogan! We went to Thomas Jefferson High School together. He was my best friend!" (*He laughs happily*)

SAM: (*Dourly*) Unfortunately, I didn't win the Academy Award.

BILLY: That didn't matter to me.

SAM: I wish I could say the same.

BILLY: What I want you to know is that I'm proud, I'm very, very proud of you and your success.

SAM: Thanks. I appreciate the sentiment. Do you like these pants?   .

BILLY: Yes, I do.

SAM: Do they match the shirt?

BILLY: Absolutely.

SAM: What about my hair?

BILLY: What about it?

SAM: Should I do anything with it?

BILLY: (*A thoughtful beat*) Like what?

SAM: Cut it differently.

BILLY: You could let the sideburns grow.

SAM: (*Stares in mirror*) That's exactly what I'll do.

BILLY: You still haven't told me why you came to Boston. Are you speaking somewhere?

SAM: Not this time. I came for two reasons, both of them having to do with you.

BILLY: I'm flattered. What are the two reasons.

SAM: Seymour phoned me a few days ago. He told me he had lunch with you.

BILLY: We see a lot of each other since he moved to Cambridge.

SAM: He said Laura left you. Is it true?

BILLY: It's true. (*Looks about*) You wouldn't have a drink for me, would you?

SAM: Perrier water.

BILLY: I was thinking of a dry chilled martini.

SAM: You still drink booze?

BILLY: (*A thoughtful beat*) No. I stopped. More or less.

SAM: And you stopped smoking.

BILLY: (*Another thoughtful beat*) Long ago. (*Rises*) I'll pour myself some . . . Perrier. (*Does so; grimly*) I spoke to Laura this morning. She's . . . living with someone and . . . Nineteen years of marriage. It's over, Sam. I haven't had the courage to tell Juliet.

SAM: Where is Juliet?

BILLY: First year at Yale. It'll break her heart. I begged Laura to . . . reconsider, to . . . come back and . . . (*He shakes his head mournfully*)

SAM: Who's she living with? Do you know him?

BILLY: He used to be married to one of Laura's friends. He's an oboist with the Boston Pops orchestra.

SAM: It figures. I never liked their music.

BILLY: When she told me she was going, I cried, Sam, like a baby. Not because she had a lover; because she said she . . . stopped loving me . . . years ago. Those were her words, and they hurt, they hurt like hell.

SAM: (*Pats him on back*) You don't have to spell it out for me, buddy. You're talking to a three-time loser.

BILLY: There's a big difference. You didn't want your marriages. I wanted mine, very much.

SAM: Don't be too sure about that. I didn't want my first two marriages, but I did want my marriage to Marilyn. She walked out on me. I went through the exact same number you're going through, the hurt, the humiliation, the emptiness . . .

BILLY: You did go through it. Sam, your coming up here to be with me because Laura left . . . Thank you.

SAM: That's what old friends are for, buddy.

BILLY: What was the second reason for your coming up here?

SAM: Maybe we should wait on that. What do you think of this jacket with this shirt? Do you think it's a good combination? (*Holds up suit jacket*)

BILLY: That's a suit jacket.

SAM: I can't wear it?

BILLY: Not without the suit pants.

SAM: I have so much to learn . . . about so many things. What about this jacket? I just bought it. It cost me four hundred bucks. (*Takes jacket from closet; puts it on*)

BILLY: That works. I like it. Now will you tell me the second reason you're here?

SAM: When we have dinner tonight. We can . . .

BILLY: I don't understand. What's all the mystery about?

SAM: What do you think of ascots?

BILLY: Ascots?

SAM: Do you like them? Are they in style?

BILLY: (*Annoyed*) Sam, what's the second reason . . .

SAM: I bought these in Brooks Brothers. Which one should I wear with the pants and shirt I'm wearing? (*He holds up three ascots*) This one? This one? Or this one?

BILLY: That one. And I should go. I don't like being manipulated . . .

SAM: No, no, don't go. I'm telling you the second reason. I am. Now. Right now. As soon as I get this on. How do you do it? Can you give me a hand.

BILLY: (*Puts on ascot for him*) Don't misunderstand me. I'm not putting down your interest in clothes. It's commendable. It is. But why do you have to play games . . . ?

SAM: How does it look?

BILLY: Nice.

SAM: Nice? Just nice.

BILLY: (*Emotionally*) What are you carrying on about? Why is this so important to you? I don't know what you . . .

SAM: Okay. Okay. Don't get excited. Calm down. I'm telling you right now the second reason I came up to Boston. (*He holds Billy's shoulders; stares directly at him*) This is something I've been thinking over a long, long time. Frankly, it's become an obsession with me. I feel it's the one insight I've had that stands up under the severest scrutiny. I feel it's the one glaring truth, the one discovery I've made, and it's going to radically change both our lives.

(*Billy waits to hear more, his mouth half open. The phone rings. Sam moves abruptly to the phone*)

SAM: I'll get to it in a minute.

(*Billy can't believe he's not going to hear the rest of it. He looks about helplessly*)

SAM: (*Into phone*) Hello? (*A beat*) Yes, Laura. You guessed right. He's here. (*A beat*) Just for a few days. (*A beat*) I stopped drinking. Thanks, anyway. One second. (*He hands phone to Billy*)

BILLY: (*Into phone*) How are you? (*A beat*) What did you decide?

(*Sam offers Billy a glass of Perrier; Billy refuses it*)

BILLY: (*Continues into phone*) That's not fair, sweetheart. Can't we at least . . . (*A beat*) You told Juliet? Without speaking to me? You are not being fair, Laura. No, you are not. (*A *beat)* Don't do this. Please. Nineteen years have to add up to more than a goodbye. *(Embarrassed; turns away; whispers a few lines that we can't hear; then puts phone down)* She's not coming back.

SAM: *(Leads him to sofa)* Sit here. Sit beside me. It was to be expected. You expected it, didn't you?

BILLY: I kept hoping . . . *(Removes eyeglasses; rubs tear-filled eyes; puts eyeglasses on again)* You wouldn't mind if I called down for a . . . a martini, would you?

SAM: This is going to surprise you.

BILLY: You would mind.

SAM: Yes, I would. But not for my sake.

BILLY: For my sake.

SAM: That's right.

BILLY: *(Clearly in need of a drink)* I'll . . . skip it.

SAM: Smart man. Would you like a carrot?

BILLY: A carrot?

SAM: *(From end table he takes plastic bag filled with clean carrot sticks)* Orange-colored vegetables are especially good for you. Carrots, yams, pumpkins . . .

BILLY: Sam, I don't like carrots. Please don't try to change me, too. I have enough problems . . .

SAM: Do I tell you the second reason for my coming up here or don't I?

BILLY: Yes, I'd . . .

SAM: Then eat the carrot. *(Angrily, Billy rips the carrot out of Sam's hand and bites into it)* Just as much as you want me to take care of myself, I want you to take care of yourself. *(Eats a carrot)* And there's nothing wrong with changing. There's nothing wrong with saying to yourself, "I've been living a lie. I've learned something from life. I'm not a horse that doesn't have the capacity to change."

BILLY: What did you learn from life that made *you* change?

SAM: The two of us aren't alone, Billy. It's happening to everyone. It happened to Robby, to Seymour, to Harold . . . Not one marriage of the members of the Hinsdale Avenue Literary Club has survived. Not one. Freddy Rutner is the only member who never got married, and he's the happiest one of us all.

BILLY: Freddy's gay. That's why he never married.

SAM: And that's why he's the happiest one of us all.

BILLY: What are you saying, Sam?

SAM: I'll get to it in a minute.

BILLY: Please do.

SAM: (*Rises; paces*) It's not our fault, Billy. It's the sign of the times. We have to change our lives because they changed their lives. And I'm not saying they shouldn't have changed. They had every right to change.

BILLY: Who's they?

SAM: Women, who else?

BILLY: Women had every right to change?

SAM: That's right. They've been put upon and knocked about for millennia. They had to change. They had to become more aggressive. They had to become fighters in order to be treated decently and with respect. But the fact remains that as a result of their changing, we have to change. It's a whole new ball game.

BILLY: Men-women relationships.

SAM: Exactly. Billy, I'm convinced heterosexuality doesn't work anymore. It's an evolutionary fossil. And it's no one's fault.

BILLY: What are you saying, Sam?

SAM: I'll get to that in a minute.

BILLY: Please do.

SAM: Look around you; look at all the marriages you know, at all the men-women relationships you know: are you jealous? Do you sincerely wish you were in the man's shoes? Living with that particular woman and having that particular relationship?

BILLY: When I was living with Laura, I didn't need to fantasize other relationships.

SAM: (*Softly, slowly*) Billy, I want you to take what I'm going to tell you in the spirit in which I'm telling it to you.

BILLY: I wouldn't take it any other way, Sam.

SAM: When you were living with Laura and everybody said you had an ideal marriage, I, I personally, was extremely happy I wasn't in your shoes.

BILLY: You didn't think I had a good marriage?

SAM: Good? I thought your marriage was the pits.

BILLY: (*A beat*) Can I ask you, politely, why you thought my marriage to Laura was . . . (*Voice cracks*) . . . the pits?

SAM: Okay. I'll put our friendship on the line. I don't think Laura loved you.

BILLY: (*A beat*) How did you reach that conclusion?

SAM: This isn't easy for me. It's . . . Okay. Okay. I don't

want any lies standing between us. There were times, buddy, when behind your back, your wife Laura would look at you as if you were smelly dog do-do.

BILLY: Dog do-do?

SAM: Dog do-do.

BILLY: How many times?

SAM: I didn't count.

BILLY: Generally. Generally speaking. Give me a number. Any number.

SAM: A thousand, two hundred and twenty-five.

BILLY: That many?

SAM: I would say almost every time I was with you two.

BILLY: How precisely did she look at me, behind my back?

SAM: Like this. (*Sam creases his face in an expression of utter repulsion, then pinches his nose and turns away from imaginary Billy*)

BILLY: I see. (*Rises, voice cracked*) Do you mind if I have another Perrier water?

SAM: No, no . .

BILLY: And I'd like another carrot stick. I'm becoming very fond of them.

SAM: I felt obligated to tell you . . .

BILLY: Don't apologize, please. Obviously Laura found me . . . insufficient or she wouldn't have left me.

SAM: It has nothing to do with you personally. They have to establish their power, their independence. I've seen it first-hand. When I met Marilyn I was still married to Leslie. Now Leslie when I married her was your ordinary domestic wimp. A perfect wife for a playwright. But after going to those conscious-raising classes and marching on Washington a few times with those women-libbers, she became so filled with anger and resentment that she was just waiting for the opportunity to put me in my place.

BILLY: Did she?

SAM: Listen to this. One night I fell asleep in Marilyn's apartment and I got home at four in the morning. Leslie was up. I mumbled some excuse about falling asleep in my producer's office, an excuse which she always accepted in the past, and I went to bed. While I was sleeping, now listen to this, she spilled a bottle of red ink all over my dick.

BILLY: Noooo.

SAM: Yes. Yes. When I got up and saw the red ink, it really scared me. It looked like blood. I thought I was menstruating.

BILLY: You didn't.

SAM: I did. I did. That was my first thought. I was in total shock. After that, Leslie changed completely, became a new person. She started arguing and screaming and fighting . . . She even took a couple of stiff swings at me. Did Laura ever hit you?

BILLY: Once.

SAM: I knew it. They're all the same.

BILLY: (*Shows Sam*) She broke this tooth here. The one with the gold cap.

SAM: Why did she hit you?

BILLY: I forgot to take out the garbage. (*Wide grin*) I'm kidding about that. That wasn't it. It was something I said about her mother. I was drunk.

SAM: What did you say?

BILLY: I said her mother had herpes. (*A beat*) And she was giving it to the Marines. (*A beat*) I shouldn't have said it.

SAM: That's still no reason for her to break your tooth.

BILLY: You're right about one thing, Sam: women have changed. There's absolutely no comparison between the young women entering my classes today and those that entered fifteen years ago.

SAM: Big difference, huh?

BILLY: Enormous. Today they're tough; very tough.

SAM: Outspoken, know what they want, abrasive, even?

BILLY: They're beyond that. Should you show any sign by word or deed that you're a sexist . . . they cut your balls off. Immediately. No second thoughts about it.

SAM: Did you see what's going on between Seymour and his second wife?

BILLY: Unbelievable. It's unbelievable.

SAM: Why did he want to marry a police sergeant?

BILLY: You got me. I had dinner at their place last Wednesday night. At one point during the course of the meal Seymour asked her if there was any butter in the house. Well, you should have been there. She looked at Seymour, her eyes bulging out of her head, and she said in what I can only describe as a deep animal growl, "Do you want *me* to go to the refrigerator and see if there is any butter in the house?" Sam, I am not a man who normally is frightened by another person. But, believe me, that woman scared the living shit out of me.

SAM: What did Seymour do?

BILLY: He looked at me, his face absolutely white, and he said something to me in a very high-pitched voice, something he hadn't said to me in over thirty-five years.

SAM: What?

BILLY: (*High-pitched, boyish voice*) "Hey, Billy, you wanna play stickball?"

SAM: Stickball?

BILLY: He had regressed to an eight-year-old child.

SAM: She did that to him.

BILLY: (*Nods*) He was embarrassed. You know what I did? I went to the refrigerator, found the butter and put it on the table.

SAM: What did Seymour's wife do?

BILLY: Very deliberately and with great exaggeration, she buttered her bread.

SAM: The bitch.

BILLY: I got out of there as soon as I could.

SAM: We have to change, too, Billy. In all respects. Eating the right foods, exercising, thinking good thoughts, it could be the beginning of a whole new life for the both of us.

BILLY: It's possible. I have a confession to make to you, Sam. I haven't . . . completely stopped smoking. Occasionally, when there's pressure, I . . . I take a quick drag. A puff, that's all.

SAM: Do you have any cigarettes on you?

BILLY: Yes, I do.

SAM: Let me have them.

BILLY: I want you to have them.

(*Billy gives pack of cigarettes to Sam. Sam drops pack on floor and stamps on it, then crumples pack in his fist before dumping it into trash basket*)

SAM: You're going to feel a thousand percent better.

BILLY: I have no doubt about it. So. You're convinced heterosexuality doesn't work anymore.

SAM: That's right. And as I said it's nobody's fault. It's evolution. It's behaviorism over genetics; a fact of our times. We just have to be honest with ourselves and come out of the closet, Billy.

BILLY: What if one has never been in the closet?

SAM: Did you see the movie *Tootsie*?

BILLY: Yes, I did.

SAM: Did you like it?

BILLY: I loved it. The screenplay was absolutely brilliant.

SAM: I thought so too. Anyway, if the movie had anything to tell us it was this: no man should be afraid to grow and let out the feminine instincts that exist in him.

BILLY: When did you decide to let out your feminine instincts, Sam?

SAM: I haven't. Not yet. But I want to.

BILLY: You want to become a homosexual?

SAM: More than anything in the world.

BILLY: What if a gorgeous pair of tits walked in here right now?

SAM: I'm not interested. Did you see *La Cage aux Folles*?

BILLY: The movie, not the musical.

SAM: I did, too. About a month after Marilyn left me and wouldn't return my telephone calls. I was jealous, Billy. What those two homosexual men had, the humor, the deep affection, the lifelong commitment to share and be part of . . . Didn't you feel jealous, too? (*Billy looks about as if he wants to escape*) Didn't you wish, if only for a minute, that you were one of those two men? (*Billy wipes his perspiring brow with a handkerchief*) Didn't you wish in your heart of hearts that you could have their kind of relationship?

BILLY: No. Absolutely. I'm not . . . I couldn't . . .

SAM: Do you want to go on with the life you have? Do you want to go on with the hurt, the anguish?

BILLY: Sam . . .

SAM: You know what you said when you walked in here today? You said you loved me.

BILLY: That was rhetorical. That was merely rhetorical.

SAM: And I said I loved you. That wasn't rhetorical. But I don't know if I could have a homosexual relationship with you, Billy.

BILLY: (*Feeling put down*) Why not?

SAM: I don't . . .

BILLY: Do you think you can do better?

SAM: It's not that. I don't know if I can cut it, the sexual part of it. As for the rest, living with you would be fun and I know we'd get along.

BILLY: So this is the second reason you came to Boston.

SAM: Yes.

BILLY: To ask me to change my life and try to have a homosexual relationship with you.

SAM: Yes. To try is the key phrase. The chances are it wouldn't work out.

BILLY: Sexually?

SAM: Yes.

BILLY: But as for the rest you don't see any problems?

SAM: None whatsoever. In fact I feel there are innumerable advantages to being gay nowadays. I know if I were gay my play wouldn't be closing after such a short run.

BILLY: What has the run of your play have to do with being gay?

SAM: You just get a more sympathetic reception, from the critics, from the audiences . . . That's how it is. Would there be any advantages for you professionally if you were gay?

BILLY: Some wonderful advantages. The head of my department is gay. As is the fellow who runs the grants program.

SAM: I'm sick of loneliness, Billy. I could move into your house or we could rent another house.

BILLY: I'm not against living together. It'll be like old times. But why do we have to turn gay? Why can't we continue to be friends, roommates, so to speak?

SAM: And do what? Get on the merry-go-round again? Look for women, have affairs, get caught in the marriage trap? I thought you understood me, buddy. I don't want that life anymore. I want a new deal.

BILLY: I do understand, but I'm not built for . . .

SAM: All I'm saying is let's try it. If it doesn't work out, we're not going to make each other miserable. Billy, be truthful now. Do you find me physically unattractive?

BILLY: Oh, no. I wouldn't . . .

SAM: Do you want me to wear a hat?

BILLY: Ahhhh, yes, that might be helpful.

SAM: (*Puts on straw fedora*) Let's just walk around the room and talk, pretend we're just meeting, becoming acquainted.

BILLY: Are we both gay?

SAM: We're both inclined in that direction.

BILLY: (*A beat*) All right. Why not?

SAM: May I hold your hand?

BILLY: Hold my hand? Why not?

(*They hold hands and stroll around the room*)

SAM: Hi.

BILLY: Hi.

SAM: Nice weather.

BILLY: Oh, yes. Delicious.

(*They swing clasped hands*)

SAM: Have you been to Key West before?

BILLY: Am I in Key West?

SAM: (*Laughs*) Where did you think you were?

BILLY: In my mother's apartment. In Brooklyn.

SAM: You have a terrific sense of humor.

BILLY: What's that? What are you doing?

SAM: I'm putting my hand around your waist.

BILLY: (*Giggles*) Oh, I thought you were trying to pick my pocket.

(*They hold each other around the waist, walk for a few beats*)

SAM: I wish time would stand still.

BILLY: I do too. This is the cheapest vacation I ever had.

(*Sam turns, puts his hands on Billy's shoulders, stares deeply into his eyes*)

SAM: Billy?

BILLY: Yes?

SAM: (*With effort*) Billy?

BILLY: Yes, yes?

SAM: May I call you Billy?

BILLY: What would you like to call me?

SAM: I . . . Shit! I can't! I'm all tied in knots! I'm sweating . . . ! (*Tosses hat away; removes ascot*) Whew, it's hard. It's too hard for me, too hard. (*Pours himself a Perrier*)

BILLY: What . . . What were you trying to do?

SAM: I was going to . . . to kiss you on the cheek and . . . I'm sorry. It's no good. It's silly, stupid . . . I shouldn't have started . . .

BILLY: (*Emphatically*) Wait a second! Wait one! little! teeny-bitty second! (*Takes glass from Sam, drinks thirstily*) It is not so silly! There's a lot going on here, Sam, that if we cut if off now, we can regret it for the rest of our lives!

SAM: You weren't . . . ?

BILLY: Turned off by you? I was. I admit it. I kept looking at you and thinking of Laura and, frankly, I felt sick to my stomach. But! But! Simultaneously with that feeling was another feeling. I was having this fantasy and I felt there was something growing inside me . . .

SAM: Your feminine instincts?

BILLY: (*Nods*) You must have planted the seed. It was an absolutely new sensation for me. But what was so weird about this . . . fantasy . . . It was like a person was growing inside me.

SAM: A person?

BILLY: (*Nods*) A very small woman.

SAM: A very small woman?

BILLY: (*Nods*) Growing inside me. And becoming larger and larger . . .

SAM: Larger . . .

BILLY: Don't interrupt me, please. I feel foolish enough as it is. Let me finish. With my mind's eye, Sam, I could see this small woman growing inside me. I saw her as clearly as I can see you. She was wearing red, high-heeled shoes, nylon tights, a short, black, pleated skirt, a white, bolero blouse, and a red pillbox hat.

SAM: She was attractive.

BILLY: Extraordinarily attractive. And all the while we were talking I was carrying on this inner dialogue with her and . . . I called her by her name. I knew her name.

SAM: What was her name?

BILLY: Shirley.

SAM: The small woman inside you?

BILLY: Yes.

SAM: (*A beat*) How did you know that was her name?

BILLY: Instinctively. I knew it. But the point is we . . . were like old friends and I was hoping, all the while, I was hoping she'd keep growing until she . . . she was me.

SAM: You had a homosexual fantasy.

BILLY: I certainly did. Sam, I'm not ashamed that there's a . . . a Shirley growing inside me.

SAM: Why should you be?

BILLY: I feel better for having . . . made her acquaintance.

SAM: You're luckier than most. You connected with your own female counterpart. That's a major breakthrough.

BILLY: Now this is going to sound very weird, but I could have sworn I heard her voice. It was a thin, tiny voice.

SAM: You probably did. What did she say?

BILLY: (*In thin, tiny voice*) "Let me out. Billy, let me out! Please let me out!"

SAM: You're starting to live my fantasy. I'm really a little pissed off at myself.

BILLY: Sam, when you were talking about how you needed to change your life and that you felt being gay was the answer, I was silently laughing at you. I was. Now I beg you to accept my apologies.

SAM: You want to keep trying?

BILLY: (*Nods*) You were right before. I haven't enjoyed my heterosexuality in years. It hurts too much. Laura hurts too much.

SAM: (*Removes jacket; rolls up sleeves*) Okay. Let's give it another try. Neither one of us has to do anything that violates his moral conscience.

BILLY: Absolutely not.

SAM: All we have to do is establish that with time and patience our normal sexual drive will be gratified . . . somehow . . . in our relationship.

BILLY: So we're not in need of women.

SAM: They go their way; we go ours.

BILLY: We don't have to . . . actually, uhhh . . . penetrate each other?

SAM: Noo. Nooooo. It's silly to think about.

BILLY: It could merely be touching . . .

SAM: I'm against penetration. It doesn't even enter the picture.

BILLY: Or hugging . . .

SAM: Oh, maybe after we've been living together for a few years . . .

BILLY: It'll be primarily polymorphous perverse sex.

SAM: That's it. That's what we should have.

BILLY: It's normal and natural.

SAM: It's what babies do.

BILLY: But if we ever go beyond that, I will not be a catcher.

SAM: A catcher? I don't get it.

BILLY: Don't you know that in every homosexual relationship there's a pitcher and a catcher?

SAM: Are the roles that clearly defined?

BILLY: Of course. And I want it understood that if push comes to shove I will not be a catcher.

SAM: Well, I don't want to be a catcher.

BILLY: Well, you have to be a catcher because we can't have two pitchers.

SAM: (*A beat*) Why not?

BILLY: Why not? Have you ever heard of a baseball team that has two pitchers?

SAM: (*A beat*) Sure. What about a relief pitcher?

BILLY: A relief pitcher is not on the team with the starting pitcher. One follows the other.

SAM: Okay, so that's what we can do. You begin as the

starting pitcher and when you get knocked out of the box, I'll come in to relieve you.

BILLY: No.

SAM: Why not?

BILLY: Because I do not want to be a catcher!

SAM: Well, you can't just say you only want to be a pitcher and you're only a pitcher. The coach decides who will be the pitcher and who will be the catcher!

BILLY: But we do not have a coach!

SAM: Yes, we do.

BILLY: Who's our coach?

SAM: I am. (*A beat*) I forgot to tell you.

BILLY: You can't be the coach and a player too. That's absolutely ridiculous.

SAM: Who said so? Did you ever hear of a player-coach?

BILLY: Who may I ask gave you the authority to be the coach of this team?

SAM: The owner.

BILLY: And you're . . . ?

SAM: The owner, that's right.

BILLY: If that's the case, I quit the team.

SAM: You can't quit the team. We have an oral contract.

BILLY: No, we don't.

SAM: Yes, we do. You promised to live with me.

BILLY: It'll never stand up in court. Nev-er!

SAM: Okay, don't get excited. Here's what we can do. You're the starting pitcher. I'm the starting catcher. But as soon as you get tired, or show signs of weakening, or throw more balls than strikes, *you* become the catcher, I become the pitcher . . .

BILLY: Sam, why do I have to become the catcher? If I get tired and weaken, why can't you send me to the bullpen?

SAM: Didn't you yourself say there has to be a pitcher and a catcher? If I'm the pitcher and if I send you to the bullpen, where's my catcher? Who the hell do I pitch to, will you answer me that!

BILLY: (*A beat*) Why don't you use the third baseman?

SAM: (*Looks about bewilderedly, then*) You want me to pitch to another man?

BILLY: It may be the answer to our dilemma.

SAM: Bring a third baseman into our relationship?

BILLY: Yes.

SAM: What about the rest of the team? (*Billy doesn't re-*

spond) Do you want me to bring in a shortstop, a left fielder, a center fielder, a first baseman . . . ? Do you want me to bring seven more men into our relationship?

BILLY: If that's . . .

SAM: Don't you think the bed's going to be just a little too crowded?

BILLY: Sam, this is silly. We don't have to go into it now. I was premature in bringing it up. We may never go any further than polymorphous perverse.

SAM: I couldn't agree more.

BILLY: In any event, we must be brutally honest with each other as to our likes and dislikes.

SAM: No question about it.

BILLY: Is there anything you'd like me to do with *my* appearance?

SAM: Yes. I'd like you to grow a beard.

BILLY: A full beard?

SAM: Yes. And don't trim it on your cheeks or under your chin. I don't like trimmed beards.

BILLY: All right. Anything else?

SAM: Yes. I can't stand the way you dress.

BILLY: I always thought . . .

SAM: I didn't want to hurt your feelings.

BILLY: What don't you like about the way I dress?

SAM: Your colors invariably match. Your shirts match your socks; your ties match your jackets; your pants match your shoes . . .

BILLY: You don't like matched clothes?

SAM: I hate matched clothes. It drives me crazy.

BILLY: All right. I won't do it anymore.

SAM: Thanks. And see if you can't stop buying fashion design jeans.

BILLY: You don't . . . ?

SAM: Hate them. *Haaaate* them!

BILLY: Anything else?

SAM: No. What about me?

BILLY: (*Wags finger at him*) Don't you ever, ever, so long as you're my boyfriend, pluck your eyebrows again!

SAM: I . . .

BILLY: I won't have it, Sam; I won't. Do you know why?

SAM: Laura.

BILLY: Constantly. Constantly. Constantly plucking her eyebrows. She used to send me up the wall, plucking those eyebrows of hers as if they were chickens.

SAM: No more plucking, Billy. I promise. What else?

BILLY: When did you shower last, Sam?

SAM: Do I have bad body odor?

BILLY: Bad? No, it isn't bad. But what does the word toxic mean to you?

SAM: It could be the clove of garlic I eat every day.

BILLY: It could be.

SAM: I'll speak to my nutritionist about it.

BILLY: Please, do.

SAM: Maybe there's a vitamin substitute for garlic.

BILLY: I sincerely hope so.

SAM: I'll take care of it. I promise. When do you think we should . . . meet again?

BILLY: You don't have to go back to New York, do you?

SAM: I have nothing there.

BILLY: You might as well move into my place, the sooner the better.

SAM: I can pack in ten minutes. Billy, there is one thing you're going to have to promise me. You're going to have to make a commitment to me. If I fail at this relationship there's nowhere for me to go. My commitment is total. Is yours?

BILLY: How . . . How can we commit when we . . . have no idea how . . . how it'll turn out?

SAM: For better or worse, isn't that how it's said?

BILLY: Sam, you're rushing me. You lived with this decision for a long time. I can't be rushed.

SAM: Then maybe we should wait. I can't let myself go emotionally if you . . . (*The phone rings. They exchange an apprehensive stare. Sam picks up phone*) Yes? (*A beat*) He's still here, Laura. (*Hand over mouthpiece*) She wants to talk to you. (*Billy turns away to look through window*) Billy. (*Billy turns to him*) Don't let me down. Please.

(*He hands Billy the phone*)

BILLY: (*Into phone*) Yes, Laura. (*A beat*) Are you serious? (*A beat*) What happened? (*He looks nervously to Sam*) Is that the truth? (*A beat*) Yes. (*A beat*) A half hour. (*He mumbles a few lines that we can't hear then puts phone down*) Sam . . .

SAM: (*Not looking at him*) Don't . . . Don't say anything. I just want you to know that you . . . you hurt me. More than she hurt you. You hurt me.

BILLY: I'm not . . . I've never been as strong-willed, as in control of myself as you have, Sam. I don't have your resolve and determination. I don't. (*Impulsively, he snatches crumpled pack of cigarettes from trash basket, picks out a mangled cigarette, and lights it with lighter*) If one had to find a reason why you achieved the success you have while I'm caught in this academic bullshit . . . That would be it. (*Sam still does not turn to look at Billy. He busies himself at suitcases or merely stares through the window or at wall*) I can't help myself, Sam. She . . . Nineteen years. I can't . . . Not now. I have to give it another chance. I have to. (*A long beat*) Forgive me . . . buddy. (*He quickly moves to door, opens it*)

SAM: (*Turns*) Billy! (*Billy turns to him*) If you walk out now, there are no second chances with me.

(*Billy hesitates, wants to say something but feels it's futile. Perhaps he gestures, helplessly. He exits, shutting the door behind him.*

Sam exhales a weary sigh, drinks some Perrier, paces a moment, stops to stare at his reflection in the mirror. He doesn't dislike what he sees. He buttons his shirt collar then goes to closet, pulls out an expensively tailored jacket, and puts it on in front of mirror, turning this way and that.

Suddenly an idea comes to him. He takes a slip of paper from his wallet: on it is a telephone number. He dials the number, biting anxiously on his lip. Then into phone; forced brightness)

Hello, Seymour. Guess who? (*A beat; forced laughter*) That's right. How are you, buddy? How are you doing?

(*Sam glances at his reflection in the mirror as he talks on the phone. He straightens his clothes, grabs his straw fedora, puts it on, angles it this way and that, etc. Then into phone*)

I'm just in town for a few days and I thought maybe we could get together. (*A beat*) That . . . That'll be terrific. I am sorry about you and . . . and your second wife. It sounds like it was a catastrophe. (*A beat*) I'm anxious to see you too, Seymour. Yes, yes. There's so much we have to talk about. I don't know where to begin . . . Well, I have been trying to change my life. So far no success. But . . . Just talking to you . . . I feel better already . . .

(*During the above, the stage darkens and the curtain descends*)

The End

Julia Kearsley

BABY

Julia Kearsley

British playwright Julia Kearsley was born in Bolton, Lancashire, in the 1940s. In her midteens, she moved to Leeds, where helped by Alfred Bradley, she started writing and became involved in amateur dramatics. At that time, she also wrote peotry and short stories for radio.

In the late 1960s, Ms. Kearsley moved to London, where her first experiences in professional theatre encouraged her to start writing for the stage. After leaving London, she taught briefly in schools for the mentally handicapped in Scotland; this experience led her to write her first stage play, *Wednesday,* in the 1970s. *Wednesday* was performed at the Bush Theatre in England in 1979 and subsequently at the Liverpool Playhouse. Other productions of *Wednesday* followed in Sweden and Denmark. *Wednesday* is a ninety-minute play about a lower-class mother's efforts to cope with a mentally retarded son and an irresponsible daughter. Presented in New York in 1983 by the Hudson Guild Theatre, *Wednesday,* starring Sada Thompson and John Cunningham, was cited by the *New York Times* critic Frank Rich as an "arresting new play . . . grotesquely funny . . . [and] strangely moving."

The same descriptions might be applied to *Baby,* Ms. Kearsley's dark comedy-drama, published for the first time in this anthology. *Baby* explores the disturbing relationships of a young British girl coming to grips with puberty and her own unhappy circumstances. *Baby* was first performed in 1980 at London's ICA Theatre.

Ms. Kearsley's latest play, *Waiting,* is based on the case of the "Yorkshire Ripper" and is set in an area of her homeland that she knows well.

Characters:

ALEX, *late thirties*
SANDRA, *nearly thirteen*
DERRICK, *late thirties*

Scene:

Early evening. A bedroom with a single bed pushed against a wall on which are photographs of various pop groups. At the foot of the bed is a small cupboard and, at the side, hi-fi equipment. This latter is overlooked by a very large photograph of one particular pop idol wearing dark glasses and appearing to have a halo round his head. Next to the hi-fi is the door into the room, closed and locked. At the other side of the room are a wardrobe, drawers with a small mirror on top, a couple of large cushions for chairs, and a paraphernalia of clothes, records, and magazines scattered throughout the room. Generally, the place is something of a mess.

A record is being played at top volume while Sandra blow-dries her hair, which is long, in front of the mirror. She is nearly thirteen years of age, about five feet in height, wears a T-shirt over jeans and nature treck shoes, and is inclined a little to puppy fat. Throughout the play, she gives the impression of lagging behind in her mental and emotional development compared to her physical appearance. Her face is attractive, large eyed though not too dreamy. Her general expression, despite a sometimes impressive glare, is a questioning one.

Over the noise of the record, someone is heard kicking at the door. When Sandra hears this, she switches off the hairdryer and pulls out the plug. After standing defensively for a few seconds, looking at the door, she reluctantly unlocks and opens it.

Alex enters, smoking and holding a drink in her hand. There must be no physical resemblance between her and Sandra. Alex is a tall woman in her late thirties, dressed also in jeans and shirt, but they are a more sophisticated version of Sandra's attire. She wears a scarf knotted over the shirt and various rings. She is tired and in the aftermath of a row with her husband.

Sandra turns her back on Alex, who leans on the door to close it, then comes into the centre of the room. Sandra saunters over to her bed, wrapping the flex round her hairdryer. Alex stands, an obviously unwelcome guest, while the record blares on. It is not switched

off. They both wait until it has finished. Silence.
Neither will look at the other.

ALEX: He wants you to go down.
SANDRA: (*Half reclining on her bed and looking at the photographs*) I'm not.
ALEX: Says you've got to.
SANDRA: I know.
ALEX: What's up with you?
SANDRA: I'm not. (*Alex turns and looks at her*) I'm listening to records.
ALEX: Have you gone into bloody exile up here?
SANDRA: (*Muttering*) Better than listening to you two.
ALEX: What?
SANDRA: Nothing.
(*Pause*)
ALEX: You look like somebody's lost dinner.
(*Sandra gets off the bed and puts her hairdryer away in the cupboard. Alex looks across at the photograph over the hi-fi*)
ALEX: He's been dead over a month.
SANDRA: (*Slamming the cupboard shut*) Still hear his voice.
ALEX: You're not in mourning, are you?
SANDRA: He'll live forever.
(*She goes back to reclining on the bed and stares at Alex. Alex suddenly kneels on her haunches, tired. She looks for something on which to stub out her cigarette, can't find anything so finishes her drink and stubs it out in the empty glass. She rubs her eyes wearily*)
SANDRA: (*Disapproving*) You won't make it for the midnight film. You'll be lucky if you're still around for the eight-thirty.
ALEX: (*Not looking up*) It's already started, hasn't it?
SANDRA: Has it, hell, it's only seven o'clock.
ALEX: Oh God. (*She gets cigarette and lighter out of her shirt pocket and lights up another cigarette*)
SANDRA: I can't breathe in here. (*Alex doesn't reply*) Are you not going out?
ALEX: Go and speak to your father.
SANDRA: He's bad tempered, him.
ALEX: He's got reasons, Sandra.
SANDRA: I haven't done anything.
ALEX: He wants you.
SANDRA: I'll only get yelled at.

ALEX: Earning your own living then? (*Sandra looks away*) If you want to bite bread, you put butter on it.

SANDRA: I might be off out anyway.

ALEX: There'll not be any bread, rate things are going.

SANDRA: He's different now.

(*Alex stands up and walks away*)

ALEX: (*Bitterly*) You've changed. When I first arrived, he was God in this house. Stuck to him, you were. A limpet on a rock. I couldn't get a word, a smile.

SANDRA: That's daft.

ALEX: He wants you to go to university.

SANDRA: I know a woman who went to one, she's working in a bar.

ALEX: (*Turning on her sharply*) Are you drinking?

SANDRA: No.

ALEX: Sandra! . . .

SANDRA: I'm not! (*Suddenly aggressive*) You're always drinking, you!

ALEX: What?

SANDRA: We've had to get another bin for all the empties.

ALEX: You little liar, you . . .

SANDRA: (*Racing on desperately*) Did you go to Rambles at lunch? Bet you didn't dare have chicken, he was bad up last year, him.

ALEX: Who was?

SANDRA: Barman. He was out at back shooting crows.

ALEX: It's news to me.

SANDRA: He was.

ALEX: God, anything to do with what I fancy.

SANDRA: (*Imitating*) Oh, darling, let's go to Rambles for a pint and crow-in-a-basket!

ALEX: *I'm* big enough to like a drink. You're a puritan. Off your mother that. And maudlin, I still remember. I had a job on every year with you crying over that bloody crib at Christmas.

SANDRA: (*Turning away*) I'd never go to Rambles.

(*Pause*)

ALEX: (*Smiling slightly*) Do you still want to be a missionary?

SANDRA: (*Sulky*) No.

ALEX: Well that's something.

SANDRA: Changed my mind at Malta.

ALEX: Malta?

SANDRA: I can't get a tan.

(*Alex smiles to herself. She goes over to Sandra's bed*)

ALEX: Your hair looks nice anyway. Why won't you speak to your dad? (*Silence. Sandra leans over and switches off the record player*) Why? What's with all these moods? (*Silence*) Come on. Tell me. Sandra. I'm not something dragged in off the street. You've started, haven't you? (*Sandra gets off the bed and walks away from her. Alex follows*) Why won't you tell me? I look after you. Have you told *her*? Your mother? She's never off that phone.

SANDRA: (*Awkwardly*) I haven't started.

ALEX: She can't help you long distance. You only see her twice a year. Anyone can pick up a phone.

SANDRA: I like talking to her.

ALEX: It's me you should talk to. I'm here, not in Scotland. I'm responsible for you. I've got a right.

SANDRA: (*Turning to her*) Will you give me a couple of quid? I want to get a record.

ALEX: You ask *him* for money.

SANDRA: I'm not going downstairs.

ALEX: Time for you to be having your periods. I'll take you to the doctor.

SANDRA: He'd laugh at you.

ALEX: No, but you'll be crying if you end up pregnant because you don't know what the bloody hell you're doing.

SANDRA: You're daft, you.

ALEX: Sandra, why won't you talk about it?

SANDRA: (*Distressed*) I haven't started, I haven't, honest!

ALEX: Listen, I only want you to . . .

SANDRA: Leave me alone!

(*Pause*)

ALEX: Do they talk to you about sex at school?

SANDRA: All the time.

ALEX: You're going to be a woman.

SANDRA: I'm me, I'm me, mind your own business!

ALEX: (*Mocking*) What's me?

SANDRA: Me, that's all!

ALEX: Grow up, Sandra.

SANDRA: Just because you've had a row with my Dad.

ALEX: (*Weary*) It doesn't matter what you think you are. (*She walks away*)

SANDRA: (*Aggressively, still upset*) You don't know. You don't know what I think!

ALEX: Don't use towels when you do start, use tampons. They're cleaner.

SANDRA: I haven't started!

ALEX: I'll show you how to do it.

SANDRA: I keep telling you, I haven't, I haven't! Are you deaf? (*Alex has her back to Sandra and is examining the photograph*) I don't have to be like you. There's something else waiting. Something.

(*Alex suddenly notices the halo on the photograph*)

ALEX: Bloody hell, Sandra . . . have you painted that on? (*Sandra doesn't answer. Alex turns to her*) You have, haven't you? (*She turns back to the photograph*) You daft bugger.

SANDRA: I did it after he died. It looks nice like that.

ALEX: What have you done it for?

SANDRA: *My* photograph. (*She goes over to it, as if to protect it from Alex*) I wanted it different.

ALEX: Think he's a saint, do you? He was in prison once for stabbing somebody. Who was it, I . . .

SANDRA: Road manager.

ALEX: Nice saint. Did he kill him?

SANDRA: No, he tried to. He wanted to kill everybody. It wasn't because he hated people. He didn't start out like that. He was nice. (*Warming to her subject*) But he kept on seeing machines in his head, taking over. The only thing he could hear all the time was them clattering and whirring. And he said the sun was going to die and everything run by these machines and nobody able to sleep because of the noise in their brains. We'd go mad slowly and all the blood and water would be drained from our bodies. (*Alex stares at her, bemused. Sandra shows her an L. P. sleeve*) It's his last cover, that. A computer in a junk yard. See?

ALEX: (*Taking it from her and looking at it*) Is this what you spend your money on? It's horrible.

(*Sandra takes the sleeve from Alex and puts it back*)

SANDRA: (*Staring at Alex*) Sometimes I see people like skeletons. (*Looking at the photograph*) I wonder what colour his eyes were?

ALEX: He was mad. Drugged himself to death.

SANDRA: (*Defiantly*) It's not mad, doing that. He wasn't bothered about life.

ALEX: Good job. His didn't last long.

SANDRA: (*Indignant*) He was twenty-three! (*Turning back to the photograph*) Nobody ever saw his eyes. He'd been touring

America for three months on the road, and when he got back he was ill, he couldn't walk. They had to cancel a show. And his roadie had a go at him and he turned around and stabbed him. It wasn't because of that. It's just he was his friend and he didn't want him to see these machines, like he had. But he lived, anyway. (*She wanders away, talking half to herself*) I hope I don't see them. A lot of his records are about that. But some of them are different. I think he felt lost. He couldn't do half what he wanted to do.

(*She sits down on a cushion and looks meditative. Alex stares at her, thoughtfully, then walks over to the cushions and stands looking down at her*)

ALEX: He's only another bloke. You've got to try thinking about other things.

SANDRA: Is that why you went to night school?

ALEX: Do it while you're still young.

SANDRA: You were going for ages. Ages and ages and . . .

ALEX: All right.

SANDRA: (*Dreamily*) I wish I could see his grave.

ALEX: You've got to know where you're setting off to in life, if it means taking a bloody map with you. (*Sandra starts to make a low moaning sound*) Don't leave it all too late and end up in a bloody mess because you'll . . . what the hell are you doing? (*Sandra sounds like an animal in pain*) Why are you making that noise? I'm telling you something important.

SANDRA: I want to get my voice lower.

ALEX: (*Walking away*) A woman can't afford to make mistakes.

SANDRA: It's too high. (*She moans again*) I'll be a man then. (*More moaning*)

ALEX: Oh stop it, Sandra. What do you want a deep voice for? After the change, it'll drop anyway, you'll end up sounding like a man, if nothing else.

(*Doors are slammed angrily downstairs. Alex and Sandra look at each other. Alex opens the bedroom door and peers down the stairs. A door slams again*)

ALEX: Go down like I told you.

SANDRA: He's stopped now.

(*Alex closes the door*)

ALEX: (*Leaning her head against the wall*) He's built a row of houses and nobody's buying any of them. You've got to have people in houses.

SANDRA: Are they all empty? Every one?

ALEX: Every single one.

SANDRA: Empty. Empty houses. I bet he keeps driving past them, crying.

ALEX: It's the bank he cries about. He drives past his bank very fast. (*Coming back into the room*) Well, you've had more than I had at your age. A nice home.

SANDRA: I never had a cat.

ALEX: What do you want a cat for? (*Sandra shrugs*) I got my two a cat once, a little kitten it was. They found it one morning hanging off a tree outside the gate, a piece of string round its neck. Kids next door had done it. I tackled their mother, she said it was an accident. But she knew. That's the kind of bloody neighbourhood we lived in.

SANDRA: Everything's rotten to you. (*Alex looks puzzled*) Why don't you go cut your throat?

ALEX: What?

SANDRA: Cats are very beautiful. They've got eyes that shine in the dark, their fur's soft when you stroke it, there are loads of them everywhere, and the only one you remember was hung.

ALEX: What do you want me to do?

SANDRA: You're always miserable, I don't know why you bother talking.

ALEX: (*Pointing to the photograph*) What about him, then? Dracula. Draining blood and machines clanking round his brain! . . .

SANDRA: He wanted to change the world!

ALEX: He was off his bloody rocker.

SANDRA: (*Angry*) You don't understand. It's all in his songs. You have to listen to them. He had like a vision. He didn't just stand there, he . . .

ALEX: He couldn't, according to you.

SANDRA: He went all over the world. Everybody was making money out of him, using him, drugging him, breaking him up into little bits and he couldn't sing anymore but he kept on writing! . . .

ALEX: (*Flatly*) He's dead. And you're no bundle of joy neither. Think of the way *you* talk. You don't see life as being all that good, do you? Do you?

SANDRA: Ask your own kids. Why should I tell you anything? You never tell *me* anything. You just talk.

ALEX: What do you want to know?

SANDRA: Nothing. (*A door downstairs slams twice. Alex opens the bedroom door again, becoming slightly nervous. Derrick can be heard shouting her name. Sandra suddenly seems desperate*) What were you like at school?

ALEX: (*Watching the stairs*) School? I hated that place.

SANDRA: I don't like it either. They just waste your time, don't they? Always on at you to do what you can't do, and what you know you can do, they don't bother.

ALEX: I was black and blue half the time. (*Derrick shouts up to her again. She calls back*) She'll be down in a minute, she's just finishing her homework! (*To Sandra*) You'd better go down, love, I think he's serious.

SANDRA: I bet you weren't like me. At school.

ALEX: No I wasn't.

(*More noise from downstairs*)

SANDRA: Oh shit! (*She gets up and moves restlessly to the other side of the room*)

ALEX: (*Still watching the stairs*) Who's teaching you bad language? Is it your stepfather?

SANDRA: He doesn't like me.

ALEX: He's an antique dealer, isn't he?

SANDRA: That's why he doesn't like me. He says all the best ones are here. (*Imitating a Scottish accent*) "You English, you're the greatest looters in the world, did you know that?"

ALEX: (*Alarmed*) He's coming up here! You're in for it now, you are. (*Sandra quickly runs to the door, closes it and locks it*) What you doing that for? (*Sandra puts the key in her pocket and moves away from the door*) Sandra? . . .

SANDRA: I don't want him coming in, do I?

ALEX: He's your dad! (*Sandra doesn't answer and won't look at her*) And I bet it's not you he'll have a go at neither when he finds that door locked.

(*Derrick tries the door and Alex moves nervously away*)

DERRICK: It's locked, I can't get in. (*He bangs on the door*) Come on, open up.

ALEX: Sandra, give it to me. (*She tries to get the key off Sandra*)

SANDRA: I wish you'd stayed downstairs.

DERRICK: Are you talking about me? (*He bangs on the door again*)

ALEX: (*Shouting to him*) Sandra's a bit upset!

(*Alex and Sandra are struggling for the key*)

DERRICK: You said she was doing her homework. What's the matter with her?

SANDRA: He wants to see somebody, him.

ALEX: He wants to see *you*.

(*Derrick bangs on the door again*)

ALEX: Derrick, love, could you come up a bit later?

DERRICK: Open the bloody door!

ALEX: I can't.

DERRICK: Open it, I'm not asking again!

ALEX: (*To Sandra*) You'll have to let him in.

(*Sandra pushes Alex away from her and unlocks the door. She flings it wide open and walks away to the foot of her bed, without looking. Derrick is standing at the open door, a bottle of wine and an empty glass in one hand. He is tall, good looking in an obvious way, perhaps slightly over the hill. He is dressed in sweater and casual trousers. His feet are bare. He walks slowly into the room, obviously still angry, looking from Alex to Sandra. There is a tense, nervous atmosphere. He suddenly looks down*)

DERRICK: I've got flat feet.

ALEX: (*Relieved and annoyed*) Bloody hell.

DERRICK: Never noticed 'til now.

ALEX: It's rotten, that.

DERRICK: (*Going to her*) Just trying to be original.

ALEX: You've never been original. I'm on Valium.

DERRICK: We were all original once.

ALEX: You don't think.

DERRICK: I remember when I walked through this house like a king.

ALEX: Banging about, frightening folk.

DERRICK: (*Holding up the bottle*) Drink?

ALEX: It's cheap, that is.

DERRICK: Is it?

ALEX: What you did, it's cheap.

DERRICK: Have some. Where's your glass. (*Alex picks up her glass full of cigarette stubs and turns it toward him*) Oh. I'll go without then. (*He hands her the glass and the bottle*)

ALEX: (*Walking away to the bed*) You don't look after me.

DERRICK: I don't know what you want, do I? (*He watches Sandra, who crosses over to the cushions, not wanting to hear. Alex flops down on the bed*)

ALEX: You couldn't give me what I want.

DERRICK: (*Turning back to her and shouting*) Well what *do* you want? What? Come on, tell me. What's the matter, Alex? Is there something you've not got? Come on. What is it?

(*Alex looks away*)

ALEX: I thought you came up to see Sandra.

(*She pours herself a drink and consumes it fairly rapidly. Derrick turns from her abruptly and watches his solitary daughter for a few seconds. He goes and sits down beside her on the cushions, wincing a little in discomfort at this. He is ill-at-ease with her*)

DERRICK: Get you a chair for in here. If you want. Would you like that? Bit more comfort.

SANDRA: (*Looking down*) No.

DERRICK: I can get you one. (*He reaches into his trouser pocket and takes out a bar of chocolate, smoothing down the pocket as he does so. Sandra glances at the candy, then looks away. He offers it to her*) Go on. It's for you.

SANDRA: (*Whispering*) I don't want it.

DERRICK: It's your favourite. Raisins in. Peace offering, this. Don't know what I've done, mind you. (*Slightly impatient*) Come on, take it. Don't make me a fool.

(*Sandra takes the chocolate from him and proceeds to eat some of it—very slowly and obviously under duress*)

DERRICK: What do you think about then? Up here? I never see you. I miss you, you know. You used to like talking to your dad. Always on the phone to me, you were. Remember? When I was at work. You liked phoning me.

ALEX: (*Sourly*) How's business then?

DERRICK: (*Sharply*) A narrow market, but a market for sellers. (*To Sandra, gently*) Hey, remember the summer when that seagull followed us everywhere we went? And we leaned over a well and his shadow floated on the water? Do you remember that?

SANDRA: It wasn't the same one.

DERRICK: You thought it was. You said "Look, Daddy, it's that bird again!"

SANDRA: Mummy thought it had drowned.

DERRICK: You're smiling (*He holds out both hands clenched into fists*) Choose one.

SANDRA: It's daft, that.

DERRICK: No it isn't. Come on. Which one do you choose? (*Sandra points to his left hand. He opens it*)

SANDRA: There's nothing there.

DERRICK: It's a wish, isn't it? Yours. You'll have to describe it to me. Because only you know what it is.

SANDRA: I can't.

DERRICK: Course you can. Tell me about it. What do you wish for? Come on, tell me, I'm waiting. (*Silence. Sandra looks*

at him almost accusingly and he glances away from her) You'll have
to grow up. It's a shame. *(He opens his right hand and looks at it)*
It's not because I want you to. You're my girl, aren't you? I'd
be lonely without you. It's not your dad wants to let you go.

ALEX: *(Muttering to herself)* Eeny meeny miny mo, sit the
baby on the po.

SANDRA: You didn't want me.

DERRICK: Who told you that?

SANDRA: Mummy did. She said I wasn't planned. And after I was born, you didn't look at me for three months.

DERRICK: Oh . . . she probably wasn't feeling well. *(He
looks at Sandra intently)* You know, Sandra, love . . . it's a very
strange thing . . . but you find out in life that what you
thought you didn't want turns out in the end to be something
you do want. Very much indeed.

SANDRA: Honest?

DERRICK: *(Awkwardly)* Honest. You look back. You look
back, you see . . . and you think how much emptier your life
would have been . . . if that had never happened to you.
That's how I feel about you.

SANDRA: Does it work the other way round?

DERRICK: What?

SANDRA: If you start off wanting something, do you end
up different?

DERRICK: *(Evasively)* I don't know.

SANDRA: *(Becoming enthusiastic)* I didn't want to go to that
concert because I was frightened of big crowds. I thought I'd
get crushed and then when I got there I was really glad, It was
the best time I ever had, that!

DERRICK: Good!

SANDRA: Funny, isn't it, and when you don't want to go? I
bet if I'd really wanted to, I wouldn't have enjoyed it, and I
had a great time, it was really great! . . .

DERRICK: *(Relieved at her change of mood)* You see? Your
dad's always right, isn't he? Think what you miss, sitting up
here on your own.

SANDRA: It was great!

DERRICK: Aren't you glad I've come to see you?

SANDRA: Really great.

DERRICK: Aren't you? Am I still your number one? Sandra. Eh? *(He leans toward her and she looks away suddenly)* Sandra. You're getting very pretty, you know. You like me, don't
you? You like your dad? *(He hugs her to him but she is obviously*

disturbed by this) Sandra? . . . You do, don't you? . . . Sandra?
. . . (*She nods her head but won't look at him*) That's my girl! (*He stands up and his tone becomes hearty, slightly forced*) Great! That's really great! (*He ruffles her hair*) . . . Hey! Sandra. Come here to your dad . . . (*He pulls her to her feet although she is trying to get away from him*) What's your weight now? Bet I can still carry you on my shoulders! . . . (*He bends down to lift her, seizing her waist from behind*)

SANDRA: (*Panic-stricken*) No! No, I don't want you to, stop it! . . .

DERRICK: Come on, let me try. I won't hurt you. (*He has to struggle to keep hold of her*)

SANDRA: I don't want you to!

DERRICK: You're not too big yet, I can still . . .

SANDRA: No don't, don't . . . leave me alone . . . DON'T!
. . .

(*She is almost hysterical. Derrick stops his attempts to lift her. She moves away from him in a manner that implies revulsion and leaves him crouching on the floor, staring at her. His mood has changed*)

DERRICK: What's up with you?

SANDRA: (*Shakily*) Nothing.

DERRICK: What is it, Sandra?

SANDRA: I don't want you to.

DERRICK: Why won't you let me near you? (*Sandra doesn't reply. She looks utterly miserable*) Answer me. (*Silence*) Sandra. I won't give you another chance.

(*Pause*)

SANDRA: I've got a raisin in my nose.

DERRICK: What? (*He stands up, bewildered*)

SANDRA: From that chocolate. It hurts.

DERRICK: In your nose?

SANDRA: It's stuck right at the top.

DERRICK: How the bloody hell have you managed that?

SANDRA: I don't know.

DERRICK: Let me look. (*He moves toward her*)

SANDRA: (*Backing away*) No, leave it!

DERRICK: (*Angry*) Don't be stupid, Sandra.

SANDRA: (*Panicking*) You won't be able to see it, honest, you won't!

DERRICK: I'm sick of this. Don't play silly games with me. Stand where you are. (*He attempts to peer into Sandra's nose*) Alex . . . Alex! . . . come over here a minute, will you. Alex!

ALEX: (*Sitting up slowly*) What?

DERRICK: She's got something in her nose.

ALEX: What?

DERRICK: Sandra.

ALEX: Who?

DERRICK: (*Going to the bed*) Sandra! She's got a raisin. Stuck. In her nose.

(*Alex looks cursorily at Sandra then flops back on the bed*)

ALEX: She's having you on.

(*Derrick turns to look at Sandra*)

SANDRA: (*Timidly*) It's come out now.

(*Silence. Derrick stares at her*)

DERRICK: (*Threateningly quiet*) Don't you ever do that to me again. (*He turns away from her and goes to the door then turns back*) I've cared about you. And there's nothing, is there? (*To Alex*) Are you coming?

ALEX: (*Not looking at him*) I might.

DERRICK: I don't know what you want, the pair of you.

ALEX: Me, I want to be finished with wanting.

(*Pause*)

DERRICK: Try and do something with her.

(*Alex raises her glass to him. He goes out, slamming the door behind him. Silence*)

SANDRA: (*Defiant*) I'd never buy one of his houses. Not if I'd a million pounds, I wouldn't.

ALEX: You're not very clever.

SANDRA: What did he come up here for?

ALEX: You could have made use of it, do you know? That was your chance to learn. One word. He'd have been at your feet. You're old enough.

SANDRA: Trying to make me look small, but I'm a giant and I'm still growing.

ALEX: I mean you're on the brink, aren't you? So make your mind up.

SANDRA: (*Turning to Alex*) I'll not be here forever. I'll go. What do you care? You'll never know about me.

ALEX: (*Sitting up*) I'll tell you what I know. There's one of two things you can do. You listen to me. Either you get yourself a career, like I told you, or if it's men you want—are you listening?—you play at being a female, you play, understand? Never mind what anyone else tells you. I know. Doesn't work with them. They don't want honesty. They want a proper female. A proper, proper female, here comes my head my arse'll follow.

SANDRA: I don't like this house.

ALEX: She's one! Lorna Doone! Never off the bloody phone. It's guilt, that is. She knows what she's done. But she doesn't play fair. Twists it round is what she does. Makes it look like I don't take care of you. It's clever, that. You've got to hand it to her, she's clever.

SANDRA: (*Turning away from Alex*) She worries about me stopping out late. I might be attacked.

ALEX: I'm your mother now. Tell her that. You see me every day, how many times do you . . . ?

SANDRA: I see her a lot.

ALEX: When?

SANDRA: I just see her, I'm telling you.

ALEX: Come off it, Sandra, twice a year, you can't . . .

SANDRA: (*Facing Alex*) I do! I see her!

ALEX: All right, when? When? When do you see her?

SANDRA: After school. She comes to see me all the time. She waits for me. We go for walks. I'll be living with her soon.

ALEX: (*Angry*) Bloody hell, I should have known. Where does she stay? That's going behind my back. It's wrong. I known she's your mother, but she's a cow. She's no right. She left you. She left you, Sandra.

SANDRA: She doesn't like me being on my own. I can go and live with her any time I like.

ALEX: Can you? (*Alex looks searchingly at Sandra, who turns away*)

SANDRA: A girl I know she got flashed on the other night.

ALEX: Oh? Has that ever happened to you then? (*Sandra doesn't answer and Alex laughs rather mockingly*) Wake you up, that would.

SANDRA: I already know.

ALEX: Do you?

SANDRA: I know what they look like.

ALEX: What who looks like?

SANDRA: Blokes. When they've no clothes on. I've seen it.

ALEX: (*Rather more alert*) Seen what?

SANDRA: Everything.

ALEX: Where? On telly?

SANDRA: No. Seen it for real.

(*Alex gets off the bed in one movement then realises perhaps she has drunk too much. She stumbles slightly then goes toward Sandra, who suddenly faces her*)

ALEX: What have you been doing?

SANDRA: I was at a party.

ALEX: When?

SANDRA: We went from a disco. I didn't drink anything. I wasn't drinking.

ALEX: When?

SANDRA: It was in a big house. Bigger than this one. He took me into a room. Upstairs, it was. An empty room. It had no curtains up. And funny wallpaper. I didn't want to go with him. I wanted him to take me home. He said he'd take me home, you see. I didn't want, I . . .

ALEX: What happened?

SANDRA: I didn't know where I was. I asked him. We went in a car. And I kept looking out of the window. But I couldn't recognise anything.

ALEX: What happened, Sandra?

SANDRA: It wasn't late or anything, the buses were still running, I could have got one, if I'd known where I was.

ALEX: (*Almost shouting*) What happened?

SANDRA: He just took his clothes off. He wasn't wearing much. (*Silence*) Do you think I should have said anything? Do you? I didn't.

ALEX: I'm going for your dad. (*She moves toward the door. Sandra follows her, suddenly frightened*)

SANDRA: What for?

ALEX: I want him up here.

SANDRA: Don't!

ALEX: He can listen to this. (*She partly opens the door, but Sandra seizes her wrist*)

SANDRA: He's not got to know. Only you.

ALEX: Let go.

SANDRA: (*Panicking*) Nothing happened. Don't tell him, Alex, don't it's rotten that! (*Alex hesitates*) I've not done anything, honest, don't tell him, you'll get me into trouble! . . .

ALEX: You don't need me for that.

SANDRA: (*Aggressively*) I've not done anything.

ALEX: I don't believe you.

SANDRA: I've not! (*She moves away and won't look at Alex, who follows her*)

ALEX: Who do you think I am. Sandra—Winnie-the-Pooh?

SANDRA: Nothing has to happen because of that. You think everyone's like you are.

ALEX: He took his clothes off, you said.

SANDRA: Wish I hadn't said anything now.

ALEX: What did you do?

SANDRA: Keep going on at me. Tomorrow you won't be talking. (*She is still moving away from Alex*)

ALEX: What did you do?

SANDRA: Nothing. I've told you. Why should I do anything? I said to him I'm not taking mine off.

ALEX: What?

SANDRA: I sat and watched him.

ALEX: He was naked. And you kept your clothes on? That's unusual, Sandra.

SANDRA: What was I supposed to do?

ALEX: Oh, God.

SANDRA: It only hung there. He looked daft.

ALEX: It what?

SANDRA: He said he couldn't manage it or something. So I laughed. I laughed really loud. (*Facing Alex*) They go right off you if you do that.

ALEX: How old was he?

SANDRA: What's that matter?

ALEX: (*Stern*) It matters. It matters. Everything. I want you to tell me. I've got to know.

SANDRA: (*Frantically*) He should have taken me home, shouldn't he? I laughed. I laughed, me. I laughed 'til I choked. And everybody could hear. He didn't touch me. Didn't dare. He was dead scared, you could see, his eyes were rolling. I kept laughing at him. I never stopped. (*Alex, tired and not really knowing what to believe in all this, goes to pour herself another drink while Sandra hurtles on*) It's all daft. I'll not do anything if I don't want. There's lots of ways. You can kick them where it hurts. Or you can cross your legs and curl up small. You can get their eyes out if you grow your nails long. Stick a finger in your throat and make yourself sick. Or buy sneezing powder from a joke shop. Pour tomato sauce all over you and make it look like you've had a nose bleed, it's a good one that. (*Alex returns with her drink, looking wearily bewildered*) He gave up in the end. I got a lift home. Not with him. I wouldn't go with him. (*Alex sits down on the cushions, has her drink then hangs her head in despair*) . . . Nothing happened . . .

ALEX: All right.

SANDRA: Honest to God, nothing.

ALEX: I believe you.

(*Silence. Sandra, appearing worried by Alex's attitude, picks up a bag of sweets from off the cupboard*)

ALEX: Sandra, now listen to me, I . . .

SANDRA: Do you like orange balls?

(*Alex looks up, startled. Sandra offers her the sweets. She takes one, laughing quietly to herself*)

ALEX: Any colour'll do.

SANDRA: (*Relaxing*) I bet he got some stick after that. I bet they pulled his leg.

ALEX: (*Beginning to collapse*) Sandra . . . (*She spits out the sweet into her hand*)

SANDRA: Do you not like them? They taste nice at first, don't they? But you go off them after a bit.

(*At this, Alex howls with laughter, and Sandra laughs, too. Both of them are slightly hysterical. A door slams downstairs. They laugh even louder. It is some time before they begin to recover*)

SANDRA: I was lying to you. I made it all up.

ALEX: What the hell for?

SANDRA: (*Shrugging*) Wanted to see what you'd do.

ALEX: (*Indignant, relieved*) Don't try it again. It isn't as funny as you think. God, he'd have thrown me through the bloody window, I'm responsible for you. I wouldn't use sneezing powder neither. (*Looks at Sandra*) You'll be sneezing with him, won't you? He might recover before you do. (*She lights a cigarette. Sandra moves to the bed*) And don't kick him, love, they're usually ready for that.

SANDRA: Did you think I was telling the truth? Were you mad at me? (*She has taken something from under the bed*)

ALEX: (*Turning to her*) I never know what to think with you, I . . . (*Sandra is sitting next to the bed, her back to Alex. She holds up a large red scarf*) . . . That's nice. Where'd you get it from?

SANDRA: Mum. She gave it to me. (*She puts the scarf over her head so that it covers her almost to the waist, like a veil. She stands up and sings raucously*) "Whose is the blood? . . . It's blinding me" . . .

ALEX: What are you doing?

SANDRA: (*Walking near to Alex*) "I'm ripped off, friend . . . It's all in the circuits . . . Clogs the control wheels . . . I'm ripped off and blind" . . .

ALEX: What? I can't hear you. (*Alex pulls off the scarf. Sandra is clasping a doll in her arms*)

SANDRA: (*Muttering*) It's all shit.

ALEX: It's a doll, what did you say?

SANDRA: Nothing.

ALEX: (*Trying to reach the doll*) I don't remember that one. (*Sandra won't let her touch the doll. She kneels down, still clutching it to her*) Let me look at it . . . Sandra . . .

SANDRA: He's missing an arm. (*She holds the doll out in front of her; it's unclothed and has only one arm*)

ALEX: You're really friendly, you, aren't you?

SANDRA: Somebody else took it. But I got the other one and its legs. I stretched out as far as I could. He had it on stage with him. He said, "This is me." And he tore all its clothes off. And banged its head on the mike. Then he passed it round to his group. They pulled its arms out and its legs and twisted its head off. And gave the pieces back to him. And he said, "This is me. You can have all of it." I knew he'd say that. I knew. The others were all clawing on the stage, but I didn't. I just lifted my hands right up. Like this. So he could see me. And I caught all the pieces. Except that one. I caught all of them. And the others were going mad trying to get them off me. But I hung on to them tight. I put them under my jacket. You're not having them, you're not, I'm taking them home with me. And I did, I hung on like anything and then I ran. I ran all the way, they didn't catch me, they didn't, they didn't catch me . . . nobody did. (*She wraps the scarf round the doll*) He looks nice now. I've fitted him back together.

ALEX: What did he do that for?

SANDRA: I'll have to get him another arm. Have you got an old doll you don't want? Alex? Have you? (*Alex laughs and shakes her head*) I can't find any of mine.

ALEX: Hey listen, Sandra, let's go down and tell your Dad, come on, give him something to laugh about, eh?

SANDRA: I'm not telling him.

ALEX: It's only a joke, might put his face right.

SANDRA: Wish I hadn't told *you* now. (*Alex tries to touch the doll, but Sandra jerks it away from her, and loosens the scarf*) Best not to wrap him too tight, he's got to breathe.

ALEX: (*Impatient*) Let me have a look. Why can't I have a look? . . .

SANDRA: Nobody has to touch him but me.

ALEX: Sandra . . .

SANDRA: He's asleep.

(*Derrick enters suddenly through the half-open door. He now looks rather disheveled and the worse for drink. Neither of the other two has seen him*)

ALEX: (*Stroking Sandra's hair*) You make me laugh, you do. Get funny ideas, don't you? I like having a laugh. (*She suddenly sees Derrick, who has walked up behind her*) Well I never, Lord of the Flies, back again.

DERRICK: What the hell are you doing?

ALEX: Have you seen this? (*To Sandra*) Show him your doll.

DERRICK: She's too old for dolls.

ALEX: You'll never guess how she got it, she . . .

DERRICK: She's too old!

ALEX: All right.

(*Sandra turns away from them and huddles over the doll, but they don't really seem to be aware of her despite talking about her*)

DERRICK: You'll not get what you want, Alex. You're trying to turn her against me. It's you. It's you. I'm everything to that kid. She loves me.

ALEX: (*Standing up*) I'm up here because you asked me.

DERRICK: What have you been saying to her? Why can't I touch her?

ALEX: I've been on your bloody side.

DERRICK: I'll tell you something, I fought for that kid, Moira wanted her off me.

ALEX: You didn't fight for mine.

DERRICK: She kept phoning her when she knew I'd be out of the house, waiting for her after school, promising her God-knows-what if she'd go and live with her. (*Sandra goes to the bed with her doll and lies down*) I got the law on my side, I had to do what was right, stop her from seeing Sandra . . .

ALEX: Oh, you would!

DERRICK: I had to do it, but she hated me for it, Sandra did. I've never told you, it took me a year before she came round. I worked at it, you see. I worked bloody hard with that kid. And I got her on my side in the end. I fought for her and I got her! . . .

ALEX: Where are my two then?

DERRICK: I'll not lose her now, I'm telling you, Alex, you listen! . . .

ALEX: You dangled her in front of me when I couldn't have my two, you used her, you . . .

DERRICK: You try anything on with me, I'll break your bloody neck!

ALEX: You didn't fight for mine.

DERRICK: Leave her alone, just leave her alone, that's all I'm saying! . . .

ALEX: God I can pick 'em, I can pick 'em!

DERRICK: (*Moving closer to Alex and lowering his voice*) She'll see right through you, you know that, don't you? She's my daughter.

ALEX: But you've let her down. You're not capable of loving anybody, you.

DERRICK: (*Incensed*) Is that what you've been telling her about me?

ALEX: She knows that now, she knows.

DERRICK: Is that what you've been telling her?

ALEX: Don't try making up for it with money, you're running out of the stuff . . . (*Derrick makes a threatening move and she jumps away*) She's on to you, Derrick, you're a rotten father, you are, you're worse than the one *I* had! . . .

DERRICK: (*Shouting*) What about *you*?

ALEX: What?

DERRICK: What about you?

ALEX: I've done nothing.

DERRICK: That Christmas.

ALEX: Christmas?

DERRICK: Christmas.

ALEX: What bloody Christmas?

DERRICK: You never came home, did you, you never came home. She waited for you, ten years old she was, Christmas, not a phone call, not a present . . .

ALEX: You liar! . . .

DERRICK: I didn't tell her! . . .

ALEX: I phoned, I phoned twice.

DERRICK: I didn't tell her, I said you had a sick friend . . .

ALEX: He *was* sick! (*Derrick grabs hold of her to hit her*) She's watching you, Derrick, she's watching you! . . .

DERRICK: Shut up, shut up, shut up! . . .

ALEX: Look, look at her face, she's watching, she's watching, look at her! . . .

DERRICK: Shut up!

(*They struggle briefly. He throws her away from him and she falls on to the bed, almost on top of Sandra, who cries out. Silence. Alex sits up shakily, on the verge of tears*)

ALEX: I've got a headache.

DERRICK: (*Suddenly embarrassed, his anger gone*) . . . Have we got anything downstairs? (*Alex doesn't answer*) I don't know where they are. You'd better have a look . . . (*He turns toward Sandra, who is still huddled with her doll on the bed. He goes to her*) . . . All right, are you? It's just a quarrel. Married people they do that. Can't always get on, you see. It's nothing . . . You coming down with me? (*Sandra looks fixedly at her doll. Derrick glances round the room, not knowing what to say*) . . . We need extra space, you know. It's too cramped. Could build an extension downstairs. More room for your stereo. Well . . . see how things go eh? . . . (*Looking at her again*) . . . Okay . . . (*He goes to the door then turns to Alex*) I'll look for something for you . . . (*Derrick exits. Silence. Alex suddenly rushes to the door and slams it shut. She leans against it*)

SANDRA: What did you marry him for?

ALEX: He was a wild boy. And he jumped up and down.

SANDRA: I'll never marry, me. I'm more interesting than anybody I know. (*Alex comes back into the room. Sandra starts playing with the doll*) I don't mind talking to him. I don't. But he shouldn't try and hold me. It's not right, is it? He shouldn't touch me.

ALEX: What?

SANDRA: You're always saying that. What, what?

ALEX: Talk sense then.

SANDRA: He's always staring at me. And he makes excuses to get near me. When you're not here. I have to lock the bathroom door. And sometimes I can hear him outside. Waiting. Breathing. I've got thin ears, you see. He says to me, "When are you coming out, Sandy? I want you. Come out here, Sandy" . . . Mummy calls me Sandy . . . (*She stops, as if expecting Alex to say something*) . . . Once he made me cry. And I was sick all down his shirt. I don't think people should look at you when you've no clothes on. It's not like they're looking at *you*, somehow.

ALEX: What happened to you at that party?

SANDRA: (*Staring at Alex*) I'm going to dress dead colourful, me. In a rainbow.

ALEX: Something must have happened. Sandra . . .

SANDRA: I'll shine like anything, and they'll all go blind when they see me.

ALEX: You've not told me the truth.

SANDRA: I don't like it. I'm me. I shouldn't be touched!

ALEX: He's your dad.

SANDRA: I'll jump off the roof, I'll fly! . . .

ALEX: You don't talk . . . you don't say those things about him, it's not natural, he's your dad, he . . .

SANDRA: He should leave me alone, shouldn't he?

ALEX: He loves you.

SANDRA: He's got you for that.

ALEX: What?

SANDRA: Right up your street.

ALEX: You don't know what you're talking about.

SANDRA: I do know, I do, I do.

ALEX: What? I've asked you, haven't I? What do you know, Sandra?

SANDRA: I've got pains, I've got them all over.

ALEX: Have you been messed around with?

SANDRA: Can you not give me an old doll, can you not?

ALEX: If anybody's touched you, I've got to know about it, I . . .

SANDRA: Nothing happened, nothing, I've not said anything happened! . . .

ALEX: (*Exasperated*) You live in a fantasy, you, you don't know what's real, you say the first thing that comes into your head, you . . .

SANDRA: It's just I'm fed up being in this house, I can't see anything out of the window. I liked the other one best, when I was little, it got more sun.

ALEX: When Mummy was with you, is that what you mean? Mummy, Mummy, Mummy. Is that it? Is that what all this is about? You want to go back to her, don't you?

(*Sandra starts to cry, burying her face in the doll. Alex goes to the bed*)

ALEX: Sandra? . . . (*She sits on the bed and pulls Sandra toward her*) Come here. What's the matter? Gone off your dad, have you? Come here to me. I want you to like me and then I can help you. Protect you. I'll tell you what it's about. I'm on your side, love. Never mind what I said to him, he's a man, isn't he? You've got to box clever with them, even when you love them, that's life, you see. Shouldn't expect too much. That's your trouble, isn't it? You've worshipped him. No bloody good worshipping. Expect nothing, love, and you won't be disappointed. We'll stick together, you and me. I'll show you. I'll show you how to beat them, don't worry. Get them on their bloody knees. You'll do it. Not worth crying over. You'll do it. You've still got time. Live for yourself, Sandra. Don't let the buggers get you down. (*She kisses her forehead. Sandra is still tearful*) That's my blessing on you. (*She stands up*) I'm going downstairs, now. I've been up here long enough. (*She goes to the door*) You come when you feel like. (*Smiling at her*) I'll be waiting.

(*As Alex opens the door, she bends down casually to tidy up a pile of clothes, cushions, etc. She suddenly notices a corner of a cloth showing from under a cushion and pulls it out. It is actually a piece of an old towel with red stains on it. She examines it closely for a moment. Sandra, who has been watching her, sees what she has found and looks tense. Alex sniffs the cloth*)

ALEX: This is blood. (*Turning to Sandra*) Have you hurt yourself? (*Sandra stares at her, but doesn't answer*) Here, love . . . Here, what is it? What have you done, what's happened to you?

SANDRA: (*Evasive*) Nothing. You've not got to look at it. (*Pause*)

ALEX: (*Suddenly realising*) Oh God! . . . (*She goes to Sandra and grabs her arm*) Come here, you, I want to talk to you. (*She yanks her off the bed, Sandra pulling against her*) I know what this is. I know. Come here, Sandra, you don't need that! (*She pulls the doll away from her*)

SANDRA: No don't, he's still broken, don't, Alex!

(*Alex throws the doll onto the bed and drags Sandra away. There is still a struggle*)

ALEX: What's the matter with you? I've been on at you for months. You told me you hadn't started.

SANDRA: You shouldn't come up here, it's my room, you've not to disturb me.

ALEX: (*Pushing the towel at her*) Look at it. Go on, look at it. Tell me what it is. You know. What is it, Sandra?

SANDRA: You're hurting.

ALEX: Look at it.

SANDRA: It's not mine.

ALEX: It's blood.

SANDRA: It's not mine.

ALEX: Blood, Sandra, it's blood!

SANDRA: It's not mine, it's not mine!

ALEX: You know what it means?

SANDRA: I'm not going downstairs.

ALEX: You're a woman, you can have babies now.

(*Sandra breaks away from her and rushes to the bed, seizing the doll and hugging it to her again*)

SANDRA: (*Hysterically*) Don't want to be touched, don't want you staring at me, you're all daft, I'll be sick down there, I will, I'll be sick! . . . (*She runs to the picture*) It's my room, I want to listen to him, I can listen to him up here, I can see him, I can see him in my head, he's dead now and I've got to remember him, I've got to, and I'm not going to any parties, they're all daft at parties, I'm not going, I'm stopping here with him, I'm stopping here, I'm stopping here . . . (*Alex seizes her and shakes her*) . . . I'm stopping here, stopping here . . .

ALEX: Sandra!

SANDRA: Stopping here, stopping here! . . .

ALEX: There's something wrong with you.

SANDRA: I want to stop here.

ALEX: (*Holding out the towel*) Tell me about this.

SANDRA: (*Shaking her head violently*) Not mine, not mine, not mine! . . .

(*Alex lets go of her and stands helplessly*)

ALEX: I don't know what we've done. Wake up, you.

SANDRA: What for?

The End

Carol K. Mack

HALF TIME AT
HALCYON DAYS

Carol K. Mack

Carol K. Mack is a New York playwright, an alumna of the New Dramatists, and a current member of The Women's Project Anthology of The American Place Theatre. In 1983, her play, *Territorial Rites*, which had been a finalist in both the Susan Smith Blackburn Prize competition and the CBS/FDG Contest (sponsored by CBS Television and the Foundation of the Dramatists Guild), was produced by Julia Miles at The American Place Theatre. *Territorial Rites* was published in Volume 2 of The Women's Project Anthology.

Concurrently, Ms. Mack's one-act play, *Postcards*, was produced by the Ensemble Studio Theatre in its 1983 Marathon Series of one-act plays. Earlier, *Postcards* had won the University of Jacksonville Award and had been produced at the university and in a Florida festival. A companion piece, *Gazebo*, received one of the John Gassner Memorial Awards in 1982. Together, these one-act plays constitute a pair entitled *Islands*.

In 1983, the Actors Theatre of Louisville commissioned two short plays from Ms. Mack. One, *High Tech*, appeared in the group's Liberty Mini Fest; the other, *Half Time at Halcyon Days*, is published here for the first time. The author reports: "*Half Time* was triggered by a personal reaction to a three-day stint in a health spa and what is obviously an overreaction to thermal wraps."

Among Ms. Mack's other plays are *A Safe Place*, winner of the 1976 Stanley Drama Award, which premiered at the Berkshire Theater Festival Playhouse in association with the Kennedy Center for the Performing Arts in 1981; *Survival Games*, produced on the second stage of the Berkshire Theater Festival Playhouse in 1980; and *Esther*, produced at The White Barn Theatre Foundation by Lucille Lortel in 1976 and Off-Broadway in 1977.

In other media, Ms. Mack has written a novel, *The Chameleon Variant*, with scientist-collaborator Dr. David Ehrenfeld, first published in 1980 and subsequently published in paperback in the United States, England, and Germany. She has written short fiction for *Moment* magazine; a number of educational film strips and a television pilot project for Joshua Tree Productions; and five original musicals for children.

Most recently, Ms. Mack has completed a full-length play entitled *American Dreamer* and was commissioned by Julia Miles to write a one-act play, *The Magenta Shift*, under the auspices of the National Endowment for the Arts. She is re-searching material for a historical play that takes place in eighteenth-century Vienna, and she is also working on a couple of film scripts.

Carol K. Mack is a graduate of Mount Holyoke College, where she studied playwriting with the late Denis Johnston (formerly of the Gate Theatre in Dublin, Ireland, and father of Jennifer Johnston, who has contributed plays to the 1981 and 1983 volumes of *The Best Short Plays*). Ms. Mack dedicates *Half Time at Halcyon Days* to the memory of Denis Johnston and his wife, Betty Johnston.

Ms. Mack also has studied acting with Uta Hagen and currently resides in Manhattan with her husband and three children.

Characters:

BABS, *attractive, slim, complusively neat; enunciation bubble-clear*
GLORIA, *older, smoky-voiced, down-to-earth*
SCHATZY, *feisty, good-hearted; Cub Scout den mother*
CASSIE, *cheerful, off-beat, romantic; direct, childlike clarity*
SONDRA, *thin, tense woman with oversized glasses; a "Color Therapist"; sincere manner and lots of eye contact*
VOICE OF RECEPTIONIST, *airline stewardess*
VOICE OF FOUNDER, *ancient Floridian*
VOICE OF MISS LUCY, *German accent*

(NOTE: *The three taped voices on the public-address system are important because these voices represent the real environment of Halcyon Days Spa. There is also Muzak-type music.*)

Scene:

The stage is an exercise room in the Halcyon Days Spa. Upstage is a series of climbing rungs. A ballet barre runs along one side. A stack of mats is in one corner and a can upstage holds a dozen batons. The fourth wall is a mirror in which the characters see themselves and address themselves during the play. Rolled up out of sight above the climbing rungs is an illustrated chart that can be pulled down for demonstration. If possible, there are a few rings hanging from flies, but these are not necessary. What is necessary, however, is constant movement and use of mats, batons, flying rings, ladders, etc., for warm-ups and exercise throughout entire piece (even when not indicated in the text).

There are two exits from the exercise room: the upstage exit leads to the rest of the spa. The other, opposite the ballet bar wall, leads to the offstage dressing room. Whatever colors are used in this exercise room should uphold the philosophy of Haylcyon Days; lots of Mylar and some pink neon. There are two huge plastic plants in opposite corners.

(NOTE: *For "Tenafly, New Jersey," substitute any familiar regional suburb.*)

Precurtain:

When the houselights are at full, the following announcement begins on the PA system. As the house fades to black and the stage is slowly flooded with pastel light, a voice, with the quality of upbeat elevator music, continues to address the audience.

VOICE OF RECEPTIONIST: Good Morning and welcome to all of you here at Halcyon Days Spa. *Please* remember to breathe deeply and rhythmically during the following announcements: first our Silver Spa Trophy to the Cincinnati group now departing for having lost between them a total of three hundred and ninety-four pounds and sixty-seven inches! Good work, girls. Second, a very Happy Birthday, Miss Schlactman. Will she please come to the desk for her present? Miss Schlactman to the desk, please. And last but not least, a Happy Half Time at Halcyon Days to Babs, Gloria, Schatzy, and Cassie from Tenafly, New Jersey. Ladies, you have five more days to beat Cincinnati! *(Babs enters. She wears a pink leotard and her own pink leg warmers, a pink ribbon in her hair. When she looks in the mirror, she tends to cock her head like Shirley Temple. Now she stands center stage and silently and appreciatively mouths the PA system's words)* Now, what do we do first at Halcyon Days? We chase away the BUNs. . . . For you newcomers, BUNs are Bad Ugly News. And *how* do we chase away the BUNs? With the GTs, girls. *Gooood* Thoughts. OK. Let's start our day right. What's first?

BABS: *(Blissfully, eyes closed, arms straight out at shoulder height)* SUS-pension.

VOICE OF RECEPTIONIST: Yes! *(Bab's eyes blink open with surprise that the PA system may have heard her voice)* We all suspend our cerebral systems. This is hard at first and must be practiced daily. By the way, you'll find all this information in Chapter One of our ground-breaking Spa Book: *Private Parts. If* you have accidentally dropped your copy in the whirlpool, there are additional free copies at the desk. Ready now? *(Babs nods)* Now, everybody, think of *your* mind as a balloon. A big balloon. And EVERYBODY fill up that balloon with the *tiniest* thought you can muster, no bigger than an eyelash, and now let that eyelash just reach *alllll* the space in your *balloooon.* GOOOOOD!

(Babs smiles, exhaling a long breath, and Gloria enters carrying clipboard)

GLORIA: *(Glumly)* Hi, Babs, at it already huh?

BABS: My goals are real high, Gloria. How're you doing with your GTs today?

GLORIA: GTs, GTs?! Who could have a GT while starving to death? Huh, tell me.

BABS: You're not trying.

GLORIA: My body *refuses* to send one good thought to my brain. It's on a hunger strike. All it sends up is: Give me fudge! Give me fudge!

BABS: (*Disgusted*) Well, I feel fabulous.

GLORIA: Yeah? Well, maybe I'm not cut out for this place. Maybe you have to give them better raw material.

BABS: What a BUN! Gloria, you know what's wrong with you, you'll pardon my saying so, but you have no faith at all! Look at me. Just look. Do I look wonderful?

GLORIA: You look pretty much the way you did when you *got* here.

BABS: That's what I mean. You don't want to believe they can perform miracles. But I know I look more gorgeous. More . . . (*Hunts for word*) More! (*She swings her leg easily on barre*) It started with little pops in my thighs. Pop . . . pop . . . And *now* I am absolutely carbonated!

GLORIA: Maybe you are our group miracle, OK.?

BABS: Maybe . . . did they start your ultravitamins yet?

GLORIA: You kidding? All they give *me* is a spoonful of bran and a couple a carrot curls. I'm a rag. A *rag*! I may black out in aerobics. (*Overdramatically, from mat*) Listen, Babs, I put my last will and testament in my locker. I want you to know in case.

BABS: (*Indignantly, walks to Gloria*) Gloria, that is another BUN thought. No wonder you're not responding to the program. Look, here's what they gave me. (*She sits, spreading her legs like a dancer and easily bending over them to examine her box of vitamins. Gloria watches, valiantly containing envy*) Did you ever see such beautiful vitamins? This one's for my hair gloss, and this is the famous magaspa purple . . . the orange one I can't remember, and the green they didn't say . . . But you know what?

GLORIA: No, what?

BABS: I feel . . . totally *new*! (*Holds out box of vitamins*) Here. Take some.

GLORIA: (*Doubtfully*) You think they could help me? I mean *look* at me. Look at me. What could help?

BABS: (*A beat of frank appraisal*) I don't know. Maybe you better talk to Dr. Hawkins. You don't look terrific.

GLORIA: I'm afraid they'll take away my coffee.

BABS: You have *coffee* in your room? You *do*, don't you?

GLORIA: Babs, I'd have to crawl from class to class . . . please don't start. I know it's a toxic waste, but right now it's the only fluid still running through my veins! . . . Babs?

(Babs gives Gloria a baleful glance as the ding, ding, ding is heard of the PA system. They both listen)

VOICE OF RECEPTIONIST: Reminder, ladies, before you empty your balloons completely, please do your morning checklist. *(Babs and Gloria, each in her distinct style, get their pads and pencils. They respond with "uh huhs" and "yups" to below questions as they check off)* Have you had your chat with Dr. Hawkins, medical supervisor? Have you gone to your weigh-in? Have you confirmed your appointments with our herbal wrap attendants, Beatrice and Charlene, who've been with us since inception? Have you checked each of your individual salon treatments: Jojoba, steam? Bleach? Nails? Scotch hose? You have? *Goooood.* Now you are ready for Class One. Class One is about to begin. *(Babs and Gloria put their pads down and start to take mats from the corner when the mellow voice goes on)* Remember, ladies, ALWAYS wear your name tag someplace on your bodies. This is a Safety Rule. We do not allow strays on the spa premises. Without your name tag, you could be mistaken for a stray and put to sleep.

(Xylophone twinkle ending, click off. Gloria, alarmed, immediately checks her body for her name tag, a startled expression on her face, and she glances at Babs, who is blithely taking a baton from the can)

BABS: *(Casually)* Where's Miss Lucy I wonder? She's usually early.

GLORIA: Wait a second? Did I detect a tiny BUN in your voice there, Babs? I bet if you check the mirror, there'll be a little frown line right between the eyes.

BABS: *(Goes anxiously to mirror)* Oh . . . Oh, dear . . . *(Exhales)* There. All gone. *(Remains close to mirror and the following, an interior monologue unheard by anybody else, establishes the convention throughout the play)* Hi, beautiful!

GLORIA: *(To mirror)* If I could only get the *bottom* of me to the *top*! Oh, well . . . *(Bending to touch toes and then walk a "hanging walk" around to loosen up)* The best thing is I can't see myself when I bend over.

BABS: *(To mirror, unheard by Gloria)* Not one speck of lint anywhere. I wonder . . . how do they *do* it? At home every morning Lawrence sabotages my mirror with droplets of shaving cream. One droplet can cloud a whole mirror . . . Oh, Babs, look now. Get a GT going quick. Empty . . . empty . . . Breathe and empty.

VOICE OF RECEPTIONIST: That's better! Breathe and empty. Breathe in the good air. Breathe out the bad. Breathe in the good air, breathe . . .

BABS AND GLORIA: (*Joining in*) Breathe in the good air. Breathe out the bad.

VOICE OF FOUNDER: (*Interrupting*) Give me that . . . Gosh dern it, give it to me! *You* gosh dern idiot, give me . . .

(*The interruption is ended abruptly by a severe squawking noise and then a click off*)

GLORIA: (*Reacting to weird sounds*) What was *that*! I wonder who's on the desk this morning?

(*Cassie enters. She crosses the space with a blissful smile at Gloria and Babs and finds her "spot." She sits crosslegged facing mirror but obviously not seeing herself. They follow her movement*)

BABS: (*Casually, doing leg lift*) Hi, Cassie.

GLORIA: (*Seeing Cassie does not respond, walks over to her. Pointedly*) Hi, Cassie. How *are* you today, Cassie?

CASSIE: HI!

GLORIA: (*Squatting next to her*) How're you feeling, Cassie?

CASSIE: (*Wrinkling her nose cheerfully*) Hi.

GLORIA: (*To Babs*) That just does it! Every time you talk to her she says "hi." That's it. Watch this (*Babs turns reluctantly from mirror*) Cassie. Class One has been cancelled due to a fire in the dressing room. We have four seconds to get out alive! . . .

CASSIE: (*Friendly, blissful*) Hi.

GLORIA: You try!

BABS: (*Holding out box of vitamins*) You want a vitamin E, Cassie?

CASSIE: Hi. (*She rolls into a ball*)

GLORIA: (*Really worried, pacing*) See?! She curls up like a hedgehog and stays that way unless Miss Lucy gives her exercises. She *does* the exercises, I'll give her that, but she knows them by heart so they don't really count. How are we going to get her back to Tenafly? What will Frank say? I asked Miss Lucy yesterday: what's with Cassie, she's kinda strange. Miss Lucy said, there's nothing *wrong* with Cassie, she's just perfectly *happy*!

SCHATZY: (*Enters fast and aggressively gives each woman a*

locker room jab. She wears a towel and a whistle around her neck) I hope I get a good workout! I'd better get a good workout or I'm gonna go home and smash skulls. I'll tell you that herbal wrap makes me crazy! You have one yet?

BABS: (*Running her hand sleekly over her body*) It's not for my body type.

SCHATZY: They keep wrapping me up like a mummy in boiling hot rags! It's doing bad things to me all over! Where's Miss Lucy? (*Focuses on Cassie*)

GLORIA: We don't know. (*Looking worriedly at Cassie*) Schatzy? What do *you* think happened to *her*?

SCHATZY: (*Fast look to see if they're alone, takes them into huddle*) I think Frank had her fixed up. I think this is all a *plot*.

BABS: (*Astonished*) What? Her *hus*band Frank? Schatzy, he's in New *Jer*sey.

SCHATZY: You don't know how these things are done! I think Frank got Dr. Hawkins to *do* something to her, (*Quick look behind her*) and I'm next!

GLORIA: What?

SCHATZY: (*Nods knowingly*) If I come in here and roll in a ball, you just call the police, OK?

BABS: (*Sophisticated "cool"*) Calm down, Schatzy. This is Halcyon Days! She probably just took too much steam.

SCHATZY: (*Combative*) Yeah? Well, I happen to know that Frank's got a cousin on staff here which is WHY you may remember that our group got this big discount?

GLORIA: That's true. They sure gave us a bargain rate!

SCHATZY: OK. Now who is this cousin? Doctor Hawkins! And he has got her on enough stuff to melt a bull in heat! Look at her, Babs, she's a veggie! (*She snaps her fingers at an unresponsive Cassie*)

GLORIA: (*Wringing her hands*) Well, Frank's gonna be shocked when she gets home! She's just gonna sit and read cereal boxes all morning!

SCHATZY: That's exactly what he *wants*! That's what I'm telling you.

BABS: (*Exercising, oblivious*) Why don't you just accept this as part of the Spa Plan?

GLORIA: (*Reluctantly*) Miss Lucy says she's happy. She looks happy. But the thing is, what's she happy *about*?

SCHATZY: He could go to prison for *life*. I mean is this a walking coma or what? Now you guys know how close Frank is to my Ralph. Like *that*! You understand what I'm saying? If

I come in here like a turnip, you call the police *and* the FBI *and* the FDA and you get the son-of-a-bitch I live with a life term, you promise me that?

GLORIA: I promise.

SCHATZY: Scout's honor?

BABS: Take some deep breaths, huh?

SCHATZY: (*Sniffs, starts climbing upstage rungs*) When we all got here last week I ad*mit* she was a little strung out.

BABS: (*At bar, arms raised, baton held overhead, in cool voice*) She was wired.

SCHATZY: But that's 'cause she was working so hard to find herself!

BABS: One minute she's writing the Great American Novel and the next she's into Tai Chi . . . and her children? There seem to be many more of them than there really are.

GLORIA: (*On her mat*) It's just the finger painting on the walls.

BABS: How many *are* there anyway?

GLORIA: Just four. It's only she likes them to *express* themselves—so the house looks a little like cave paintings.

BABS: Exactly! Exactly like a cave, that's so true. And she tells *me* I'm a compulsive cleaner.

GLORIA: (*Thinking*) It's not the house. It was her idea about reincarnation that got out of hand. She thought she had been too many great women of history. Pocahontas was the last straw.

SCHATZY: Look! (*She literally leaps to Cassie's defense by jumping from top rung like Peter Pan*) Frank married her for better or worse, and if he doesn't like the mess or all the women she thinks she *was,* well then let him talk it out. Right? Boy, I thought there was something fishy when he agreed to spring for this trip. And my Ralph? . . . Since when has he ever even bought me a birthday present!?

BABS: Speak for yourself, please. I mean, Lawrence agreed to my coming with you all and *he* thinks I'm perfect. He even said as I left, "Honey, you just be sure to come back as perfect as you went out."

(*She checks the mirror while Schatzy and Gloria look at each other uncomfortably. Babs sees them in mirror and looks away tensely*)

VOICE OF RECEPTIONIST: (*Friendly reprimand*) Is everybody breathing? Dr. Hawkins to the dining room please. *Immediately,* Dr. Hawkins!

(*Gloria, Babs, and Schatzy all put one finger to the side of their noses and breathe deeply through one nostril, change fingers and do other nostril)*

GLORIA: Hey! Wait a minute. Where's Cassie's bag?

SCHATZY: I stepped over it in the dressing room . . . Gloria?

GLORIA: (*Has run to offstage dressing room, calls from offstage*) If she unrolls, just keep her busy! (*Babs and Schatzy begin doing knee-bends on either side of Cassie, wondering*) I think I found it! Yup! Look at this. (*Gloria reenters*) Look at this! A lotta weird-looking capsules. No label. This bottle is definitely involved! Here's what I'm going to do. I'm going to keep this bottle away from Cassie, no matter what. OK?

BABS: Sure.

GLORIA: Tell no one!

SCHATZY: We're in this together, Gloria.

VOICE OF RECEPTIONIST: Will Miss Schlactman *please* report to the desk. Miss Schlactman please report to the desk.

(*Clicks off. The upstage door opens and Gloria immediately hides the bottle behind her as the trio looks guiltily toward the door*)

SONDRA: (*Enters backwards, all in beige, leotard and tights and wrap dance skirt. A beige chiffon scarf is knotted at her neck and floats as she walks. She turns, surprised to see them, and immediately smiles graciously*) Hello, everybody. I'm sondra with a small "ess."

ALL: (*Not all at once, tentatively*) Hi . . . ?

SONDRA: (*Evenly, flatly, nearly by rote*) I'm your color therapist. It's the cutting edge of personality work. You probably haven't heard of it yet, but it's very hot, not in New Jersey but elsewhere. Have you had your color analysis yet? (*She looks around but they are speechless. She selects Babs as the most apt to respond*) All right then. Take a color. Say grape. Some people are basically grape. Like you . . . I'm sorry, your name is?

BABS: Babs.

SONDRA: Babs, you are definitely grape. You see, grape and plum are winter . . . you are a winter or late fall person. My*self*, I tend to be early spring. I CANNOT wear olive. Olive is poison.

BABS: What color *are* you?

SONDRA: (*Immediately*) Beige. I'm beige. The most important thing is not to fight your color! It's a cosmic influence on your world view. You're familiar with the expression: "through rose-colored glasses"? Now that is a lay term for the color-complex which includes your peach through pink and the early summer personality that is usually cheerful.

BABS: *(Resisting)* I always thought *I* was pink.

SONDRA: Never.

(Gloria walks away with a disbelieving head shake and lies on her mat)

BABS: Oh, but I . . . my bedroom is all pink and I . . .

SONDRA: This is what happens when *non*professionals make decisions without prior training. You are absolutely plum. Have you experienced fatigue lately?

BABS: Yes, but I started ultra vitamins on Day One and I . . .

SONDRA: *(Touching her scarf)* Oh, dear. Being on the cutting edge has frustrations. Babs, listen to me, you're supplementing for nothing. You are simply not PINK. If you go around thinking you're pink, you'll get depressed because your spectrum is out of whack!

BABS: But Dr. Hawkins himself said that . . .

SONDRA: I'll speak to him immediately.

SCHATZY: *(Not buying. Belligerently)* Whaddyathink my color is, *son*dra?

SONDRA: *(Without pause)* Aubergine.

SCHATZY: *(Taken aback by immediate response)* Yeah? And Gloria? That's her lying down.

SONDRA: She's blue. Pale, pale, silvery blue, with a soft mature gloss over a basic intensity.

BABS: *(To mirror)* I don't know who she is, but I know I'm pink!

SCHATZY: How about HER? *(Points to Cassie)* Cassie!

CASSIE: *(Looks up, wreathed in cherubic smiles)* HI!

SONDRA: Hello. Well, you're slightly . . . mixed. I'm getting a strong yellow but there's a tint. Let me work on you a bit, Cassie.

CASSIE: Hi.

SONDRA: Hi. I'm afraid your friend is a bit murky.

SCHATZY: *(Beginning to be curious, tomboyishly shy)* What IS aubergine?

SONDRA: A rich, silky brownish color. Near raisin.

SCHATZY: *(Not happy with her color)* Can people ever get to be other colors?

SONDRA: Well, if I'd met you several years ago, you might have been green. That happens a lot with raisin.

SCHATZY: *(Shifts weight, nodding)* You think this has anything to do with my being a den mother for the Cub Scouts? I'm thinking woods and uniforms, you know, and peanut butter . . . and tavern nuts and beer. Not for the kids but for my husband Ralph . . . and then the dogs. Both beagles . . . Plus, now that I think of it, I was named after my dad's dachshund!

SONDRA: You have a natural aptitude for this field yourself.

SCHATZY: Oh, yeah? (*Wistfully*) I'd sure like to be green again.

GLORIA: (*Sitting up*) Do you get *paid* for this?!

SONDRA: As I said, I'm on the cutting edge . . .

GLORIA: But are *you* on the *staff*? You're not on my checklist.

SONDRA: (*Flatly*) Blue people have problems with new concepts and belief systems. Even as children. Gloria, did you *ever* believe in the Easter Bunny?

GLORIA: Oh, come *on*!

BABS: (*To break tension*) Maybe we should begin without Miss Lucy. I mean, if you don't mind, sondra.

SONDRA: Not at all!

BABS: Miss Lucy is usually punctual.

SONDRA: She's crimson.

BABS: You mean . . . ?

SONDRA: The entire staff has undergone color analysis. Miss Lucy asked me to meet her classes . . . But I never thought I'd meet a rainbow! (*She smiles winningly at all*)

GLORIA: I don't believe this! You're right! BODY is *everything* to Miss Lucy. She's a health nut.

BABS: (*Conciliatory to sondra*) *She* means . . . Miss Lucy says that a body in perfect condition IS the meaning of life. And it's hard for Gloria to imagine Miss Lucy checking out other philosophies.

SONDRA: (*Sweetly*) Well, Babs, maybe Miss Lucy had a lot of wrinkle-producing BUNs in her balloon because she was fighting her color!

SCHATZY: No offense, sondra, but it's lousy sportsmanship talking about Miss Lucy behind her back, so I vote we get started. OK, kids? (*She blows her whistle*) UP, Cassie!

CASSIE: (*Stands*) Hi . . .

SCHATZY: Let's go. Grab a place where you can see yourself and . . . we all know this exercise by now so let's REACH . . . REACH . . . REACH . . . (*All face mirror and hold arms overhead. The reach is done by reaching with alternate arms while placing weight on the balls of opposite feet. As all do this exercise, Schatzy begins an interior monologue to mirror. Her speech is unheard by the others*) Gosh! I must've shrunk one and a half inches! (*Looks hard at mirror*) Now I'm losing my boobs! Uh oh . . . At my age and my sex I may be mutating into a Cub Scout! (*Sighs at her reflection*) How'd it start? Maybe since I learned all the scout cheers and I can pitch a tent and start a fire with sticks . . . Most of the time I'm with people under four feet tall in army uniform in the woods of New Jersey. That could be it! Maybe I adapted to my habitat—like a tree frog!

BABS: (*Interior monologue to mirror*) If there was a prize for just *being* . . . I'd win this room for sure!

GLORIA: (*To mirror, to herself*) BLUE?! . . . It's new . . . is it true . . . does it help? . . . Would a stomach tuck do?

SCHATZY: (*Thinking to mirror*) Maybe Ralph doesn't want me anymore 'cause to him I look like a Cub Scout which would make him kind of a perv . . . could it hurt to try this place? Who would've thought the ceiling could move UP . . . I wanted a couple of curves is all . . . golly! Look what's happening! . . . REACH . . . REACH. (*Finishing exercise aloud*) REACH . . . and RE-lax. (*All drop arms a second and then*) OK, troop, let's all do the Shrugs. And UP, up, up, forward, back, forward, back and one and two and . . .

CASSIE: (*Sweetly sings in sync*) I went to the animal fair. The birds and the bees were there . . . The big baboon, by the light of the moon . . .

SCHATZY: AND arms out, shoulder height . . . breathe and stretch. Hands in fists and make little circles . . . one and two and three . . .

(*All do arm circles*)

GLORIA: (*Outloud to Schatzy, who exercises near her*) Schatz, I don't know. The other day this woman in my office, she tries to fix me up. She says to this guy, divorced. She says, "I want you to meet somebody very, very special." *He* says he'd be glad to meet any chick she knows. *She* says "Gloria is not a chick, she is very, very special." SHE decides he isn't good enough for me. One more weekend shot to hell.

SCHATZY: Keep up the arm circles, you never know.

GLORIA: You're right. Next month she's got a cousin visiting who she says is very sensitive, sixty, a bachelor . . . who recently lost his mother and his hair and his car and his *cat* all in one week! Which SHE says has made him even more sensitive.

SCHATZY: Sounds interesting. Let's do the arm lifts. OK, everybody?

(*All switch to an exercise that involves arms straight out at shoulder height, hands touch shoulders and then arms up and back out and so on*)

GLORIA: (*Interior monologue to mirror*) Can Gloria get this body in shape for Donald? And does she care? Oh Lord, I *want* to care, I *want* to care, I want to be*lieve* but I'm blue! On top of everything else I'm blue! This is it! I have done the Pritikin and TM and computer singles . . . so let it work, I want it to work, I want it to work, make it work, make it . . .

SCHATZY: (*Stopping her train of thought*) Gloria? What's with you? You stopped. You tired? (*Noticing Cassie wandering in circle*) Cassie? What're you doing, honey?

CASSIE: (*Walking around the room, looking*) I'm a . . . where's my bag? I'm looking for my . . . I have a . . . it's time.

SONDRA: She's looking for something.

(*Gloria, Schatzy, and Babs all look guilty*)

GLORIA: Cassie? What is it?

CASSIE: I have to . . . there's a bottle in my bag . . . anybody? (*Exits to dressing room*)

SCHATZY: (*Abruptly*) Let's get the mats out! Keep her active!

(*They all get mats. Cassie reenters and they all stop to listen. She clutches her large tote bag*)

CASSIE: (*Cheerfully, directly to her friends*) Some very, very famous people dreamt about me last week! The dreamers all told their analysts who then told *my* analyst *not* to tell me because it would go to my head . . . Bu-ut, he told me anyway! OK. You're all *dying* to know who dreamt about me, OK. Carolyn Kennedy, Robert Redford and Jerzy Kosinski to name a few . . .

GLORIA: She sounds like herself again! Cassie, are you OK?

CASSIE: I feel all right. (*Looks around*) Where *am* I?

BABS: Class One. Halcyon Days Spa?

CASSIE: Oh. Then where's Miss Lucy?

SCHATZY: Late. We have a visiting staff member.

CASSIE: Hi ya'.

SONDRA: Hi. I'm sondra, small "ess."

CASSIE: (*Shaking her hand*) *Small*-ess. Is that American Indian?

SONDRA: No, I'm a color analyst.

CASSIE: (*Cheerfully, matter-of-fact*) I just wondered 'cause a couple of lives ago I was Pocahontas. I died young because of the climate change and manners . . . I couldn't deal with the manners over there! You're probably thinking: what's she talking about, the British are so polite! Well, not back then. They stared at me and pointed rudely at my headdress . . . Well, anyway, Frank doesn't like me to discuss that particular incarnation in detail, although between us, it was one of my best *short* lives.

(*Schatzy gently intervenes as sondra is staring open-mouthed. She pats Cassie on the shoulder*)

SCHATZY: Hey, Cas, let's do some more warm-ups, huh, kid?

BABS: (*Sits, suddenly, feeling the full impact of what sondra said earlier*) I'm not doing one more exercise. I've *had* it. If my problem is this pink business, then I'll deal with it entirely differently from now on. (*She angrily unties her pink ribbon and pulls off her pink leg warmers*) I never liked my personality anyway. I wore myself out being perky all the time. I think that's why Lawrence roams around wherever he can find a welcome. You don't have to pretend you don't know. (*Defiantly, standing*) And so when I go home, I'll go home PLUM. What do you think, Schatzy?

SCHATZY: (*Edgy, feeling sorry for Babs*) Whatever you say, Babs.

BABS: (*Getting bitchier*) I think maybe if I'm not pink, Lawrence won't play house so much at Gloria's . . . that's what I think.

GLORIA: (*Exploding*) You're starting that again? Because the guy gets spaghetti sauce on his shirt, it's a federal case. A thousand restaurants in New Jersey serve spaghetti, Babs, not just me! Shalimar I could understand! But spaghetti sauce?!

BABS: (*Controlled*) I also happened to see his car parked in front of your building. (*Severely; intensely*) Do you know that the three hardest stains to remove are blood, chocolate, and spaghetti sauce?

GLORIA: You know you really piss me off?! *Don't* exercise if you don't want to. I don't know why you came with us anyway since you're so goddamn perfect! Some of the rest of us have to make the most of the ten-day spa plan, let me tell you!

BABS: (*With a withering all-over glance*) I'll say. It's a good thing you can do it al dente.

GLORIA: (*Moving in*) Why you . . .

SCHATZY: (*Blocking her*) Break it up. OK. OK. Now, Babs, Gloria, let's shake hands and get to work . . . (*Babs and Gloria shake their hands in the air as if at an exercise command, glaring. They walk to opposite sides of stage as Schatzy stands, nonplussed by their interruption*) Let's try to get some work done on the waistlines . . . OK, kids?

(*Schatzy blows whistle, and they all begin revolving torso exercise that involves circling upper torso with fists on hips, elbows out*)

GLORIA: (*To mirror, interior monologue*) Babs! With her pale pink house. Which *I* sold her when it was gray! And me . . . my one and a half with my real estate percentage on *all* their houses . . . put together! Yeah! And now I'm using up my vacation time for what? To go back to meals for one? Pretty soon meals on wheels. Lawrence, once a week tops, the thrill of Tenafly! Lawrence, the suburban night crawler! The scene couldn't make it to R-rated!

SCHATZY: (*Noticing Gloria's movements are different*) Gloria, hey, you with us?

GLORIA: (*Stopping, directly to Schatzy*) Listen, do you really think Halcyon Days could make a difference in my destiny? The truth. "Destiny" is Chapter Four. After you get on top of your BUNs with your GTs, rearrange your bod, and redesign your personality, then that is when you "Seize Your Destiny." Did you get up to that part?

SCHATZY: No. I'm only up to the end of the bod. But look, Gloria. What have we really got to lose? Except . . . have you noticed my boobs lately?

GLORIA: (*Puzzled*) No . . . ?

SCHATZY: (*Nods*) That's what I was afraid of. Well, look, let's do the "rump bumps," all right? (*Pats Gloria's shoulder*) We can talk about Destiny tomorrow.

GLORIA: Sure. It can wait. The tush is NOW and destiny? Well that could be five years down the road. (*She sits cooperatively, ready for the exercise. So do all*)

BABS: (*Sweetly, loudly from across room*) I'm sorry, Gloria. I keep forgetting how very lucky I am to be me and how you . . .

GLORIA: (*Ready to murder Babs*) HOW I WHAT?!

BABS: Never mind. I'm not here to have some ugly scene

with you. No BUNs for me, thank you very much. (*She breathes ritually through one nostril and then the other*)

SCHATZY: (*Noticing Cassie is still standing up, seemingly asleep, stands, pokes her on shoulder*) Cass, last one down's a rotten egg! Cass? Wake up honey.

CASSIE: (*Directly, hand on Schatzy's arm*) Oh. I keep having this dream. I get on a bus and the bus driver's kind of neutrally hostile, you know: regular. I pay my fare and sit down. The passengers are all staring straight ahead and suddenly I realize I don't know where I'm going. I have no idea *why* I got on this bus in the first place! So I walk up to the bus driver to ask HIM . . . then I realize that of course, he's not gonna know why I got on his bus . . . ?

BABS: (*Practical*) Of course not, Cassie. You're the one who has to know where you're going. That's always been your problem. You're so busy looking backwards that you never get ahead.

CASSIE: (*Sitting next to Babs, admiringly*) You know you're *right*?! Babs, I never heard you say anything so profound.

(*Babs smiles, pleased at the compliment, and she sits alertly on her rump, legs straight out. So do all. During the following soliloquy, all do exercise with arms extended straight out as they "walk" forward and backward on their buttocks*)

BABS: (*Speech in sync with movement to mirror as she travels downstage and upstage, unheard by others*) All this concentration on the lower torso is good for the brain. It's all the circulation. I am having more thoughts than I ever had before. Cassie is right. For one thing I think I really hate Gloria. I know she knows all about Lawrence and me and how we divided the house down the middle with a string. What a nerd *he* is. My God, I hate the suburbs. I never wanted kids. How did they all do it? Kids are messy. *Having* kids is messy. I saw that film on natural childbirth! Yuck. I hate the sight of blood. I hate watching people eat spaghetti. All Lawrence wants is babies and spaghetti. He used to be so sweet and smell like talcum powder. I hate Cassie's house because the walls are always wet and you trip on toys in the hall. And there are *children* all over the furniture! Don't tell me four. I counted eighteen last time I tried to walk in the door. Maybe other peoples' children have moved in and she doesn't even know it!

GLORIA: (*To mirror*) Maybe I shouldn't diet for Lawrence or for Donald, whoever he is. Maybe I should do it for *me*— Gloria! I'm not half bad.

SCHATZY: (*Cutting into Gloria's train of thought and everybody moves into new position*) OK, everybody, let's do "The Hydrant." (*All get on all fours and do an exercise that involves extending alternate legs behind and swinging them out and back and down*) What kinda magic? I'd be better off toasting marshmallows. Ten days! Oh, yeah! And if I go home with green hair and seven feet tall, would Ralph notice anyway? He doesn't even *see* me! I could be a dustball . . . Only Lawrence notices me. What a wimp! He smells like *tal*cum powder. A real turn off, and he hasn't missed anybody in town! (*She stands, and everyone else continues what they are doing*) Lately, whenever I'm chopping wood, I get this really clear vision . . . (*Romantically*) that I open a hotel for women who have murdered their husbands . . . nothing fancy. And only if they have a real good case . . . I *see* it! The front lobby is filled with women! I'm behind the front desk. The rule is when you register you have to say how you did it. Then you get your room for life. But it isn't like a jail. It has an ocean view and a really strong sense of community! (*Worried*) I put away the Swiss army knife last month. Then the steak knives, but last week every time I spread the peanut butter with a spoon I still saw this hotel in my mind . . . I know what it's gotta mean. I wonder if Lizzie Borden ever had these visions.

CASSIE: (*Brightly at her side*) Nope, she never did. (*She kisses Schatzy on the cheek*) I think it's fabulous!

SCHATZY: (*Bewildered; embarrassed*) Did I talk out loud?

CASSIE: Schatzy, how long have we been friends and neighbors, huh? And besides I am nearly clairvoyant . . .

SCHATZY: No kidding. Listen, you weren't ever Lizzie Borden, were you?

CASSIE: No, I was never a killer. But I knew Lucrezia pretty well, 'cause the Borgias were big in town.

SCHATZY: (*Looking at Cassie a beat*) Don't you, uh, get burned out remembering all those past lives?

CASSIE: (*Looks down*) Takes your mind off the present, you know.

SCHATZY: I can't understand why it bugs Frank. I mean he's got *his* thing, him and Ralph sitting there like a couple of rocks in front of the TV chugging beer . . . so what's it to him?

CASSIE: He's jealous 'cause, see, he's part of the present. I think he could handle a real other guy better than the ones in the past. He thinks I'm mental.

SCHATZY: (*Loyal*) Well *I* think you add a lot of color to the community. Better than anything playing at the Cinaplex in the mall! Cassie? Do you really think you *were* all those ladies?

CASSIE: (*Swallows*) Well, I've memorized the back of Frank's neck, and to tell you the truth, I'd rather be Cleopatra.

SCHATZY: I could see that.

CASSIE: (*Mischievous grin*) The hotel has an ocean view, huh?

SCHATZY: (*Really embarrassed*) Yeah.

CASSIE: That's such a neat thought to tuck away for when you're unloading the station wagon! Don't worry about it, Schatz, imagination never hurt anybody.

SCHATZY: (*Doubtful*) You're sure?

CASSIE: Especially in New Jersey. What would Dorothy have done in Kansas without Oz, huh?

SCHATZY: I see . . . she wouldn't have been in color.

CASSIE: You got it. Schatzy, the answer isn't in Ralph, it's (*Pointing to her head*) here.

VOICE OF RECEPTIONIST: Class One. Class One. May I have your attention please? I have a little BUN announcement, so breathe deeply and rhythmically during the following. Our Miss Lucy has met with a small accident and will never return, BUT here's the GT, stand by for a substitute instructor . . .

VOICE OF FOUNDER: (*Interrupting*) Just a minute, just a goshdern minute . . . listen to *me*!

VOICE OF RECEPTIONIST: (*After scuffle with microphone sound*) Oh, dear, our founder is a little low on *her* GTs today because her Secret Formula seems to have been misplaced . . .

VOICE OF FOUNDER: Spies! We got spies here . . . All over the place! Nazi bastards! Took my stuff!

VOICE OF RECEPTIONIST: (*Mellifluous voice slightly flustered*) Oh, dear, as you all know, our founder's Secret Formula has won her the title of Miss Ponce de Leon, among other things, and so if any of you *happen* to find a bottle of unmarked pills, *please* bring them to the desk immediately. And breathe! (*Click off*)

SCHATZY: (*Immediately*) I'd like to run by that one more . . .

BABS: (*Cutting in, clapping her hands sharply*) Let's keep going. Let's do it the way Miss Lucy would want it.

SCHATZY: (*Looking at Gloria*) Wait a minute, where do you think she *is* anyway?

GLORIA: Yeah, what exactly do they mean accident? What kind of "accident"?

SONDRA: (*Wringing her hands*) Oh, dear, oh, dear! Oh, dear!

CASSIE: sondra?

BABS: (*Clear and annoyed*) Our energies should be aimed right now at perfection. You are wasting time. Now how would Miss Lucy deal with this . . . yes! I know! Let's all have a look at The Neglected Lady! (*She crosses upstage and pulls down the shade with a flourish, looking at all intently*) There!

GLORIA: Wait a minute, Babs.

BABS: Gloria, *you* better take a careful look at her. Think about it. This could happen to certain people. (*She whacks the shade with her baton. On the shade is an illustration of a woman's torso in really bad condition. The woman is headless and all the bad spots are pointed at by arrows and exclamation marks in bright inks*) Now, what is that? (*She officiously hits the illustration again*) That happens to be Hanging Arms. If we don't do our Reaches every day, we will all have Hanging Arms. OK. Cassie, tell us what that condition is exactly.

CASSIE: (*Obediently, spelling bee style*) Hanging Arms is like having swamp moss grow from your armpit to your elbow only it's flesh color and it wobbles when you move and eventually you have to wear long sleeves all the time: Hanging Arms.

BABS: Exactly. And *this*? (*Hits the chart with baton*) Gloria?

GLORIA: Neck Wattles.

BABS: Dewlaps!

GLORIA: OK, Dewlaps. Babs, will you cut this out?!

BABS: (*Insistently going on*) And *this*, my friends, is Pectoral Sag, so let's do our presses, OK? And these? The only good news is you can't see it when you sit on it.

SCHATZY: Whaddyasay we roll her up and start moving.

BABS: Please don't interrupt. I'm down to Flabby Thigh, Dropping Knees. Look, this is *war*—not kid stuff. This tremendous force against us is no less than Nature itself! I'm talking about gravity, erosion, and T-I-M-E! My God, sometimes I think you people don't understand at *all* what we're up against. Now pliés. First position. Come on, the cellulite is multiplying as I speak!

VOICE OF RECEPTIONIST: Class One. Class One. One more little BUN, ladies, are you breathing deeeeply? Due to a computer irregularity, there has been a tiny mixup in the Tenafly individualized program. But the GT is we can fix it right now. The megavitamins labelled "Babs" are meant for Gloria, who should take three of each NOW, if she is still within reach of my voice. Gloria, take three. Gooood! Babs, no more diet dinners for you, only massage and loofa. Schatzy, NO MORE herbal wraps. They were scheduled for Cassie. Here's a big GT bonus, girls, because of our computer errors we will give you free, at no additional charge, five extra whole days at the spa, or if you prefer, a year's subscription to the beauty magazine of your choice, plus a freezer full of airplane lunches!

(*During above, each reacts with little grunts of approval, disapproval, astonishment, or relief*)

GLORIA: (*Outraged*) What's going *on* here!

VOICE OF RECEPTIONIST: Remember to breathe rhythmically, everybody . . . and will Miss sondra Schlactman *please* report to the desk *immediately*. Happy birthday, Miss Schlactman, wherever you are, and *please* come to the desk for your present. Thank you.

(*Ding, ding, ding. Click*)

SONDRA: (*Freezing with fear*) Oh, my God, I can't go!

GLORIA: (*With surprise as all look at sondra*) You're sondra Schlactman?

SONDRA: Was.

CASSIE: Is it your birthday?

SONDRA: No . . . no, they just want me to go to the desk. It's a trick.

BABS: Wait a minute. I thought you were on staff here.

SONDRA: (*Automatically*) Yes! . . . No . . . I . . . Listen, I was a guest just like you . . . I was with the Cincinnati contingent. I couldn't leave . . . I . . . see I lost my name tag! (*Looks around but nobody understands*) Now I'm a stowaway.

BABS: A stowaway?

SONDRA: (*Confiding urgently*) I'm not really a color therapist. I was a medical illustrator. Nearly one month I've been incognito. They keep calling me to the desk . . . but I . . . One whole month I've been living off melba toast crumbs, used tea bags . . . No, don't look at me that way. I'm fine. I'm fine. I used to weigh over two hundred pounds. Yes, that's the truth. I am over two hundred pounds of the Cincinnati weight loss!

GLORIA: Oh my God!

SCHATZY: (*Simultaneously*) Gee!

CASSIE: (*Simultaneously*) Wow!

BABS: (*Simultaneously*) Goodness!

SONDRA: (*Having a breakdown*) It works! (*Nodding her head rapidly*) Halcyon Days has made me what I am. You *can* live on carrot peelings and . . . well *I* can, but of course I'm beige and we have strong wills . . . and, oh, my God, what am I going to do?

GLORIA: Just go to the desk, sondra. What's the big deal? Just tell them you lost your name tag.

SONDRA: You CAN'T, no, I can't possibly, no . . . I . . .

CASSIE: Hey, it'll be all right. You're just a guest here.

SONDRA: No, I can't, I'm too scared . . . you don't . . . the founder's crazy.

BABS: Don't be ridiculous.

SCHATZY: (*With a sharp look at Babs, sympathetically*) Come on, I'll go with you. It'll be fine.

SONDRA: But you don't understand . . .

SCHATZY: Honey, you can't hide out here forever. You're thin enough already . . . come on! (*She has taken sondra's arm firmly, and they exit through upstage door*)

BABS: Here, Gloria. You're supposed to take three of each right now. I'm surprised they could make a mistake like that.

GLORIA: (*Wolfing pills*) You are?! How about Cassie's pills?

BABS: (*Suddenly intent*) May I see that bottle?

GLORIA: (*Hands it to Babs*) Here.

BABS: Unmarked! Cassie, how did you get this bottle?

CASSIE: Uh . . . I used to know that.

GLORIA: You think they did any permanent damage?

CASSIE: It's hard to tell with my mind. Maybe erased a life here or there.

BABS: (*Clasping bottle to chest*) An unmarked bottle. This belongs to the founder.

CASSIE: I remember now. This tiny old lady wheels past me on Day Two. She looked like an old apple, like the ones you sometimes find under your radiator? She's singing to herself and when she sees me, she stops her wheelchair and stares at me real hard. She asks me where I'm from. I tell her. She kind of smiles and she says: "OK, I'm going to let you go, but watch out for the kamikaze." So I stand there wondering what she means and when she wheels away, that bottle falls off her lap. I guess I got her pills mixed up with mine . . . That's the last thing I remember.

GLORIA: So her so-called Secret Formula is just some horse dose tranquilizer. Of *course*! It makes her think she's whatever she wants to be, she's blitzed out all the time.

BABS: To *her* it's Secret Formula. And that's what's important.

VOICE OF RECEPTIONIST: Class One, Class One. We have a BUN loose. This is a safety announcement! Our founder has escaped and is somewhere in the spa. She is *in* a wheelchair, *may* be armed, and *is* dangerous. Please do not panic. Remain in your scheduled activities till further notice. We'll have a GT any minute now. Breathe please. Thank you. (*Click*)

SCHATZY: (*Enters, pale and shaken, a can in her hand*) Guys?

GLORIA: Schatzy, what's wrong? You look awful.

SCHATZY: This ain't spray net, kid.

BABS: What?

CASSIE: Where's sondra?

SCHATZY: (*With control*) They . . . put her to sleep.

GLORIA: What are you talking about?

SCHATZY: Like . . . cats and dogs . . . I mean like no pulse. One spray and . . . just ZAP. sondra is probably with Miss Lucy.

CASSIE: You mean they . . . ?

SCHATZY: I mean when they said they don't allow strays . . . I tried to explain but . . . Oh, my God, you know this lunatic will do anything to protect her Secret Formula. She thinks if you don't have a name tag you're some kind of spy. Like from Revlon.

CASSIE: Take it easy . . .

GLORIA: Let's get out of here. Concentrating on the body is one thing, stepping over them is something else.

BABS: (*Picks up can gingerly*) Lethal spray net, goodness! That's awesome.

GLORIA: Babs, we're talking homicide, honey, put it down. It's not spray net anyway, it's some kind of aerosol poison like Agent Orange or something.

CASSIE: (*Shocked*) What kind of morals do they have around here? You know Halcyon Days is not above the law.

BABS: Oh yes it is. Perfection is a state beyond New Jersey. This is something none of you understand. Except me. (*She looks at can*) A spray and the Secret Formula. The keys to the kingdom. The power can be mine. "Seize Your Destiny." (*Trancelike, she sings very quietly walking toward mirror, the spray as her bunch of roses and the bottle as her scepter between thumb and forefinger*) "*There* she is . . . Miiisss . . . Amer . . . ica . . . There . . .

CASSIE: (*Commandingly breaking trance as others look on horrified*) Babs, give me that can this minute.

BABS: (*Sweetly*) No, Cassie, first I'm going to try it on the plant.

SCHATZY: Come on, Babs, put it down. The plant is *plastic*. All the indoor plants at Halcyon Days are plastic. It's dangerous stuff . . .

BABS: (*Ignoring Schatzy, sprays the large plastic plant. Immediately, the plant falls over. She watches it, then*) Oh good*ness*! But if it only kills plastic, then what happened to sondra and Miss Lucy?

SONDRA: (*Enters upstage, embarrassed and breathless*) I fainted. I'm under stress. (*Cassie and Schatzy hug sondra*) Listen, Gloria, this plankton is for you. It has your name on it. Beatrice and Charlene just gave it to me. You were supposed to take it before meals so you wouldn't feel hungry, and the computer gave it to some poor lady who swelled up and got left in the herbal wrap too long. They can't *find* her!

GLORIA: Oh, my God. Listen, I think we better split before anything else happens!

SCHATZY: I *knew* that wrap caused shrinkage!

(*PA system clicks on*)

VOICE OF MISS LUCY: Help me. Vill somebody help me. This is your Miss Lucy! I'm locked in ze computer center mit some maniac! HELP.

VOICE OF FOUNDER: Give me back my formula, you foreign invader! Your government won't get you out of this one!

VOICE OF MISS LUCY: Pleeese somevon unlock ze computer room *door*. She tinks I'm un spy!

VOICE OF FOUNDER: I don't care if you're an extraterrestrial creature or if you're straight from Moscow, you hear me? I know you're all after my Secret Formula! I'll go straight to the *President*. Can't get this goddamn machine to dial the President!

(*Awful zilch noise as machine clicks off*)

BABS: (*After a stunned silence*) The real crime is that such a paradise as this could be mismanaged. (*Very Marilyn Monroe*) It seems wrong, somehow.

CASSIE: Babs, honey, it's *all* wrong. There's some real crazy things happening around here, and I vote we go home, now, where we belong.

BABS: (*Has been thinking hard*) Who do you think is at that desk? Who do you think locked Miss Lucy in the computer room?

SONDRA: I think the founder did it by mistake. She's the

one who messed up all the computerized programs looking for spies.

SCHATZY: Maybe the computer did it, from the desk. You know like the garage door gismo.

GLORIA: Yeah, like the thing that turns your lights on when you're away.

CASSIE: This place isn't for us. It isn't *real!*

SCHATZY: Too many mirrors, who wants to know?

GLORIA: I'll never eat another carrot.

CASSIE: I miss my kids. Let's go home!

BABS: But I really do love Halcyon Days. (*She looks at them all somewhat distantly*) I think I was born to live here. It's so very clean and lint-free, and it smells so nice. I think it will look better pink . . . And I think I could run it very well.

(*Pause. They all take in the finality of her decision*)

SCHATZY: Babs, what'll we tell Lawrence?

BABS: Oh. Well, tell him he can take the string down and, maybe . . . well, Gloria, if you're interested . . . Anyway, tell him I got lost. That's exactly what he told me to do. (*Slight bitterness, sharply remembering*) His last words to me were: "Babs, get lost." (*She looks at each of her friends after confession*)

GLORIA: (*Feeling terrible for Babs*) Listen, Babs, can we send you anything?

BABS: I'd like my trimline telephone and my neck pillow . . . that's all I need. (*Generously*) You could all *stay*, you know. They've given us a whole half time free.

SCHATZY: I have to regain my inch loss, Babs. And you know what? I'm going back to school to become a color therapist.

CASSIE: Really?

SONDRA: She should. She has a natural aptitude for it. That's the truth.

GLORIA: I have to get back 'cause I have a date with Donald.

CASSIE: Who's Donald?

GLORIA: He's this cousin of a friend of mine. He's totally unattached and has had some interesting life experiences. He could be the one!

SCHATZY: I don't know what I'll do with the troop when I'm in school.

CASSIE: (*Friendly*) Leave them with me. I want to do the whole house over in play dough. Also I have this gorgeous idea for a wall mural that will take a lot of kid power . . . it'll be a kind of abstract study of Man from the Beginning. We'll start in the rec room and work up to the attic. Maybe Frank will help.

SONDRA: I guess they'll be missing me soon, in Cincinnati . . .

BABS: (*Her eyes misting*) *I'll* miss *all* of you a whole lot! Even you, Gloria.

GLORIA: I know. Look, I'll check on Lawrence but I plan to keep my apartment. I was thinking it's true the meal's for one, but on the other hand it's when you want to eat it, know what I mean?

SCHATZY: Yes!

BABS: But, will you all come visit? I mean, when I get it all fixed up?

SCHATZY: We could have a team reunion next year, how about it?!

BABS: On the house, OK?

GLORIA: Terrific!

CASSIE: It's going to be beautiful, Babs, lots of luck!

BABS: Thank you! (*She exits*)

VOICE OF RECEPTIONIST: Class One is over now, ladies. Check your individual programs for Class Two. And a reminder for your balloon: if you have not had your Before and After photo taken, go to the Photo Salon as soon as possible or it will be After before your Before . . .

(*Sudden sound of spray on microphone followed by sound of electronic zilch*)

NEW VOICE: (*This is a nasal, angry voice*) What the heck do you think you're doing, lady? Look what you did, you killed the tape . . . look at it. It's *melting*! They should have the guests here screened more carefully. My Gawd, now what am I supposed to do up here?

VOICE OF BABS: (*Calmly*) Look, kid, if all you can do is lip sync for a tape loop, you're in big trouble. You are *fired*!

NEW VOICE: Yeah? Who says?!

VOICE OF BABS: I says. Your act isn't good enough for Halcyon Days! (*Closer to the stewardess, but clearly Babs*) GOOOOD afternoon, everybody, this is your new director, Babs! I'm going to be here on hand to welcome all of you individually today, right here at the front desk with our sweet old founder and our own Miss Lucy. The GT is that the Secret Formula has been returned and from now on there will be no more BUNs on these premises! (*The women onstage look at each other, roll mats, replace batons, pick up totes, and by the time Babs ends the following announcement, the stage is empty and flooded with pastel light as at opening) Please* remember to breathe deeply and rhythmically during the following announcements: first, a hearty congratulations to the dozen ladies from Tulsa for their record-breaking inch loss of one hundred and four! A Happy Birthday to you, Mrs. Brockaway, do come to the desk for your present, please. And now for a relaxing musical interlude between classes while you all empty your balloons . . .

(Muzak-type music up and, slowly, lights fade out)

The End

Joseph Hart

HIT AND RUN

Joseph Hart

Joseph Hart made his playwriting debut in 1977 in the tenth-anniversary edition of *The Best Short Plays* with his compelling drama about a family of Irish-Americans, *The Dark Moon and the Full.* Originally performed Off-Off-Broadway at The Cubiculo theatre in 1974, *The Dark Moon and the Full* was again performed in 1976 by The Irish Rebel Theatre, also in New York.

Hit and Run is one part of *Triple Play,* a baseball trilogy first performed Off-Off-Broadway at the American Renaissance Theater and later chosen as the inaugural production of the Philadelphia Festival Theater for New Plays. Reviewer Mimi Torchin, viewing the premiere for *Other Stages,* is lavish in her praise: "The writing is sublime and the performances inspired. . . . The details of characterization are impeccable . . ." William Raidy, writing for the *Newhouse Syndicate,* is equally enthusiastic: *"Hit and Run,* which describes the reunion of two once well known ballplayers several decades after they hung up their uniforms . . . is a strong picture of a man who, despite all the personal wounds he got playing the game, is still secretly 'looking for his team.' . . . [the play] which among other things shows Joseph Hart's remarkable talent for dialogue and strong characterization, hits home."

The author was educated at Fordham University, where he graduated with a B.A. in English literature, and at New York University, where he received an M.A. in theatre. Equally adept as playwright, director, actor, and teacher, Mr. Hart is playwright-in-residence at the Mason Gross School of the Arts, Rutgers University. He is also master teacher of ensemble acting technique, as well as the founder-director of the Shoestring Players, Rutgers's resident experimental theatre for children.

In addition to his work at Rutgers, Mr. Hart is a member of the playwrights' unit at the Ensemble Studio Theatre in New York. He has also been playwright-in-residence at the Aspen Playwrights Conference and "In-The-Works," the new-plays festival of the University of Massachusetts at Amherst.

Mr. Hart's work as both a playwright and a director has been the subject of interviews on television and radio, as well as articles and reviews in the *New York Times,* the *Washington Post,* the *New York Daily News,* and other major publications. Other produced plays by Mr. Hart include *Lot's Wife, Wiglaf, A Myth for Actors,* and *Simon of Cyrene.*

As an actor, Mr. Hart has appeared with the New York Shakespeare Festival, the Heritage Theatre, Rutgers's Professional Repertory Company, New York University's Youtheatre, as well as on radio and television.

Mr. Hart lives in Highland Park, New Jersey, with his wife, Vicki, an actress, and his two daughters, Rebecca and Megan.

Characters:

CARL
ROY
VOICE OF ANNOUNCER

Scene:

New York City. The present. A hot midday in early June. The scene is the cellar of an unfinished high-rise office building. The walls show unpainted plasterboard and exposed cinder blocks. The floor is littered with the debris of construction. Leading down from the street level above is a stairwell of reinforced concrete steps.

In the corner of the room opposite the stairwell, Carl is lying under some pipes, working their joint with a wrench. He is a thick-set, graying, middle-aged Italian. His arms and shoulders are swollen with strength, but his waistline sags under years of neglect and the legacy of too many beers. Except for moments of laughter, his face is set in an expression of dogged determination. As he works, a portable radio nearby blares a stream of "golden oldies" rock 'n' roll. A baseball bat with a taped handle and rawhide thong leans against the wall near the stairwell.

After a few moments, a figure descends the steps. This is Roy, a middle-aged black man, also overweight. In contrast to Carl's rough work clothes, Roy is well turned out in expensive slacks and a flashy sports coat. He enters on tiptoe—a difficult maneuver for him—and his face is lit with an expression of excitement and mischief. He carries a six-pack of beer wrapped in a brown paper bag. Carl does not notice his approach.

ROY: (*Suddenly*) Hey—hey—hey—little hustle—hustle—hustle—outta shape—outta shape—'round the track—'round the track!

CARL: (*Struggling*) What the hell!

ROY: Gimme some laps—gimme some laps!

CARL: What the hell's going on here?

ROY: There's one thick-headed dago here's gonna have to fight for his job this spring!

CARL: (*Recognizing him*) Jeez-zuz!

ROY: Hustle—hustle—hustle!

CARL: I'm seeing a ghost!

ROY: Seeing a *spook*!

CARL: Big black spook!

ROY: Fat black spook! (*He throws out his belly*)

CARL: (*Touching it*) What's this? What's this?

ROY: Two-twenty-three! (*Feeling Carl's paunch*) What's this?

CARL: Two-o-nine!

ROY: Couple wrestlers here!

CARL: Tag team! Whadda you say?

ROY: No way—making a *comeback*! (*He leaps into position as if to field a bunt in baseball*) Here you go. (*He uses the package as a baseball*) Little bunt down the third base side—takes it bare-handed. (*Flipping the package to Carl*) Here comes the play at the plate! (*He mimes a bad slide at Carl*)

CARL: (*Slapping him across the rump*) Out!

ROY: Ouch!

CARL: Clinched the pennant!

ROY: Broke my ass. (*Rubbing*) Boy, where'd you get your glove—U.S. Steel?

CARL: Don't rub.

ROY: (*Hands up—quickly*) Never rub.

CARL: Rub it and they know they hurt you.

ROY: Rub it and they do it to you again.

(*By now they are face to face. There is a smiling, awkward hesitation before they go on*)

ROY: (*Tapping Carl on the chest*) Hey, Mr. Hit.

CARL: (*Returning the gesture*) Hey, Mr. Run.

ROY: Got fat.

CARL: You too.

ROY: Got gray.

CARL: You too.

ROY: Got old.

CARL: You too.

ROY: So . . .

CARL: So . . . (*Then quickly*) So, how are you doing? What are you doing? Where'd you come from?

ROY: Your friends upstairs having lunch—they told me you were down here. Been tracking you down the last two weeks.

CARL: Yeah, I heard.

ROY: You heard? From who?

CARL: The guy on the *Daily News*.

ROY: Peterson.

CARL: Yeah, Peterson. He called me last week. Said you were looking.

ROY: Yeah, that's the guy told me where you were.

CARL: I said, sure—send him over.

ROY: Why didn't you call me yourself?

CARL: (*Dodging the question*) Aah, so what? You found me, right? Hey—how do you like my office?

ROY: Your office? Man, it's a cellar.

CARL: Hey—all's I need's a secretary, an air conditioner, and a wall-to-wall carpet. Here, let's get rid of this. (*Carl moves to snap off the radio as Roy spots the bat and picks it up*)

ROY: Who left you this—your decorator?

CARL: Here, gimme that. (*He takes it quickly*)

ROY: Louisville Slugger—thirty-eight ounce. I remember.

CARL: More use to me now than it ever was.

ROY: What's the rawhide for?

CARL: So they can't pull it out of your hands.

ROY: Who?

CARL: Kids around here. They know you're working alone, they come right in after you.

ROY: Bad neighborhood.

CARL: Colored neighborhood.

ROY: Same thing, right?

CARL: (*Embarrassed*) Hey—c'mon—you know what I'm talking. (*Changing the subject*) So what about you? You still with the same company, or what are you doing?

ROY: (*With a laugh*) Oh, yeah—vice-president-in-charge-of-sitting-by-the-door.

CARL: Seen you on the six o'clock news. You and Ruthie. Big dinner or something.

ROY: Al Smith Memorial.

CARL: Whatever. Must be a year ago.

ROY: Two years ago. I'm split from Ruthie going on two years.

CARL: I didn't know.

ROY: (*Shrugging it off*) What are you gonna do, right?

CARL: Welcome to the club.

ROY: Yeah, I heard about yours.

CARL: Going on ten years.

ROY: That long, huh?

CARL: Me and my old lady are living together.

ROY: Well, it's good you got a woman.

CARL: I'm talking about my mother.

ROY: Oh, oh.

CARL: Over in Flatbush. I moved back after Pop died.

ROY: Heard you had a deli in Flatbush. You went partners with somebody.

CARL: That's years ago.

ROY: Peterson said you were on the trucks for awhile.

CARL: Maybe a year. I done lots of jobs. I get the itch, you know? (*Referring to package*) What'd you bring me here?

ROY: Champagne. What's it look like?

CARL: (*Taking a six-pack of beer out of the bag*) Our sponsor, huh?

ROY: Yeah. Kinda seemed appropriate.

CARL: You remember the billboard out in left field?

ROY: Sure do.

CARL: Everytime you hit it on a fly, they'd send a couple of cases of beer to the veteran's hospital.

ROY: Yeah. Same with the cigarettes sign over in right.

CARL: I remember one game I hit the beer can three times. Next morning there's a telegram waiting for me. "Thanks for the beer," it says, "but next time you're up please hit to right field. We like to smoke while we drink."

ROY: Front office idea. Good little P.R. man

CARL: Puerto Rican?

ROY: Public relations.

CARL: Oh, geez. Shows you how construction guys think. So, make yourself comfortable. Pull up a cinder block.

ROY: (*Sitting delicately*) So—how long you working construction, anyway?

CARL: I don't know. Six months.

ROY: You like it?

CARL: It's OK. I'm quitting.

ROY: What's the matter—you don't like the rest of the team?

CARL: No, no—good bunch of guys.It's—well— it's the foreman. You know what I mean?

ROY: (*Knowingly*) Oh yeah. I think I do.

CARL: He says something. I say something. He says something back.

ROY: (*Shaking his head and smiling*) Same old Mr. Hit.

CARL: (*Suddenly defensive*) Yeah, well, you listen—there's one of our guys got mugged. Six o'clock in the morning— right outside. I mean, what kind of conditions is that to work in, I'm asking?

ROY: Yeah, yeah. I see, I see.

CARL: Yeah, everybody sees. Everybody's grumbling—but nobody's doing nothing. So I take it on myself. "You gotta get us some protection," I tell him. And right away he starts giving me bullshit. Everybody's egging me on. They won't do it themselves—but they're egging me on.

ROY: (*Smiling*) Yeah, yeah—I can see it.

CARL: Pretty soon we're chin-to-chin and somebody throws a punch . . .

ROY: *Somebody*, huh?

CARL: We won't go into that.

ROY: (*Laughing*) Oh man, just like I been there before!

CARL: (*Sharply*) Yeah, right. Like you been there before. That's right.

ROY: (*Suddenly uncomfortable*) So what happened, anyway?

CARL: I got what I wanted. Six o'clock in the morning there's a squad car out there when we're coming to work. And five o'clock at night there's a squad car there for when we're going home. So how's that sound to you?

ROY: Sounds like Mr. Hit is still fighting the management.

CARL: Yeah. (*Quoting*) "Mr. Hit—Baseball Bolshevik." You remember that?

ROY: That was Peterson wrote that.

CARL: Right after I got my release. The *Daily News*—a whole series of interviews.

ROY: You said some pretty hot stuff.

CARL: Told it like it was, that's all.

ROY: Got a lot of people uptight. They thought baseball was supposed to be the Boy Scouts.

CARL: I told them the truth. They didn't like it.

ROY: Aah, nowadays everybody's doing it. Interviews—books . . . all this behind-the-scenes stuff. Getting to be a regular fad.

CARL: I was the first.

ROY: Yeah. Maybe.

CARL: I was.

ROY: (*With a shrug, smiling*) So who keeps those kind of records?

CARL: That's how Peterson made his name—Pulitzer Prize nomination.

ROY: I don't remember.

CARL: Sure. For sportswriting. (*Deliberately flippant*) So—you see? A reputation like that—I gotta uphold it, right? Even down this place.

ROY: (*Changing the subject*) Nice and cool down here. You can say that much for it.

CARL: Yeah, maybe I don't need the air conditioner. Just the secretary.

ROY: With an air-conditioned blouse.

(*They both laugh*)

CARL: (*Handing Roy a beer*) Here, pop the cork on this champagne.

ROY: What are you trying to do—put a belly on me?

CARL: You got the belly. Let's work on the ass.

(*Roy laughs and pops the top of the can. Beer spurts into the air*)

ROY: Wooo-eee! Watch out!

CARL: That's what you get for shaking it. Watch it! (*Carl pops the top of his beer and there is another spurt*)

ROY: Like the locker room after the Series. All the beer cans. Yellowstone National Park!

CARL: Champagne.

ROY: Hah?

CARL: Champagne. Champagne for the Series. The Pennant was beer.

ROY: There were guys in the shower washing down in it!

CARL: You poured a whole bottle in my shoes.

ROY: That was funny.

CARL: Funny? Seventy-five dollar pair of alligators!

ROY: I said, "Don't worry, alligators can swim!"

CARL: I got even.

ROY: You did indeed.

CARL: (*He makes the motion of squirting a bottle*) Zzzt! Right in the front of your pants!

ROY: Next day the *News* runs this full-length picture. And there's me with this big stain on my crotch. (*Quoting*) "Mr. Run Cannot Control His Joy."

CARL: That was what's-his-name wrote that. The guy before Peterson.

ROY: He's the one gave us the two names. What was his name, anyway?

CARL: Who cares? Fuck him.

ROY: What's the matter?

CARL: Fuck all those writers.

ROY: You like Peterson, don't you?

CARL: What makes him any different?

ROY: Well, you just said yourself you were talking to him.

CARL: He called *me*. He said, "Your buddy wants to see you." I said, "Fine." End of conversation.

ROY: He likes to keep in touch with the old-timers.

CARL: I don't talk to writers no more.

ROY: He's been helping me out lately.

CARL: (*Not listening*) They write whatever is good for *them*.

ROY: Hey—you know who I saw yesterday?

CARL: Who?

ROY: Billy.

CARL: (*Interested*) No fooling. What's he doing?

ROY: Out on the Island. Bartender.

CARL: That's bad right there.

ROY: You don't know *how* bad.

CARL: His own best customer, right?

ROY: Just like we always said.

CARL: I mean, that guy never pitched a game he didn't have half-a-pint in his locker.

ROY: Win or lose—I don't remember a game he wasn't hung over the next day.

CARL: (*Sadly*) Shit.

ROY: I saw Deacon.

CARL: (*Brightening*) How's the Deacon doing?

ROY: (*Slapping his belly*) You think I'm bad?

CARL: No! That skinny little guy?

ROY: Two-fifty. He says, "I know I'm overweight. But I wear loose clothes. So at least I don't look like a house." I said, "Fine. Now you look like a tent."

CARL: I don't believe it.

ROY: I'm seeing a lot of the guys lately.

CARL: (*A pause—deliberately*) How about my old friend? You ever see him?

ROY: Who?

CARL: Our manager.

ROY: Oh. No—no—no— . . . Monahan—he's out in Cleveland.

CARL: So I heard. Does he still pee on the rookies in the shower?

ROY: That I can't tell you.

CARL: But he's still going strong?

ROY: Oh, yeah. Red-hot pennant race.

CARL: (*Bitter laugh*) Well, well. Ain't life shit.

ROY: No—I mean, it's the players I been seeing. The old lineup.

CARL: What's the matter—you getting sentimental in your old age?

ROY: You mean Peterson didn't tell you?

CARL: Tell me what?

ROY: Well, I was kind of hoping he'd say something.

CARL: I told you—I don't talk to writers.

ROY: Well—no—you see—I'm on the committee this year. You know, Old-Timer's Game.

CARL: (*Slight pause—eyeing him*) You are, are you?

ROY: Yeah, sure. July 18. Been rounding up the guys. You know, getting commitments . . .

CARL: (*Offering another beer*) You want one of these?

ROY: I'm fine.

CARL: Before it gets warm. Finish your first one.

ROY: Chug-a-lug?

CARL: Chug-a-lug.

(*They chug-a-lug the remains of the first can and proceed to pop the second*)

ROY: So anyway—let me tell you. The committee I'm on—we come up with the theme for this year. The Subway Series. That's what we're calling it.

CARL: Subway Series.

ROY: So?

CARL: So?

ROY: So what do you think?

CARL: I think it sounds good.

ROY: I mean what do you think about you? You know—knock the rust off the spikes . . .

CARL: No way . . .

ROY: Let out the old belt line . . .

CARL: No way . . .

ROY: Oil up the old mitt . . .

CARL: No—no—no way . . .

ROY: Man, I made myself a little promise before I came down these stairs. I said this here is one thick-headed dago son-of-a-bitch. But I ain't going back up those stairs less'n he tells me yes.

CARL: You got your sleeping bag with you?

ROY: I'm serious.

CARL: You got your portable toilet?

ROY: Lookit, man, we got Billy and Deacon and . . .

CARL: Good for them.

ROY: You're the last one and we got the whole lineup. You're number nine.

CARL: I'm number three thousand two hundred.

ROY: Man, you're sore about something happened fifteen years ago!

CARL: Three-two-zero-zero. That's my number. That's my lineup.

ROY: Now just hear me out—just hear me out. The Subway Series. The two New York teams. You played two World Series yourself, right?

CARL: Three.

ROY: Three. So we got it all figured. We're introduced from the center field gate. The people at home see the old film clips—flashes . . .

CARL: Sounds good—I might watch it.

ROY: Hey man—come on . . .

CARL: I said no.

ROY: I mean it's not even like we're asking you to do it for nothing.

CARL: There's money? Good. Let them give me the three thousand two hundred they owe me.

ROY: Hey come on—stop showing your age.

CARL: *My* age? What are *you* talking—with your stories of this one and that one? Old-Timers Game!

ROY: Difference is I remember the good things. You— you only remember the shit.

CARL: No—no, that's not true.

ROY: Just listen to yourself.

CARL: There's good things, too. I remember the good things, don't worry.

ROY: (*Quickly—almost pleading*) Then that's all I'm say-ing—all I'm asking. The good things. Nine guys the people still remember—the plays we made—The World Series— Old-Timers Game!

CARL: Can't do it, man.

ROY: Fifteen years!

CARL: (*Quoting by rote*) "Disability—resulting-from-an-in-jury—

ROY: Fifteen years ago!

CARL: "—*resulting-from-an-injury*-shall-not-impair-the-right-of-the-player-to-receive-his-full-salary-for-the——pe-riod-of-such-disability-or-for-the-season-in-which-the-injury-was-sustained."

ROY: Yeah—yeah. Swell.

CARL: "—*the-injury-was-sustained*." Don't say nothing about *how* it was sustained, *where* it was sustained, *who* gave it to me.

ROY: I remember your interview.

CARL: Just an injury. That's all. Words of the contract.

ROY: (*Muttering*) I don't believe this. The same old bull-shit.

CARL: What?

ROY: Never mind.

CARL: What do you mean, "The same old bullshit?"

ROY: I remember the interview. Why don't you just put it to music and sing it?

CARL: What's your problem, anyway? You get a little bored sitting around your big fancy office? Figured you'd come down and see your old Dago buddy? Thank him for all the records he helped you set?

ROY: Hey, listen, man, if that's how you're gonna be . . .

CARL: How *I'm* gonna be? How are *you* gonna be?

ROY: Look, you want me to leave? Is that what you want?

CARL: Suit yourself, buddy.

ROY: OK. I'll leave.

CARL: Yeah, sure, leave.

ROY: OK. I'm leaving.

CARL: Go ahead. Another twelve years we'll pick up the conversation.

ROY: (*Stopping*) Is that how long?

CARL: That's how long.

ROY: It's not that long.

CARL: Don't tell me.

ROY: Figure after twelve years a guy would be glad to see you.

CARL: All right, I'm glad to see you, all right?

ROY: No, you're not. You're still sore.

CARL: I'm not sore.

ROY: Don't tell me.

CARL: You're the one who's sore.

ROY: What am *I* sore about?

CARL: What do *I* know?

ROY: What the hell are we talking about?

CARL: I don't know. You got me all confused.

ROY: She-it.

CARL: Drink your beer.

ROY: You too.

(*They both sit on their cinder blocks, hunched toward each other, sipping their beer. It is a moment before they speak*)

ROY: (*Peeling off his sports coat*) Getting hot. Can feel it even down here.

CARL: It's not the heat. It's the humidity.

ROY: (*Sudden gasp*) Wooo-weee!

CARL: What's the matter?

ROY: Asthma. Little touch.

CARL: (*Concerned*) Since when?

ROY: Since all the time.

CARL: I didn't know that.

ROY: Oh, yeah. Feel it worse than I used to. Good old inner city—gave me something to remember it by.

CARL: You want for me to go get you something?

ROY: No—no, I'm cool. (*Flapping his shirt front*) They say it may thunderstorm this afternoon.

CARL: My knee didn't tell me yet.

ROY: Knee still bothers you, huh?

CARL: Not much. When it does, I think of Monahan. *That* bothers me.

ROY: You know, a day like this I'm all sealed up in my office looking out the window. Ninety degrees outside— seventy degrees inside. I cannot believe that we used to be playing hit-and-run baseball on days like this.

CARL: It's so hot I seen a dog chase a cat and both of them were walking.

ROY: Monahan's old line.

CARL: (*With a snort of disgust*) Forget I said it.

ROY: Well, the beer's still cold. That helps.

CARL: Where'd you get it?

ROY: Up the corner. Little place.

CARL: Puerto Rican guy.

ROY: Used to be an old Jew. That's going back years. I used to live around here, you know.

CARL: You were saying.

ROY: (*Grandly*) "One-hundred-fifty-fifth and Eighth Avenue. A boyhood lived in the shadow of the Polo Grounds!"

CARL: That's what you said on the news.

ROY: What news?

CARL: Long time ago. Six o'clock news.

ROY: Hey, you been keeping tabs on me?

CARL: Public information. I'm one of the public, right?

ROY: I don't remember it. Must be when I got my release and went with the company.

CARL: You still with the same company, right?

ROY: Oh, yeah. Sure.

CARL: Good job, huh?

ROY: Oh, yeah. It's good.

CARL: What is it you do, anyway?

ROY: Public relations.

CARL: You got some kind of title goes with it?

ROY: I told you. Vice-president-in-charge-of-sitting-by-the-door.

CARL: Cut the shit.

ROY: Here—I'll tell you what I do.

CARL: All these years on Madison Avenue—I thought you'd have your own company.

ROY: I'll explain. Say there's a prospective account my company wants to get.

CARL: OK . . .

ROY: So it's my job to romance the dude. Wine and dine—soften him up. I take him to lunch. Very fancy—very impressive. Maybe the dude's from Jersey—who knows? Well, anyway, along with me goes this young guy—all smiles and pinstripes and carrying an attaché case. So we meet the account and I introduce myself, and right away it's, "Hey, didn't you used to play—" And I say, "Yes." And he says, "I remember this one play—" and I say, "I remember that one too." And on and on, blah-blah-blah, till the waiter's clearing the main course, and the pinstripes opens his attaché case.

CARL: That's it?

ROY: More or less.

CARL: So who likes work—right?

ROY: Yeah, sure, who likes work?

CARL: I mean it's money—right?

ROY: Yeah. Uncle Sam and Ruthie split it up between them.

CARL: What happened? Your wife got the judge on her side?

ROY: Let's just say she got everything she asked for.

CARL: Mine, too. And you better believe she asked for everything. You see the kids much?

ROY: I see them.

CARL: But not so much. Not like at first.

ROY: No, not like at first.

CARL: First few months you got ants in your pants.

ROY: Making big red circles on the calendar. Every second Sunday, rain or shine.

CARL: Circus, zoo, roller coaster . . .

ROY: Gotta be special every time. Racking your brains to make it special.

CARL: It's all such bullshit.

ROY: You can't keep it up.

CARL: You get sick of it.

ROY: I mean, it's a terrible thing to say . . .

CARL: It's the truth . . .

ROY: But it's the truth . . .

CARL: They get sick of it too.

ROY: I mean, I'm supposed to be their father, you dig? I'm coming on like the fucking Pied Piper.

CARL: Every Sunday—like some kind of religion. After a while we're just going through the motions.

ROY: What I wouldn't give just to be sitting over their homework or digging up the backyard.

CARL: Ah, it's sad, you know? Nobody wins. Maybe they shouldn't allow divorce between married people.

ROY: So who's gonna get divorced—single people?

CARL: I mean, with kids. Married people with kids.

ROY: I think the beer's starting to get to you.

CARL: *Me?* You.

ROY: (*Protesting*) No—no . . .

CARL: (*Protesting*) Takes more'n a couple of beers . . .

ROY: Listen, you sure it's OK, I'm sitting around like this?

CARL: I'm on my lunch.

ROY: OK.

CARL: Business lunch.

ROY: Oops. Forgot the attaché case.

CARL: Forgot the guy in the pinstripes.

ROY: Forgot the dude from Jersey!

(*They both laugh*)

CARL: Anyway, the foreman's too scared to come down here. He thinks the bat's for him.

ROY: What time is it? (*Checking his wristwatch*) Hey, it's getting near that time. Let's give a listen. (*Roy gets up and moves toward the radio*)

CARL: What are you doing?

ROY: They're playing that big series in Chicago. Chance to catch a whole game on them.

CARL: Not on that radio.

ROY: What's the matter?

CARL: I don't talk to writers and I don't follow baseball.

ROY: (*Disbelief*) Hey—come on . . .

CARL: Haven't seen a ball game in . . . oh, it must be eight or ten years.

ROY: You're jiving me.

CARL: No, *man*, I ain't jiving you. You put on whatever you want to hear. Only I don't want to hear no ball game.

ROY: Well, whatever you say.

CARL: Whatever I say.

ROY: (*Finding a soul music station*) Little music. Nice music.

CARL: (*Not pleased at the choice*) Whatever you say.

ROY: (*Sitting*) Good young team this year.

CARL: I'll take your word.

ROY: Good kid in your old spot.

CARL: Yeah, huh?

ROY: Good hands—good arm.

CARL: Can he hit?

ROY: He's OK.

CARL: I said, can he hit?

ROY: Well, he can't hit with you.

CARL: I'm not surprised.

ROY: (*Luring him*) Not yet anyway. (*Carl looks up*) They're starting to make comparisons.

CARL: Who's making comparisons?

ROY: Peterson had a whole column a while back. You catch Peterson's column?

CARL: No, I didn't catch it.

ROY: It was very interesting.

CARL: What's he hit, this kid?

ROY: Two-ninety—three hundred.

CARL: (*Snort*) Didn't get that playing no hit-and-run.

ROY: No—no, that's true. Not like you had to do it.

CARL: I had to swing at the worst kind of garbage, just to move you down to second base.

ROY: Yep-yep, that's true. Mr. Hit got the job done.

CARL: And I *still* batted over three hundred. Three years in a row.

ROY: I remember.

CARL: Like to see this kid do that.

ROY: Well, like I said, he can't hit with you.

CARL: You said, not yet.

ROY: Well, they're starting to make comparisons.

CARL: (*Eagerly*) Listen—you remember that game against Chicago? First game of the Series.

ROY: I'm on first, you're at bat, and they got what's-his-name—that kid . . .

CARL: Burly.

ROY: Burly. He's pitching for them.

CARL: All season long he's been hearing about us. Hit-and-run—hit 'n' run . . .

ROY: So that's what he's looking for now—the old hit-and-run.

CARL: Five times you start running . . .

ROY: Five times you foul it off and I gotta come all the way back to first.

CARL: Meantime, Burly's getting cross-eyed. He don't know who to look at—you or me. He figures we're going for number six sure.

ROY: Only we don't.

CARL: He tries to pick you off first, and he's so fucking wild he throws it into the seats.

ROY: And I'm just standing there—*standing* there! Two feet flat on the bag, watching this little white ball sail six feet over my head. The umpire just waved me down to second. I couldn't even run, I was laughing so hard.

CARL: Next pitch he threw me, he didn't have nothing on it. Big as a basketball. I gave it a shot down the left-field corner.

ROY: And I scored from second. End of ball game.

CARL: End of Burly. Back to the minors.

ROY: He was decent, too. We must have broke his spirit.

CARL: He was stupid. Can't be stupid and pitch. You can be stupid and umpire.

ROY: I was thinking of using that film clip.

CARL: Film clip?

ROY: That same play. You know—for Old-Timers Game.

CARL: (*Condescending*) Oh, yeah . . . Old-Timers Game.

ROY: Each player we introduce. We show a film clip. Something he was famous for.

CARL: Well, that's a good one. Like to see it myself.

ROY: (*A deep, sad sigh*) Only too bad we can't use it. No need for it now.

CARL: Hey, look, will you please knock it off . . .

ROY: Not saying a word . . .

CARL: Like these pipes I'm working on—drip—drip—drip all morning on my head.

ROY: I'm just sorry you feel so ornery.

CARL: Me? *You.* What's the matter—you on the rag or something today?

ROY: (*Innocent*) Not saying a word . . .

CARL: Maybe you're not getting enough lately.

ROY: Never mind that.

CARL: (*Teasing*) That your problem, huh? All those long-legged models from Madison Avenue—they starting to run too fast for you?

ROY: Hey, don't worry—Mr. Run still got his legs.

CARL: Hey—you remember down Florida? Spring training? That bar in the hotel?

ROY: What'd we used to call it?

CARL: The Olympic Village.

ROY: (*Laughing*) The Olympic Village!

CARL: One of those hookers would spot a ballplayer coming in the door . . .

ROY: Zap! Right off the stool like a sprinter!

CARL: You remember that one girl?

ROY: The whole lineup. One right after another.

CARL: We drew straws. I was last. By the time I got in . . .

ROY: (*Laughing*) Oh, boy . . .

CARL: (*Sadly, shaking his head*) Should've saved my money—done it to the catcher's mitt instead.

ROY: That's one I missed.

CARL: How'd you miss? She musta took on the batboy.

ROY: Man, she was white—you dig?

CARL: She was a whore.

ROY: Don't matter to them Florida crackers. Monahan said to me, "Son, you keep your pants on tonight, or tomorrow morning I'll find your ass out in that oak tree."

CARL: Well, I guess that's one line not even Jackie Robinson crossed.

ROY: This was years after Robby. It was still bad.

CARL: So, you're making up for it now. All those models and . . .

ROY: Not so much any more.

CARL: G'wan . . .

ROY: It's like the old philosopher says . . .

CARL: What's the old philosopher say?

ROY: Don't eat where you shit. (*Shrugging off the memory*) I was crazy that way for a while. Then Ruthie found out. Beginning of the end. How about yourself?

CARL: (*Reluctant*) Aah, I'm OK. Every now and then.

ROY: Nobody special.

CARL: One. Once.

ROY: Yeah?

CARL: She said, "Let's get married."

ROY: Oh.

CARL: I said no. She said goodbye.

ROY: Once burned, twice shy.

CARL: Something like that.

ROY: One time on our honeymoon me and Ruthie are in bed together. She said, "Do you want me to get on top?" I said, "Sure, baby. You're bound to get there sooner or later."

CARL: Aah, nobody's on top in that game. Only the lawyers.

ROY: The lawyers and the ad men.

CARL: The ad men?

ROY: First day I went with the Company—I'll never forget. Me and all the new guys are sitting in the president's office. He said, "Gentlemen, our company specializes in promoting products for men. We are an ancient and honorable fraternity. We have discovered the great gift of turning sex into gold."

CARL: Pretty funny.

ROY: It's true.

CARL: Yeah, I guess you must see a lot of gold, huh?

ROY: Me? Bush leagues.

CARL: Don't bullshit me. Sharp-looking clothes, big fancy office . . .

ROY: I'm telling you—bush league. Nothing like what it could be. Listen to me . . .

CARL: (*Offering another beer*) Here.

ROY: I got this idea.

CARL: Pop a top.

ROY: I'm OK.

CARL: C'mon—c'mon. Before it gets cold. (*Correcting himself*) Hot.

ROY: You're doing OK.

CARL: It's not the beer. It's the heat.

ROY: (*Smiling*) It's not the heat. It's the humidity.

CARL: So, what are you saying?

ROY: I got this idea. I'm thinking about it the last two weeks.

CARL: Yeah, so?

ROY: There's this new account—see? Two weeks ago I

took him out to lunch. You know—the usual scene—just like I was telling you. Well, when him and the attaché case get to talking, that's when I'm supposed to shut up. Only this time I hear something made me take notice. You see, this guy's bringing out a whole line of men's products. He's shopping around for somebody to do his advertising. Playing it real cute—going from this one to that one. It must be millions—whoever gets it.

CARL: I got the picture.

ROY: Anyway, I'm listening to our guy and he's getting nowhere fast. They're talking up a new line of after-shave and cologne, and—well—do you know what sells a product better'n anything else? I mean, they made studies. Do you know what it is?

CARL: What?

ROY: The name, man. The name.

CARL: The name, huh?

ROY: Sure, like this after-shave and cologne. It could be made outta cow piss and flowers. The right name and—bang!—everybody's gotta have it.

CARL· (*Innocent*) I thought by law you had to list the ingredients.

ROY: (*Pushing ahead*) So dig it. The guy's telling about his after-shave and cologne. And he's saying things like, "I want to appeal to the outdoorsman—blah, blah, blah—I want a name that's gonna grab them by the balls." And all of a sudden I hear my own voice. I mean, it's like I don't know where it came from. You know what I said?

CARL: What'd you say?

ROY: "Hit-and-Run."

CARL: Hit-and-Run.

ROY: After-shave and cologne. Hit-and-Run. Get it?

CARL: Yeah. OK.

ROY: You like it?

CARL: It's OK.

ROY: He liked it. I could tell he did.

CARL: So you made a sale. Good for you.

ROY: Well—no, no—not quite.

CARL: I thought you said the guy loved it.

ROY: He liked it. He did.

CARL: So what's the problem?

ROY: Well—I mean—there's a lot of things to consider.

Like, for instance, how and when the product ought to be introduced.

CARL: (*Working his beer*) You'll figure it out.

ROY: Oh, *I* got it figured. You want to hear how I got it figured?

CARL: You want to tell me?

ROY: (*Cautioning him*) Now, we're talking money—right?

CARL: (*Puzzled*) You started to.

ROY: I'm getting to it. Money in the bank. *Hit-and-Run.* You and me.

CARL: (*Startled*) What? How?

ROY: National television—Monday Night Baseball—July 18—Old-Timers Game.

CARL: Oh, come on . . .

ROY: Thirty million people watching . . .

CARL: Come on . . .

ROY: Twenty-four hours later . . .

CARL: You just don't quit . . .

ROY: *Twenty-four hours later* we're running the commercial. You, me, the product . . .

CARL: Shit . . . (*He is on his feet*)

ROY: (*Following—tapping both Carl and himself in turn*) "Hit" and "Run"—*Hit-and-Run!*

CARL: You just don't know when to fucking quit!

ROY: You wanted to talk money . . .

CARL: I told you already . . .

ROY: Well, here's money. Big money! There's DiMaggio and his coffee—Mantle and his hairspray . . .

CARL: Yeah, yeah—good for them.

ROY: Now us. *Hit-and-Run.* Sexy name—me and you . . .

CARL: Sexy? Couple of pork chops like us—what are we supposed to sell?

ROY: Man, I got it all planned—TV, radio . . .

CARL: What—you *planned* all of this and I'm only just now hearing about it?

ROY: Well, no—no, you see, it's not definite yet.

CARL: It's *not* definite?

ROY: It's an idea. Million-dollar idea.

CARL: Shit—getting all worked up over nothing.

ROY: I can sell it—I know I can.

CARL: So what's stopping you . . . ?

ROY: The guy—the account . . .

CARL: Only leave me out of it . . .

ROY: He's off in Europe for a month. And I gotta be careful in my own company. There's other guys—like wolves—I mean—this is a whole new thing for me.

CARL: Yeah, yeah—"Vice-president-in-charge-of . . . " I know all about it.

ROY: Besides, before I can sell it to anybody, I gotta sell it to you.

CARL: (*Patting Roy's shoulder*) Well, boy, you're batting out of your league. You need your man in the pinstripes.

ROY: (*Sharply—no nonsense*) Now, lookit, man—don't shit me. You *need* the money, don't you?

CARL: (*Flaring*) I don't need *nothing* outta baseball!

ROY: Not outta *baseball*!

CARL: Only what I had coming to me—that's all I ever wanted!

ROY: All right—OK—just tell me this—what'd you have to settle for?

CARL: I didn't settle! The lawyers settled.

ROY: What—your salary minus thirty-two hundred— what's that? Eighteen, nineteen?

CARL: I had all of it coming. And I could've got them for doctors and medicine and—"Disability resulting from an injury . . . "

ROY: I know all about it. What I'm saying—if you're looking for money do you know how much you can make? One minute—prime time . . .

CARL: (*Almost shouting*) It's not the money!

ROY: Then, what, then? What the hell are you talking about?

CARL: More than money! What—what do you take me for anyway? You think I'm no different from you?

ROY: What's that supposed to mean?

CARL: Money, money, money—million-dollar idea . . . !

ROY: You think that's what I'm pushing so hard for? Money?

CARL: Then *you* tell *me*.

ROY: Because once in twelve years I open my mouth. And it's good! And I ask myself, what am I doing all this time, sitting by the door?

CARL: OK—OK! Then you know what I'm talking. Money—money don't mean nothing for itself. (*A declaration*) Money's what other people think of you.

ROY: That's Monahan.

CARL: Huh?

ROY: That's his old line.

CARL: Me—I'm saying it.

ROY: You got it from him.

CARL: I didn't get nothing from him. (*Pointing at his knee*) Only this.

ROY: Every spring—contract time. "Money's what other people think of you."

CARL: Well, it shows you what they thought of me, don't it? Didn't even get what was coming to me. Didn't even get my contract.

ROY: You got a chance now to make a hundred times . . .

CARL: It's not the same thing . . .

ROY: A thousand times . . .

CARL: Find somebody else . . .

ROY: There's nobody. Nobody else. You're the other half.

CARL: You want to know the trouble with you? Do you? You're living in the past. (*Roy gives a sudden bitter laugh*) Don't laugh. I mean it.

ROY: You and Ruthie. (*Mimicking her*) "You libbin' in de past. You libbin' in de past!"

CARL: Right—she's right . . .

ROY: Got so I started feeling guilty. Like I had a prison record or something. Took all the pictures off the wall. Put them in a trunk. Put the trunk in the cellar. Locked it. Piled junk on it. The past is dead. Bury it!

CARL: Right—right . . .

ROY: I can't!

CARL: I can!

ROY: Man, don't you get it? It's the only thing we got that still works!

CARL: No—no—not me . . .

ROY: You're a liar!

CARL: (*Stunned*) I don't like how you talk.

ROY: Too bad what you don't like.

CARL: What's the matter? You drunk or something?

ROY: Me? *You!* Drunk the last fifteen years . . .

CARL: You all finished?

ROY: Man don't even know how drunk he's been!

CARL: Look, if you're all finished . . .

ROY: I ain't finished till I get what I came here for!

CARL: I am all finished with baseball!

ROY: Then what are you keeping tabs on me for? What are you quoting Monahan? What are you so jealous about this new kid?

CARL: Hey—hey—hey—lookit, why don't you go back up to Larchmont and recycle your beer cans?

ROY: (*Loud and taunting*) Mr. Hit . . . !

CARL: (*Rushing to snap off the radio*) And turn off this fucking music . . .

ROY: The Baseball Bolshevik . . . !

CARL: How do you people listen to such shit?

ROY: All these years—job after job . . .

CARL: Just get the hell outta here!

ROY: I know what the man's been looking for! I know!

CARL: Go ahead!

ROY: He's been looking for his team!

CARL: (*Savagely, his hand gripping his right knee*) You see this? You see it? *This* is what I got from my team! The end of my career.

ROY: You did that to yourself.

CARL: Monahan did it with his cleats!

ROY: After *somebody* threw a punch!

CARL: He benched me!

ROY: He was the manager. You were slumping. He had a right to put you on the bench.

CARL: He put me on the bench because I opened my mouth!

ROY: Nobody asked you to open your mouth!

CARL: Nobody else had the guts! His first year managing—right off the bat he's abusing the rookies, telling the old guys like us we had to fight to keep our jobs.

ROY: He was still the manager!

CARL: Well, now, ain't you the good little batboy.

ROY: (*On the defensive*) I testified for you. I saw the commissioner.

CARL: Sure, you did. (*Mimicking*) "Well, suh, Mr. Commissioner, ah don't rightly know what happened . . . Yes, suh, maybe he did throw the first punch . . ."

ROY: I did what I could. It was different those days. A colored ballplayer . . .

CARL: My old buddy. My teammate. Hit and Run.

ROY: We had to be on our toes all the time.

CARL: I turn around and where is he? Zap! He's gone—he ran!

ROY: They were always watching—pressure all the time . . . !

CARL: You ran!

(*They are chin-to-chin now, the image is that of a violent argument, player and umpire, in a baseball game*)

ROY: Somebody always looking to get you fired . . . !

CARL: You ran!

ROY: Just what the hell'd you know about any of that?

CARL: You ran out on me!

ROY: Mother-fucking, thick-headed . . .

CARL: And what are you? What are you? Uncle Remus! No . . . !

ROY: Son-of-a-bitching dago . . .

CARL: No—no—Tom! Uncle Tom! (*Slapping him hard in the chest*) Hey, Tom—how you doing?

ROY: (*Knocking his hand away*) Get your hands off . . . !

CARL: You watch what you do!

ROY: Watch yourself!

CARL: Get out of here!

ROY: Man, I'm telling you . . .

CARL: (*Taking up the bat*) Here, see this? See it? Wanna know what it's good for?

ROY: Watch out with that!

CARL: (*Prodding Roy's chest*) Gets rid of the muggers . . .

ROY: Watch it . . . !

CARL: Fat, black muggers . . . !

ROY: Watch it now . . . !

CARL: Get the hell outta here! (*He gives a hard shove with the bat as Roy kicks out at him in self-defense. Carl takes the blow on his bad knee. Roy pulls back, upsetting the cinder block stools and beer cans as he tumbles to the floor. Carl drops the bat as he hops around the room, holding his bad knee. Hopping*) Mother . . . !

ROY: (*Floundering*) Fucker . . . !

BOTH: *Shit!*

CARL: The knee—the same fucking knee!

ROY: (*Genuine concern*) Oh, Jesus . . .

CARL: The knee!

ROY: I got your knee?

CARL: You got my knee!

ROY: The same fucking knee?

CARL: Shit!

ROY: I'm sorry.

CARL: Shit!

ROY: I wasn't trying to kick you in the knee.

CARL: The hell you weren't!

ROY: I swear to God. I was trying to kick you in the balls.

CARL: Well, I'm almost sorry you missed. (*He stands still and tries, very gingerly, to straighten his leg*)

ROY: Can you straighten it out?

CARL: (*Still in pain*) I'm all right.

(*Roy goes to Carl and crouches in front of him. He begins to massage the injured knee gently in his powerful hands. The image is that of the team trainer attending a hurt player. Carl does not resist the attention. Roy is still breathing heavily from the exertion*)

ROY: I mean, I didn't mean to get you on the knee.

CARL: It'll be OK.

ROY: Walk on it.

CARL: Don't worry. I can shake it out. Here. (*He sets himself as if in a batter's stance and gives his leg several sharp shakes*)

CARL: Sometimes it helps to do this.

ROY: (*Noticing*) Hah!

CARL: What?

ROY: What you just did.

CARL: What about it?

ROY: It's how I used to tell if you were going after the pitch or not.

CARL: How could you tell that?

ROY: Your right knee. If you were swinging away you'd give it a little shake.

CARL: Little shake?

ROY: Like just then. (*Carl repeats the move*) There. That. Yeah.

CARL: I never knew I did.

ROY: Didn't want to get you self-conscious. Oh, sure. And what field you were hitting to—and whether you were nervous or not . . .

CARL: You could tell all that?

ROY: Every move. I'd study you like a book. I'd get half a jump on the pitcher when we played hit-and-run.

CARL: (*Delighted*) No fooling?

ROY: I had your moves down better than Ruthie's.

CARL: Ah, gee, now—kiss me, will you?

ROY: Oh, fuck you.

(*Carl laughs as Roy continues to study the knee. Slowly, he reaches out his hand and lets it rest very lightly on it*)

ROY: (*Quietly*) I didn't mean to get you there.

CARL: It's OK.

ROY: I'm sorry, man.

CARL: Yeah . . . yeah, me too. I'm sorry. (*He lays his hand on Roy's shoulder and gives it an affectionate squeeze. Roy's labored breathing stifles a sob*)

ROY: Oh, shit . . .

CARL: What's the matter?

ROY: (*Fighting back tears*) Shit, shit, shit . . .

CARL: What are you crying . . . ?

ROY: I don't know.

CARL: (*Moved*) Hey—come on . . .

ROY: All of a sudden.

CARL: All this memory lane stuff.

ROY: Must be.

CARL: C'mon. (*Humoring*) What are you crying over, your lost youth?

ROY: (*Forcing a laugh*) Maybe I'm crying 'cause I never lost it.

CARL: Yeah.

ROY: You know?

CARL: Oh, yeah.

ROY: I mean, what do you do when all the big things in your life happened way back in the beginning? What do you do?

CARL: You spend the next fifty years knowing how the first line in your obituary's gonna read.

ROY: (*With a smile*) I hate to tell you, but I think Monahan said that.

CARL: (*Sheepish*) Yeah. He did.

(*They laugh quietly together. There is a muffled rumble of thunder followed by the sound of a hard, sudden rain on the street outside*)

CARL: Here it comes.

ROY: Just like the man said.

CARL: Good. Break this weather wide open.

ROY: Give some room to breathe.

(*They remain in close physical contact for a few moments. There is no talk, only the sound of the rain from above. After a pause, Carl moves off, walking about the cellar, flexing his knee from time to time. Roy is lost in his thoughts*)

CARL: (*Suddenly*) So. What do you think—this million-dollar idea of yours. Does it have a chance, or what?

ROY: It's got a chance.

CARL: (*With a shrug*) OK.

ROY: Just like that?

CARL: Well, what do you want me to say? You want me to give you an interview?

ROY: (*Laughing*) No-no. Not the kind of interview you give.

CARL: Tell me the truth—you don't think nobody's still sore?

ROY: (*Reassuring*) Man, I'm telling you . . .

CARL: I mean all that "Bolshevik" stuff . . .

ROY: It don't matter . . .

CARL: That was Peterson. He wrote what was good for *him*.

ROY: You mean you really didn't say none of it?

CARL: No, I said it. I said it. (*Shaking his head—a little sadly*) I just didn't know it would last so long.

(*Roy approaches, and the two men stand facing each other as they did at the beginning. Roy lightly slaps Carl on the side of the arm*)

ROY: (*Smiling*) Hey. Hr. Hit.

CARL: (*Returning the gesture*) Mr. Run. (*There is a self-conscious pause—then quickly*) So—you think your ball game's rained out, or what?

ROY: They're playing in Chicago.

CARL: Go ahead. (*As Roy starts toward the radio*) Hey, how you doing? You got your wind back and everything? You doing OK, huh?

ROY: Yeah—yeah, I'm cool. How's the knee feeling?

CARL: (*Reaching down to rub*) OK—little stiff . . .

ROY: Don't rub.

CARL: (*Hands up—quickly*) Never rub.

ROY: Rub and they know they hurt you.

CARL: Rub and they do it to you again!

(*Both laugh as Roy walks to the radio and sets his hand to the dial*)

ROY: You ready for this?

CARL: I'm ready

(*Roy switches the radio on. Immediately, the stage lights lower on the scene in the cellar, and Roy and Carl face front isolated by a spotlight. Around and above them is an imaginary stadium jammed with spectators. The general roar garbles the announcer's amplified voice*)

VOICE OF ANNOUNCER: . . . pleased to welcome back . . . numbers nineteen and six . . . baseball legend . . . Mr. Hit and Mr. Run . . .

(*There is a roar of approval as Roy doffs his imaginary cap and flashes a grin. Carl hangs back slightly*)

ROY: (*Acknowledging the fans*) Just a crowd . . . same big crowd . . . you wave your cap—you give a little smile . . . you don't have to say nothing at all . . .

CARL: Sure. (*He raises his imaginary cap*) What do they want to know for, anyway?

(*The welcome continues as the lights come down and the image fades*)

(*Curtain*)

The End

Julie Beckett Crutcher

APPROACHING
LAVENDAR

Julie Beckett Crutcher

Julie Beckett Crutcher heads the New Play Program at Actors Theatre of Louisville, a position she has held since 1981. The editor of this anthology is personally acquainted with Ms. Crutcher's work as dramaturge and deeply appreciates the support she gives fledgling writers—not only those writers whose works have been selected for production in the Actors Theatre SHORTS and Humana Festivals but any writer whose promising work attracts her attention. Playwrights around the country who have submitted scripts for her consideration are delighted with the attention and respect their work receives.

Ms. Crutcher recognizes talent because she is a talented playwright. When her own play, *Approaching Lavendar,* premiered in the Actors Theatre 1983 SHORTS Festival, *Louisville Times* critic Dudley Saunders raved, "Crutcher's characters set off lively comic sparks from start to finish. The satire is good and her dialogue is often bitingly funny." *Courier-Journal* (Louisville) critic William Mootz reports, "Crutcher invests her material . . . with a precise and disquieting vision. The writing, full of trenchant humor, is sharp. As two sisters sit waiting for their father to wed yet another spouse, she gives us, in deft dramatic strokes, a sense of who they are, where they came from and the rocky emotional territory they are likely to tread in the future . . . it's a good play, and Crutcher is a playwright of bright promise."

Before joining the Actors Theatre of Louisville, Ms. Crutcher served as the administrative director of Horse Cave Theatre in south central Kentucky. In addition, she held a variety of positions at StageWest in Springfield, Massachusetts.

Ms. Crutcher is a magna cum laude graduate of the University of Massachusetts and wrote free-lance theatre reviews and book reviews as well as feature articles for a number of publications in the New England area. *Approaching Lavendar* is her first published play.

Characters:

WREN
JENNIFER
ABIGAIL

Scene:

The play takes place outside the Monsignor's office. Lights rise on Jennifer, sitting on a hardwood bench, outside a door in a rectory. Sign on the door reads, "Monsignor Kelly." The door is located in a hallway that has the feeling of age to it—heavy wood, framed pictures of bishops and popes on the wall. She sits with her hands folded. Wren, a young woman dressed much too loudly for the daytime, enters, walks down the hall, stops at the door, peers.

WREN: Excuse me? Do you work here?
JENNIFER: No, I'm sorry, I don't.
WREN: Is this the Monsignor's office?
JENNIFER: I believe so. The sign on the door would indicate that, yes.
WREN: Is there a sign? (*Peering closely*) Oh, you're right. There is. I don't have my lenses in. (*No response*) You know. Contacts? Contact lenses? I'm just blind without them, really! But this morning, God, I just couldn't put them *in*. My eyes were burning up. (*Confidentially*) Too many smoky rooms last night and all, I guess. (*Pause. No response*) Are you one of the children?
JENNIFER: Yes.
WREN: Oh, I'm so happy to meet you. Really! My name's . . .
JENNIFER: Yes. I know. I'm Jennifer.
WREN: Oh, *hi!* Isn't this exciting and all?
JENNIFER: Oh, I don't know. The thrill wears off after a while.
WREN: Aren't you going in?
JENNIFER: I don't think so. I think I'll just wait out here until it's over.
WREN: Not me! (*Pause*) He's so *romantic*, isn't he? He brought me the most beautiful roses this morning you've ever seen. I mean, he didn't *have* to do that. Sweethearts, he said,

because I was one. Isn't that sweet? (*No response*) I guess I better go in if I'm going, huh? Oohh, I just love weddings, don't you? (*No response*) Well, I'll see you later then, I guess. We're all going somewhere together. After, I mean. To celebrate. So we'll have lots of time to chat and all. (*Confidentially*) I just hope there's lots of champagne, don't you?

(*And she's gone. Jennifer shakes her head. Pause. Abigail rushes in. Her appearance is slightly disheveled*)

ABIGAIL: Jen? Jenny? Oh gosh, I'm sorry I wasn't here sooner, but the traffic was . . . Are they in there? Already? Did you see her?

JENNIFER: Yes.

ABIGAIL: What's she look like?

JENNIFER: I don't know. Healthier than the last one.

ABIGAIL: Whew. The last one looked transparent.

JENNIFER: Well, she only lived eight weeks.

ABIGAIL: Jenny!

JENNIFER: This one looks sort of extremely feminine. All ruffles and pastels. She probably serves boiled hot dogs on paper doilies.

ABIGAIL: (*Abruptly*) Oh, no! I forgot to leave Brad a note about the aluminum foil. He'll blow up the microwave or something. I maybe better go home before he gets back.

JENNIFER: (*Amused*) Oh God, Abby. You never change, do you?

ABIGAIL: (*Thinking*) Well, I joined a health club!

JENNIFER: No, I mean . . . You just got here, for God's sake, and I expect Brad can probably figure the foil out for himself, now can't he?

ABIGAIL: You don't know Brad. I just know what he'll do. He had a golf game this morning and he'll come in all sweaty and mean and he'll hit the button on the microwave and he won't look inside and he'll go to take his shower and he won't hear the explosion and then he'll come back and there'll be ground beef on the ceiling and I can't call him at the club because he's already teed off so if I leave *now* . . .

JENNIFER: (*Overlap with Abigail*) Uh-uh, Abby. Not this time. Abby, sit down. It'll be all right.

ABIGAIL: No it won't.

JENNIFER: Yes it will. And anyhow, the way these things run you'll be home before he hits the ninth hole.

ABIGAIL: Well. Maybe. I guess. (*Pause*) Can I say it's your fault if the kitchen blows up?

JENNIFER: Abby.

ABIGAIL: (*Pause*) How's Mom?

JENNIFER: In Chicago.

ABIGAIL: I *know* that. I mean, about all this, how is she?

JENNIFER: I don't think she's losing any sleep over it, Abby.

ABIGAIL: Well she should be. I mean, *I* am. I just lie there and imagine what he said, exactly.

JENNIFER: Something like, "Hello, how are you, mind if the church annuls our marriage?"

ABIGAIL: Well, that's just rude.

JENNIFER: Are you kidding? For them it's a communication breakthrough.

ABIGAIL: (*Pause*) Did you get one of those forms from the Archdiocese? That long thing with all the questions about their marriage?

JENNIFER: Yup.

ABIGAIL: What'd you do?

JENNIFER: Filled it out. Sent it back.

ABIGAIL: Oh Jen, you *didn't.* I mean, why? It's so crass. I looked at it and just threw it away and Brad said that's just what I should have done too. He just said that whether Dad's third wife got to stay Catholic or not was none of . . .

JENNIFER: Fourth. Dad's fourth wife. You forgot one.

ABIGAIL: I did?

JENNIFER: Probably the one that only lived eight weeks.

ABIGAIL: Jenny, that's not funny. (*Pause*) Brad wouldn't come today, you know. He says he won't go near them. At all. But Jen? Brad's right, don't you think. I mean, what do we know about Mom and Dad's marriage? I mean, it's not our place . . .

JENNIFER: Abby. You know Mom. You know Dad. Right?

ABIGAIL: I think so.

JENNIFER: Can you honestly tell me they ever should have been married?

ABIGAIL: But they *were.*

JENNIFER: But they're not any more. And if erasing it makes Dad happy, what the hell. Mom doesn't care. It gives her a clean slate. (*Pause*) Well, a partial clean slate. If you don't count that man she was married to for half of 1981. And I don't.

ABIGAIL: But Jenny, they had four kids. What about *us?*

JENNIFER: MaryBeth's in transit, as usual, and Tommy's at

Fendhorne, watching cabbages grow. Or something. And we're here.

ABIGAIL: Fendhorne?

JENNIFER: Yeah. It's in Scotland. Some spiritual community where they grow big vegetables.

ABIGAIL: Vegetables?

JENNIFER: Don't ask me. Ask Mom. She sent him last week after he tried to convince her to sign his share of the GM stock over to some Mormon TV station. I think it was a compromise.

ABIGAIL: Poor Tommy.

JENNIFER: Poor Tommy? He got a trip to Scotland as a reward for being a free-lance cultist, so don't go feeling sorry for *him*.

ABIGAIL: Well, Tommy's just a little mixed up, is all. (*Pause*) Probably as a direct result of all this. (*Pause*) Jenny, look. Don't you see? This annulment means Mom and Dad were never married, right, so how do you explain us? That means we're . . . well, it means we're illegitimate. It's not done. In polite society anyhow, and how can Brad and I raise our children in the church if *I'm* not in the church because I don't exist?

JENNIFER: But you don't have any children, do you?

ABIGAIL: I don't think I like this conversation anymore.

JENNIFER: Look, Abby. We've watched Dad get married twice and Mom get married once, not to mention we survived the years they were married to each other. We've got brothers and sisters we've never even met, we don't like the ones we *have* met, every family holiday means a different damn family, and on paper, our family tree looks like a Bonsai bush. All we ever get out of these marriages is a decent meal after the ceremony anyhow, so just relax about it, okay? It's just a lot of Catholic red tape. Annuling a marriage is like getting a VISA card renewed and carries about as much weight. Anybody with enough assets can do it.

ABIGAIL: You're so . . . so . . . I mean, I don't like to say this to you, but you're, well . . . you didn't used to be, but you . . . somehow . . .

JENNIFER: What, Abby? I'm what?

ABIGAIL: MEAN! You're so mean!

JENNIFER: (*Pause*) Possibly. Probably.

ABIGAIL: Oh gosh, I'm sorry . . . I didn't mean to . . .

JENNIFER: No, it's okay. You're right. (*Pause*) Oh hell,

Abby. I almost *didn't* fill out that form. But I thought about it some, and I did think about us being illegitimate, and it did bother me, for a while anyhow.

ABIGAIL: So why'd you do it?

JENNIFER: Because I just want it all to be over.

ABIGAIL: (*Pause*) What's her name?

JENNIFER: Who?

ABIGAIL: This one. The one in there.

JENNIFER: Lavendar.

ABIGAIL: Like the scent, lavender?

JENNIFER: Yeah. Like the flower, like the color, purple, you know.

ABIGAIL: (*Pause*) Do you think they'll be out soon?

JENNIFER: I don't know. I hope so.

ABIGAIL: I wonder if she'll ask us to call her "Mom"?

JENNIFER: Probably. They always do.

ABIGAIL: What'll we say?

JENNIFER: Same thing we always do. "Sweet of you to ask, but I think I'd feel more comfortable . . .

ABIGAIL: . . . calling you Lavendar. Like the *smell!*"

JENNIFER: Like the *smell*, Abby?

(*Silence as they both stare into space. Suddenly the door behind them opens and Wren scuttles out, shuts the door behind her, and scurries down the hall. Jennifer's solemn contemplation continues*)

ABIGAIL: (*Digests what she's seen and suddenly . . .*) I think I have to go home now. (*Prepares to move down the hall*)

JENNIFER: Abby, wait! What are you . . .

ABIGAIL: I think I forgot to unplug something and . . . I better remember soon . . . (*She begins to move*)

JENNIFER: (*Grabs her by the purse strap*) Abigail! What the hell's the matter?

ABIGAIL: (*Visibly upset*) I knew Brad didn't want me to see them, but I never thought that . . . I mean, how could he? How *could* he? I mean, it's one thing to not exist all of a sudden to make Dad happy, but . . . and I know because I read magazines, that Chief Justice or whatever and that Governor who's an invalid, they did, it's just, well . . . but it's just sick. It's plain not done in the place where we live and I won't be able to go to the Lilac Festival ball tonight because (*Beginning to cry*) they'll all knooow.

JENNIFER: (*Who has been trying to get a word in anywhere*) Abby, what? Why? They'll all know *what*?

ABIGAIL: They'll all *knooowww.*

JENNIFER: *What* will they know, Abby. *What!*

ABIGAIL: They'll know that Daddy . . . they'll know he . . . that he . . . (*Heavy sniffling at this point*) what he did.

(*Wren comes back up the hall*)

ABIGAIL: (*She sees Wren*) Oh, noooo.

JENNIFER: Oh, God.

(*Abigail continues sobbing, turns her back to the hall, facing the wall*)

WREN: (*To Jennifer*) Well, the least you'd think they'd do is label the loo. I bet I opened every door down there and I just thought I wouldn't make it. (*As if it were a big achievement*) But I did! (*Looks closely at the closed door*) I go in *this* door, don't I? (*Indicating Abigail*) Is she upset?

JENNIFER: I don't know. I expect so.

WREN: Did someone hurt her?

JENNIFER: She's emotionally overwrought, I think. For the moment.

WREN: Oh . . . I know what you *mean.* Weddings *do* that to some people. They're so nice. You know? Pretty, like flowers everywhere and dresses and hats and gloves? I go to zillions and cry everytime. Forever. God, I'm such a faucet. The drop of a pin and I get all choked up.

JENNIFER: Amazing.

WREN: (*Confidentially*) Sometimes even when I don't know who they are! (*Pause. No response*) Well, if she wants to freshen up later, it's downstairs, turn right and three doors . . . no, four maybe . . . on the, uh . . . (*Turns as if to simulate being in the hall*) . . . left, I think. Or the right. Well, whatever. (*Opens the door, enters, closes it behind her. Silence*)

ABIGAIL: (*Slowly turning around*) You talked to her!

JENNIFER: Well of course I talked to her.

ABIGAIL: Well, I'm not going to talk to her. Ever!

JENNIFER: I swear, Abigail, sometimes I think living in a split-level Cape Cod is seriously endangering your health.

ABIGAIL: Colonial.

JENNIFER: What?

ABIGAIL: It's Colonial. Not a Cape Cod. And they don't make Colonials split-level. Which shows you how much *you* know about it.

JENNIFER: You're right. I know nothing about it. And I intend to keep it that way, thank you very much.

ABIGAIL: You'll be sorry, with that attitude. It's not positive

JENNIFER: Thanks for the warning, Abby.

ABIGAIL: (*Pause. The dust settles. Softer*) Can you honestly tell me that it doesn't bother you?

JENNIFER: It doesn't bother me. I don't know a low-boy from a Lazy-Boy and so far it hasn't hurt me any.

ABIGAIL: Not that. I mean Lavendar's age. Doesn't *that* bother you?

JENNIFER: What about her age? I told you she was healthy.

ABIGAIL: But you didn't tell me *why* she was healthy.

JENNIFER: All I meant, Abigail, was that at least she doesn't have one foot in the grave.

ABIGAIL: Well, not *her* grave. Maybe *his* grave.

JENNIFER: Abigail. Look me straight in the eyes and tell me you're not drunk.

ABIGAIL: Don't you see what she wants? His money! She should be in jail. Oh Jenny, we have to do something.

JENNIFER: I really don't think we can *do* anything, Abigail. Nor that we'd have cause to *do* anything. Why don't we just sit here like the polite girls we are and when it's over, they'll tell us, and we can all go and have a nice lunch. You and me, Dad and Lavendar, and Lavendar's adrenally over-active daughter.

ABIGAIL: Daughter!

JENNIFER: That's right, Abigail. Her daughter. That terminal debutante who whizzed past us en route to what she referred to as the "loo." (*Pause*) It means bathroom.

ABIGAIL: That's not Lavendar?

JENNIFER: No, Abby. Lavendar is busy in there staying Catholic while marrying Dad . . . who doesn't much care about being Catholic except in as much as Lavendar *is* and wants to go to heaven, which she can now do since the church conveniently obliterated history. Think how much simpler everything would have been if Mom had just died like the others. (*Pause*) Sorry.

ABIGAIL: What's her name?

JENNIFER: Whose name?

ABIGAIL: The one who's not Lavendar, that I thought was.

JENNIFER: You seriously thought *that* was Lavendar?

ABIGAIL: Well, she came out of there, didn't she? And you didn't tell me anybody else was in there. What was I supposed to think?

JENNIFER: Oh God, Abby. How *can* you have remained so totally unassuming?

ABIGAIL: I don't know. I guess 'cause I got married so young and moved to the suburbs. And I read a lot.

JENNIFER: Maybe it's just what you read that's the problem. (*Pause*) Her name is Wren.

ABIGAIL: Wren? Well, it's . . . not like Linda or Susan. (*Pause*) She's awfully *pretty*, isn't she?

JENNIFER: I guess. If you like that sort of look.

ABIGAIL: I think most people like that sort of look, don't you?

JENNIFER: No.

ABIGAIL: Jenny? Why do we only get pretty sisters? Why don't we ever get ugly ones? I'm sick of pretty sisters that make me feel like no matter if I only ate grapefruit for a year I'd still never have a body like theirs.

JENNIFER: Would you want a body like hers, Abby?

ABIGAIL: Well, no. Not really. Well, maybe sometimes, or if I wanted to, I could.

JENNIFER: She probably gets it wrapped in avocado pulp twice a week.

ABIGAIL: Do you think Lavendar will make Dad adopt her?

JENNIFER: I doubt Wren's real interested in being adopted. I met her three weeks ago at some charity ball that Mom dragged me to because she didn't want to go by herself. She's a little like Mom, you know? Scary thought, huh? Has the same ability to completely block out reality and live for the moment. Mom's problem is that her moments are fewer and farther between. Wren's problem is that she knows nothing *but* moments. And most of them not during daylight hours.

ABIGAIL: Well, she's pretty young, yet, isn't she?

JENNIFER: Poor excuse.

ABIGAIL: Well, yes. But you don't know. Lots of girls grow up late. Look at MaryBeth.

JENNIFER: Abigail. Have you talked to MaryBeth? Recently?

ABIGAIL: Two months ago.

JENNIFER: And what did she say?

ABIGAIL: She said she couldn't talk to me right then because they were about to cut off her electricity because she hadn't paid the bill because they sent it to an old address so she never got it, but it was okay because the apartment smelled like cat urine and she was moving anyway and she'd let me know where when she got there so I could send a check to her so she could buy some milk for the cat. That was the last I heard from her.

JENNIFER: How much did you send her this time, Abigail?

ABIGAIL: Two-hundred and fifty.

JENNIFER: For the cat?

ABIGAIL: Well, she sounded so lonely . . . and lost . . . and confused.

JENNIFER: MaryBeth is lonely and lost and confused. MaryBeth *thrives* on confusion. If she ever got her life in order nobody would feel sorry for her anymore and then she'd *really* be confused.

ABIGAIL: I don't think this is a very nice discussion.

JENNIFER: Well, no. You wouldn't. But it's true, Abby. MaryBeth should either get married or get a job so she has somewhere to go at nine o'clock every morning.

ABIGAIL: She has a job.

JENNIFER: What as?

ABIGAIL: She works with orphans. Twice a week at least.

JENNIFER: And what does she do with these orphans?

ABIGAIL: Plays with them. Helps them understand how adults act.

JENNIFER: I rest my case.

ABIGAIL: Well *you* don't have a job.

JENNIFER: I'm in law school. That's different.

ABIGAIL: Well *I* don't have a job.

JENNIFER: You're married. That's different too.

ABIGAIL: Being married isn't a job.

JENNIFER: But being married to Brad is.

ABIGAIL: Well, no it's not. I mean, it's a lot of work and sometimes I get tired and the house is pretty big, too, so I have to clean and do the laundry but it's not a *job* job. It's a . . . well, it's just my life, is all, I guess.

(*The door opens and Wren emerges, looking none the worse for the time she's spent in the chambers. Her dazed expression turns to a smile as she sees Jennifer and Abigail*)

WREN: Hi again!

JENNIFER: Hello.

WREN: They sent me out. For a little while. I think I was talking too much. The Monsignor got a headache.

JENNIFER: How's it going in there?

WREN: Oh just *fine*. A little slow though, maybe. Dad keeps nodding off and all. He's so cute when he does that. Like a cute little puppy. He does that a lot, doesn't he? (*Noticing*

Abigail, who bristles but doesn't yelp at "Dad") Oh, I'm so *gauche!* We haven't met. You were upset before so I didn't want to disturb you. I'm Wren. (*Offering her hand to Abigail, who isn't quite sure whether she wants to take it or not*)

JENNIFER: This is Abigail, Wren. (*No response*) Abby, shake Wren's hand.

ABIGAIL: (*Taking Wren's hand*) How old are you?

JENNIFER: Abby!

WREN: I just turned twenty-one. Do you believe it?

ABIGAIL: No.

JENNIFER: Yes.

WREN: I just came out two years ago.

JENNIFER: Came out of what? . . . Sorry, I didn't know they still did that.

WREN: Oh, they do! You're so *funny.* That's what Dad said. He said you always made everybody laugh, even though it wasn't always funny. Well, I don't know what he meant by that part.

ABIGAIL: Dad?

WREN: Yeah. Your dad said why don't I call him Dad. Isn't that sweet? I started today, even though they're not married yet, I know, but . . . well, it's kinda weird and all, and I'm not used to it yet but . . . I didn't want to hurt his feelings or anything.

ABIGAIL: (*Pause*) I think I have to go home now.

JENNIFER: (*Warning*) Abby.

ABIGAIL: Brad will be on the third to last green and if I leave now, I can get back and pretend that I never came here and everything will be all right again.

WREN: Is Brad your boyfriend?

ABIGAIL: We're married.

WREN: Oh, that's all right. Lots of people I know get married. (*Pause*) Oops. I almost forgot. He called.

JENNIFER: Who called?

ABIGAIL: Brad did?

WREN: Yeah. A little while ago when I went to the loo and you were out here crying.

ABIGAIL: Uh-oh.

JENNIFER: What, Abby. What uh-oh?

WREN: Gosh. Maybe I shouldn't have told you.

JENNIFER: Abby, *what* did you do?

ABIGAIL: Something bad.

JENNIFER: How bad, Abby?

ABIGAIL: Pretty bad.

WREN: They said to tell you, though, that he called.

JENNIFER: What, Abby, what?

ABIGAIL: (*Pause*) I threw out his goldfish.

WREN: Doesn't David Bowie do something with goldfish?

JENNIFER: You threw out his *goldfish?* What'd you do? Flush them down the toilet?

ABIGAIL: How'd you know that, how I did it?

WREN: He eats them or something. Yuck.

JENNIFER: You took his goldfish out of the bowl and *flushed* them?

ABIGAIL: Not the bowl. The bag.

WREN: I mean, I think that's pretty gross, don't you?

JENNIFER: He keeps goldfish in a bag?

ABIGAIL: Yeah, you know, you buy them that way. In those little bags. For ninety-nine cents each?

JENNIFER: Not *live* goldfish?

WREN: Kinda like crackers, right?

ABIGAIL: You know. Pizza and Parmesan and Pretzel and Cheddar.

JENNIFER: Abby, *why* did you flush Brad's goldfish down the toilet? (*No response*) That's a pretty ineffectual way of expressing anger, Abby.

ABIGAIL: Well, I threw out some other stuff too!

WREN: You didn't just walk out and all? That's what I did once, only I came back because I couldn't start the car.

ABIGAIL: I threw out the spoon-size shredded wheat, and that kind of bread he likes that makes you have heart attacks. (*Pause*) And that's why he called.

JENNIFER: Abby, why were you mad at Brad?

ABIGAIL: Because.

JENNIFER: Because why?

ABIGAIL: Because of what he said about my family and how it embarrasses him and how I couldn't come here today.

JENNIFER: He's a jerk, Abby.

ABIGAIL: He is *not* a jerk.

JENNIFER: Abigail, Brad does not know what's right for *you.*

ABIGAIL: But he does, Jenny.

WREN: He does?

JENNIFER: But he told you *not* to come and you *came.*

WREN: That's true too.

ABIGAIL: Well, yes, but I didn't lie this time.

WREN: Once I threw a piece of chateaubriand at this guy I was with in Zelda's, in front of his agent and everything. Or maybe his editor.

JENNIFER: (*Pause*) That's very interesting, Wren. (*Pause*) Oh, Abby. I thought you were better.

ABIGAIL: Oh, I *am* better. Before if I got mad, I'd just try to pretend I wasn't and maybe buy a new chair or magazine or something, so this *is* better.

JENNIFER: But how's Brad gonna know you're angry if you don't tell him?

ABIGAIL: But I did tell him, didn't I?

JENNIFER: Abby, you threw out the contents of the pantry. That isn't *telling* him.

WREN: Well, in a way, that is.

ABIGAIL: You see, Jenny. In a way that is.

JENNIFER: But for God's sake, Abby. If you had to throw something out, why didn't you throw out something that *mattered*?

ABIGAIL: His *goldfish* matter.

JENNIFER: Oh yeah, they are terrifically vital and irreplaceable. Big deal!

WREN: Whew. I mean, aren't you afraid he'll be real ripped? I mean, I would be, if someone did that to me. Even accidentally, I would be. Wouldn't you?

ABIGAIL: Maybe . . . I don't exactly know, but . . . no . . . yeah . . . I guess so.

WREN: What I mean is like . . . well, think about it. He gets up, right, and you're gone and all, and he goes for the cereal but it's not there so he figures maybe you just forgot to buy it or something, so he decides to have some toast instead, maybe . . . So he goes for the bread but that's gone too . . .

JENNIFER: I don't think you're helping.

WREN: . . . so he figures maybe he'll get something on the way to wherever, you know, coffee *and* . . . so he goes to the bathroom to get ready . . .

JENNIFER: This doesn't concern you, Wren.

WREN: . . . and he goes to, well, *you* know, and he lifts the seat and he looks down and there's these swollen pizza goldfish floating in the bowl . . . oh, it's sooo gross.

(*The image does it, and Abigail takes off down the hall*)

JENNIFER: (*Starting after her*) Abby? Abigail?

WREN: Nothing for breakfast and crackers in the toilet! I mean, it's vintage Fellini. (*Pause*) No wonder the guy freaked.

I mean, I would, wouldn't you? (*Pause. Realizing it's futile, Jennifer returns*) Where do you think she's going?

JENNIFER: Well, I *don't* think she's heading home.

WREN: Prob'ly the loo. You know, when I threw that chateaubriand at Ryan, in Zelda's, that guy I was with? . . . he didn't call for two whole days. I mean, I thought it was pretty funny. Everybody *else* laughed. It was this benefit number they were doing there . . . Save the Trees or Save the Seals or something.

JENNIFER: Wren, I think maybe it would be best if . . .

WREN: (*Oblivious*) I forget now. All those people were so starched-in, acting dignified and all. It wasn't much of a party, if you want to know the truth.

JENNIFER: It was Save the Children.

WREN: Yeah? Well, I knew it was Save the something. (*Pause as she realizes*) Oh no! You were there? You saw me trash Ryan?

JENNIFER: I was there, yes.

WREN: Well, didn't *you* think it was funny?

JENNIFER: We were introduced, remember? I left before you started tossing meat.

WREN: We met there? Are you sure? Oh, gosh. Am I embarrassed. I do a zillion charities and all. Do you remember if I was wearing red or navy? Sometimes I can hook into it if I can focus on the dress.

JENNIFER: Wren? I know this may have eluded you, but my sister appears to be slightly upset. I don't think she's quite up to dealing with strangers right now and frankly, I don't believe this incident need concern anyone but the immediate family.

WREN: But I *am* immediate family.

JENNIFER: Not yet, you're not.

WREN: Well, practically, I am.

JENNIFER: Wren, Abigail is my sister.

WREN: She's my sister, too!

JENNIFER: Yes, well, that's true. She'll soon be your stepsister, I'll be your stepsister, and we'll all be stepsisters. But stepsisters are different from real sisters. Now I'm sure Abigail seemed relatively stable to you, but she has some problems, uh . . . *coping* sometimes, and when she gets upset I'm one of the few people she'll talk to. You probably have older brothers and sisters yourself, so you know what it's like.

WREN: I'm an only child.

JENNIFER: Oh. (*Pause*) Well then, I'll explain what it's like. You see, brothers and sisters . . . and especially sisters, I think . . . share many things when they grow up. Especially if they come from broken homes, which Abigail and I do. She's only eleven months older than I am, so we were very close. (*Pause*) Now. Divorces can be very nasty sometimes, and this one *was*, and as a result Abigail and I came to understand each other, you see? (*Pause*) And Abby is really very shy and extremely sensitive, so when something happens, like it just did, then I have to help her. And it would be easier for her if you weren't here.

WREN: (*Pause*) Why do you talk to me that way?

JENNIFER: What way?

WREN: Like you did just then. Like I was ten years old or something.

JENNIFER: (*Mock sincerity in her tone*) Did I? I'm sorry. I didn't mean to.

WREN: You do that a lot. Talk to people that way. (*Pause*) You think I'm a real flake, don't you?

JENNIFER: No. I don't think that.

WREN: Well then, you don't approve of me, or something. Do you?

JENNIFER: Look, Wren, it's not that simple. There's a lot of inherent tension here and . . .

WREN: No. It's not just that. It's something else. You didn't like me from the moment you met me.

JENNIFER: But you don't *remember* meeting me.

WREN: Now I do. I do now. And I remember thinking that you were, you know . . . pretty cold, just like all the rest of those people.

JENNIFER: Well, the situation wasn't exactly conducive to congenial chitchat.

WREN: You were trying to be cooler and more above it all than they were even. It's the same story every time. The women don't like me because I'm young and rich and pretty, and the men keep trying to kiss me when they dance with me. It's disgusting. And you were right there with them, looking disapproving and all.

JENNIFER: (*Hears Abigail coming back down the hall*) Look, Wren. I don't think this is really doing either of us any good. So why don't you just scoot back in there like a good girl and see if you can't hurry the nuptials along and I'll stay here and have mv talk with Abby and then we can all go have a pleasant lunch somewhere and after that, we'll only have to see each other once a year, and everything will be just fine and painless, like it's supposed to be.

(*Abigail is suddenly behind them*)

ABIGAIL: I couldn't find the powder room. So I went across the street to the church, but there wasn't one there . . . so I sat in the back for a while, where it was still. And then I came back.

JENNIFER: Good girl, Abby.

ABIGAIL: I'm sorry I left like that. It wasn't very polite, not to say "excuse me."

JENNIFER: It's okay. I'm sure Wren didn't take any offense. Did you, Wren? (*No response*) Well. So. Here we all are. Wren was just about to go back in there and see if she could hurry them along. Weren't you, Wren?

WREN: No.

JENNIFER: I see. Okay. Well, then. (*Pause*) Well, then. Actually, Abby, I was trying to explain to Wren about being sisters and how, sometimes, you can only talk to *me* about things. I was explaining bonding, in my fashion, and Wren was telling me how she was an only child so she didn't grasp the concept. Exactly. Essentially.

WREN: No I wasn't. I was telling you that I didn't like you because you pretend not to be something that you really are, and because you talk to me like I'm stupid. I know lots of people who have divorced parents, and you know what? You all have the same attitude and you all use it as an excuse for not having any friends.

JENNIFER: (*Pause*) You sure shoot straight when you shoot, don't you?

WREN: Yes.

ABIGAIL: Maybe I should go to the bathroom again?

JENNIFER: No, damn it, Abigail, you just sit right there and behave yourself.

WREN: You see? You just did it. Right then, ordering her around like that and all.

JENNIFER: Look, Wren. How you regard me is one thing. But whether or not I have any friends, for God's sake, is another. There is a history involved here that you can't possibly comprehend and it also determines the way I treat my sister, which is none of your damned business in the first place so I'll just thank you to kindly *butt out.*

WREN: (*To Abigail*) Gosh. Do you think I made her hate me?

JENNIFER: I don't hate anybody, for God's sake.

ABIGAIL: (*Pause*) I think maybe you do, Jenny.

JENNIFER: Just what the hell is that supposed to mean?

ABIGAIL: Well. Just that you always say you don't so fast, you know, and in most cases that indicates deep-rooted . . .

JENNIFER: Don't play analysis with me, Abigail. I pay someone to do that.

ABIGAIL: I know you do, and I'm not, really, but Jenny . . .

JENNIFER: What, Abigail, *what?*

ABIGAIL: You do. Hate some people.

JENNIFER: (*Calmly*) All right, Abby. You're so smart. You tell *me.* Whom?

ABIGAIL: Well, me, a little, because I got married where it was safer.

JENNIFER: No, Abby. You'd probably like to think that, but I could easily have . . .

ABIGAIL: And Dad, I think, because he walked out and didn't tell us.

JENNIFER: I felt anger, yes, initially, but I forgave him and . . .

ABIGAIL: And Wren, because she's right.

WREN: Well, I don't know about . . .

JENNIFER: Wren was merely repeating a much publicized generalization which hasn't proven true in . . .

ABIGAIL: And Tommy and MaryBeth because they were younger, but mostly Mom because she agreed to the annulment and made you an orphan.

JENNIFER: (*With rising intensity*) That is absurd, Abigail. I have *dealt* with that issue. It's dead, okay? It's a god-damned moot point. We've been orphans since the day Dad left, and you know it, because you were there and damn near went nuts because of it and if it weren't for me . . .

ABIGAIL: But I did go nuts, Jenny.

JENNIFER: You did *not.*

ABIGAIL: Yes I did. And you couldn't save me.

JENNIFER: (*Nearing tears*) Stop it, Abigail. Please?

ABIGAIL: It's okay, Jenny. I'm better now.

JENNIFER: (*Dissolving*) Oh God, Abby. It's not fair.

ABIGAIL: (*Comes to Jennifer and embraces her, very much the parent now*) I'm older, Jenny. I give up easier.

(*Wren moves to the two women, reaches into her purse, and silently extends a Kleenex to Jennifer*)

JENNIFER: Thank you. I don't usually cry at weddings.

WREN: I do.

JENNIFER: Especially at my parents' weddings.

ABIGAIL: That's not true, Jenny. You cried at one of Mom's weddings.

JENNIFER: That's because she was marrying a real jerk. (*Pause. Abigail shoots a look at Jennifer*)

WREN: What's it like, having a stepfather?

JENNIFER: Oh, it's okay. Pretty strange at first though. Just don't let Dad play you against your mother.

WREN: Do they do that?

JENNIFER: Not always. One of our's did all the time, but he didn't last long.

ABIGAIL: Yeah. He left after Tommy barfed all over the inside of his Mercedes.

WREN: Oh, how gross!

ABIGAIL: Well, he didn't mean to or anything.

WREN: (*Pause*) I guess you'll come to my house for Christmas now, huh?

JENNIFER: Well, Dad likes to spend Christmas with his children. Just wait until he hauls out the flea-bitten old Santa suit and pretends that we're all still in grade school.

ABIGAIL: Oh, it's nuts at Christmas. You have to start making place cards in October, and you never have the right number anyhow.

JENNIFER: But it's fun, in its way. (*Pause*) He's basically a nice man, Wren. Really. (*She suddenly jumps up*) Oh, my God. I think I heard a chair move in there.

WREN: You did? Really?

ABIGAIL: (*Jumping up*) Really? Are they really coming out? (*Moves to door and puts her ear against it*) Oh, gosh . . . they are. Oh no, what do we do? What do we do?

WREN: (*Fumbling in her purse*) Here. I brought a bag of rice. We'll throw it at them when they come out, okay? It'll be just like they're newlyweds and all.

JENNIFER: Wren, they *are* newlyweds.

ABIGAIL: I was gonna bring rice too, but all we had was this icky old cracked wheat stuff that Brad keeps around because he thinks it makes him regular. And I thought maybe it wouldn't be very nice to throw it at them. So I just flushed it down the . .

JENNIFER: Abby, would you *please* be quiet?

WREN: Here, Abby. You stand in the middle and hold the bag for us, okay? (*Everybody lines up*) Isn't this exciting? I just love weddings, don't you?

(*There is a moment of silence as all three prepare to hurl rice. An expectant, brief pause*)

ABIGAIL: (*Whisper*) Jenny? (*Pause*) Jenny, I gotta ask something.

JENNIFER: What, Abby, what?

ABIGAIL: Well, I might be wrong about this and everything, but isn't rice the symbol for fertility or something?

WREN: (*As the door begins to open*) Here they come, everybody. Start throwing. Start throwing.

JENNIFER: Oh my *God*! Don't *throw* that! Wren, don't . . .

(*The lights snap to black*)

The End

James G. Richardson

EULOGY

James G. Richardson

In February 1983, shortly before the New York premiere of *Eulogy*, James G. Richardson died in a mountaineering accident. The play, published here for the first time, is a memorial to the tragic loss of an accomplished young playwright.

Born in Gainesville, Florida, on August 22, 1945, James G. Richardson later resided in Santa Monica, California. His education included years at Phillips Exeter Academy, Duke University, and the University of Florida, where he received his M.A. During the United States action in Vietnam, Mr. Richardson served in the Armed Forces.

Following his military service, he spent a year at the American Conservatory Theatre in San Francisco. His other work as an actor included Broadway, Off-Broadway, film, and television. He was a star of the Universal Pictures series *Sierra*, as well as the CBS Afterschool Special *All for One*. He wrote for episodic television, and his work was commissioned by the PBS Workshop. He was a coordinator of the Ensemble Studio Theatre/Los Angeles Writers Workshop.

Eulogy was his most recent play, written especially for the performers Sarah Cunningham and John Randolph. The production in the New York Ensemble Studio Theatre's 1983 Marathon Series won rave reviews. Robert Massa, *Village Voice* reviewer, praising the evening of plays in the Marathon Series, writes: "The strongest [play] is James G. Richardson's *Eulogy*, in which an elderly couple clash over how and how much respect should be paid the husband's deceased brother. The dialogue is amusing and moving . . ." The play was filmed for television in 1984.

Characters:

KATHERINE ANN GRACIE, *in her late fifties*
BEN GRACIE, *about sixty*

Scene:

The play takes place in a large Victorian home in Gainesville, Florida.

The setting suggests the upstairs hallway and main bedroom of the house. There are no walls present, but their positions are made clear by such things as a freestanding door frame, center, which leads from the hallway into the bedroom. The hallway itself is delineated by an oriental runner that covers its length. At one end, stage right, is a grouping of potted plants on the floor, and beyond them, just offstage, we can imagine French doors leading to a veranda. At the other end of the hall, stage left, lighting suggests a window with northern exposure with the light filtered through the window's shutters. Also at this end of the hall is the stairway leading down to the main floor of the house. If we could see the entire hallway and railing, we would find that we could walk all around the stairwell by following the railing that surrounds it on three sides. Present onstage is the upstage side of the railing and a partial cutaway of the stage right side, and in addition, there's a suggestion of the bannister that would follow the stairway itself. Sitting on the newel post is a man's black fedora. Approximately opposite the door frame, against one of our imaginary walls, is a swan table covered with a delicate doily on which rests a crystal vase filled with yellow freesias. If we could see this imaginary wall, we would also see a mirror hung above the table.

If we now go into the bedroom and turn left, there is a dressing table and chair set against another imaginary wall, which is also the upstage wall of the hall. Set on the table are such things as an elegant comb and brush set, perfume, black gloves, a jewelry box with a string of pearls showing, a porcelain cup containing a pair of earrings, a box of Kleenex boutique tissues, and so on. Above the dressing table is another unseen mirror. To the right, as we enter the bedroom, we can imagine a large dressing closet in which sits a small vanity table with a drawer and, below it, a door. Sitting on the table is a woman's black hat. Upstage of this table is a trifold dressing screen.

The time is two o'clock on a June afternoon. At rise, we see Ben ·Gracie in the hallway. He is a handsome man, about sixty, who wears glasses that he needs only to read. He paces between the plants and the table, looks at himself in the mirror, and mutters and gestures, occasionally checking several 5 x 7 file cards that he holds. He is dressed in an expensive black suit and tie and black shoes.

In the bedroom, sitting at the dressing table and trying to get her hair to cooperate, is Katherine Ann Gracie. She is attractive, in her late fifties, with just a hint of the lion about her. She is dressed in an elegant black dress and heels. She calls to her husband through the open bedroom door.

KATHERINE: You know I hope they have chairs. Do you think they'll have chairs? (*There is no response*) I hate standing at funerals. I don't mind standing at weddings. But I like to sit at a funeral. (*She sees Ben pass the doorway*) You think they'll have chairs?

BEN: (*Still distractedly muttering*) What?

KATHERINE: (*Overly clearly, with a marked Southern accent*) Chairs.

BEN: Oh, yes.

KATHERINE: Good. That's good. I hope they're padded. I hate those hard folding chairs.

BEN: Yes.

KATHERINE: (*After a pause*) The coffin won't be open?

BEN·   They cremated him, honey.

KATHERINE: (*Amazed at what she has just heard*) What?!

BEN: Cremated. They cremated him.

KATHERINE: (*Scandalized. She gets up and joins him in the hallway*) They did! (*And now interested*) They did?

BEN: Yes.

KATHERINE: (*She turns her back to him and presents him with the ends of her pearl necklace, which he is expected to fasten for her*) Imagine that! Cremated.

BEN: Marlene had to watch. Awful thing, really. Terrible hing.

KATHERINE: (*Again, not sure she's heard right*) She what?

BEN: She had to watch.

KATHERINE: She did?! They made her?

BEN: (*Now finished fastening the necklace*) Well, somebody had to. She said it was her last gift to her father.

KATHERINE: (*Moving to the hall mirror to make sure the necklace is hanging properly*) Some gift. I couldn't have done it. Imagine, Marlene, his own daughter. (*She puts on her earrings, still using the mirror*)

BEN: She did it out of love, honey.

KATHERINE: Well, I suppose so. I hated the man, but I still couldn't have watched him burn. (*She's finished surveying herself and starts to go back into the bedroom. She pauses outside the doorway*) Well, maybe I could. (*She goes to the vanity*)

BEN: (*Following her into the bedroom*) Katherine, please, he's not even in the ground.

KATHERINE: (*Opening the vanity table door and getting her clutch bag*) What's that got to do with it? He's dead. He can't hear me.

BEN: Please, honey. (*He goes back out into the hallway and starts consulting his file cards once again*)

KATHERINE: (*Picking up her hat and musing*) Could you?

BEN: Could I what?

KATHERINE: Watch me burn?

BEN: What?

KATHERINE: (*Joining him in the hall*) Would you give me that as your final gift?

BEN: Christ, Katie, what's wrong with you today?

KATHERINE: Nothing, dear. Nothing. (*Consulting the mirror again*) It's a normal thought. That's a normal thought.

BEN: Well, I don't want to think about it.

KATHERINE: (*Suddenly noticing*) I should have sent this dress to the cleaners. Can you see the wrinkles?

BEN: (*Stepping back to appraise her*) You look . . . you look pretty as a picture.

KATHERINE: (*Critically, to the mirror*) A picture in need of some restoration.

BEN: Rembrandt couldn't do better.

KATHERINE: Rembrandt? Why Rembrandt? I'd say El Greco or somebody. (*She makes a face as if to imitate a cubist version of herself*) I look like a goddamn inquisitor, that's what I look like. (*Pulls her face up at the temples with her fingers*) How do you think I'd look with a lift? (*Looks*) No. A sixty-year-old Chinese blonde wouldn't work at all.

BEN: What's all this b'iness with the mirror all of a sudden?

KATHERINE: Oh, I don't know. Old age. Funerals. Something's got me stirred up today. Nothing looks right. (*She impatiently flips the end of her hair with her hand*) Maybe I'll dye it red. Whatdaya think, old man. Could you handle a red-head?

BEN: Long's you don't take up snorin', you can do anything you like.

KATHERINE: (*Picking up her bag and hat from the table*) All right, I'm ready.

(*They start toward the stairs*)

BEN: (*Stopping*) Listen to this just a minute, 'fore we go.

KATHERINE: What?

BEN: I'm supposed to speak a few words.

KATHERINE: For Sigsby?

BEN: Yes, honey. He's the one havin' the funeral.

KATHERINE: I'm aware of that, Ben. (*Putting her bag and hat down on the table again and turning from him*) I am perfectly aware of that. I'm just a little surprised that you're going to speak at the funeral of a man who more or less dedicated his life to destroying you.

BEN: Oh, honey. Let's not start this. He was my brother and he was my law partner and it's only fitting that I say a few words over his grave.

KATHERINE: (*Moving toward the plants*) Over his urn.

BEN: What?

KATHERINE: His urn. When you're cremated you get an urn, not a grave.

BEN: Well, they're burying something. Maybe they're burying the urn.

KATHERINE: (*Looking out through the French doors offstage*) No doubt. Dot can barely set a table, no reason to expect her to have any taste at a funeral. (*Coming back to him slightly*) She could at least *scatter* the ashes. You don't *bury* ashes, you *scatter* them. She could scatter them on the Gulf (*Gesturing to the veranda off right, then a slight pause*) or at the Mall. (*Very pleased with herself*) That would be nice. In memory of his many *civic* contributions.

BEN: Katherine, shut the hell up, now! You're talking about my brother.

KATHERINE: Yes, indeed, I am.

BEN: Will you just listen to this for a minute. And try and imagine that you're not his sister-in-law.

KATHERINE: (*Starting in to the bedroom*) All right. Come in here where I can sit down. I don't like to stand up for speeches either. (*She sits at the dressing table*)

BEN: (*Calling after her*) No, honey. Just sit here. (*Going in after her*) I can't give a eulogy in a bedroom.

KATHERINE: Why not? You practice your summations in the bedroom.

BEN: Summations are intimate. (*He picks up her chair almost out from under her and brings it out, setting it just outside the doorway in the hallway*) It helps to imagine that the jury and I are all there in the bedroom. Eulogies are public. Think of Brutus, think of Pericles. (*During this, she has sat on the chair, where he placed it, and he has moved toward the railing. Now he turns and appraises his setup*) I need all this hallway. (*He once again scoops up the chair and sets it down at the end of the runner, stage right*)

KATHERINE: (*Chairless, standing*) The things I have endured for your career as a public speaker. Where do I sit?

BEN: (*Invitingly*) Just down there.

KATHERINE: (*She has crossed almost to the chair, now stops briefly*) Pericles! (*She passes around the chair and right on to the plants while saying*) Is this all right, or shall I go out on the veranda? Give you more range. (*Gestures like a Greek statue*) Perhaps it'll seem more Greek.

BEN: No. That's fine. Just fine. You just sit down in that nice *padded* chair.

KATHERINE: (*Sits after adjusting the chair's position to suit herself*) All right, dear.

BEN: (*Nervous again, looks at his cards*) I won't use the cards. I just want to check 'em a minute here. (*Reads, then moves to the stairwell*) I think the grave, or the hole or whatever, will be . . . (*Looks around for a suitable location, settles on the stairwell itself*) say it's here . . . And the crowd is out there. (*Gesturing vaguely beyond and to the right of the stairwell*) Preacher Gordon's right here. (*At the head of the stairs*) And Dot and Marlene and the kids are here up front. (*He has gone over to the right of the stairwell and "placed" them. Now he returns to the railing and puts his cards away and his glasses in his jacket breast pocket. Now he addresses his imaginary audience quite cheerfully*) Well . . . afternoon, friends. Dot and Marlene asked me to say a few words about Sigsby, and you know I was never a man to turn down a captive audience. Something I learned from Sigs. When we were kids he used to tie me up and make me listen to *his* speeches. So I guess I'm finally getting even. (*He stops and talks to Katherine*) You think that's all right? I don't want to be too solemn about it, but I don't want to be irreverent either.

KATHERINE: I think it's fine. Evokes those memories of childish sadism that we all cherish.

BEN: No, seriously.

KATHERINE: I think it's fine.

BEN: You do?

KATHERINE: Yes. It's fine.

BEN: Okay. Good. (*He puts his glasses back on and checks his cards briefly*) I don't know why I'm so damn nervous. (*As he pockets both the glasses and the cards*) So, anyway, the b'iness about the captive audience. (*Goes back to addressing the crowd*) I'd like to take just a few minutes to talk about Sigsby Lancelot Gracie, who was my older brother and my law partner and my lifelong friend. To quote the bard, you might say I come to bury Sigsby, not to praise him. (*Katherine lowers her head to hide her reaction to this*) Because Sigsby doesn't need praise. I don't need to tell people who were his friends and neighbors for the last sixty-eight years that Sigsby was a fine and distinguished member of this community. He graduated from the University of Florida Law School in 1939. He and the beautiful Dorothy McGinnis were married that year. He settled down to practice law, but the war intervened. He served for four years—"four years, two months and eleven days" he used to say. He didn't much like the army, but he was a good officer. He landed at Guadalcanal and Okinawa with the 244th Light Infantry Brigade and was awarded the Distinguished Service Cross for his bravery in battle.

In 1946 Sigsby came back to Gainesville and resumed the practice of law, which he continued until his health forced him to retire three years ago. He was a member of the First Presbyterian Church, a Sunday School teacher for twenty-one years, a past Exalted Ruler of the Benevolent Protective Order of Elks, a member of Kiwanis. He was a Rotarian and a Moose. He was president of both the Junior Chamber of Commerce and the Chamber of Commerce, and was twice Quarterback of the Fighting Gators Quarterback Club. He was a loving father, grandfather, and husband. And he was a brother. When I say he was a brother, I don't just mean that he was *my* brother. I mean that he was a brother in the Christian sense. And he was his brother's keeper. (*Brief pause*) There's a saying in law school that the A students make professors, the B students make judges, and the C students make money. Well, Sigs was about a C minus student in law school, and what Sigsby made were friends. Not that he wasn't a fine practicing attorney, he was. But everywhere I went in this county I'd meet people who remembered him for some act of generosity, for some kindness. To quote the bard again, "He was a man, all in all, we will not see his likes again." (*He bows his head very briefly, then looks to Katherine*) That's it. (*Takes out his handkerchief and wipes his upper lip*) What'd you think? (*Makes a point*) Objectively?

KATHERINE: (*After a moment's hesitation*) I'm surprised you didn't go ahead and nominate him for sainthood.

BEN: (*Not seeing her irony*) There aren't any saints in the Presbyterian Church. It's the Catholic Church has saints.

KATHERINE: That's a good reason.

BEN: Do you think it's okay?

KATHERINE: (*Gets up to look for her gloves on the hall table, and not finding them there, goes into the bedroom to the dressing table. All the time, she's avoiding the issue*) I'm really a very poor person to ask. (*She picks up the gloves*)

BEN: You're the only one available.

KATHERINE: (*Thoughtfully, putting one glove on*) Yes, I guess I am.

BEN: (*When she says no more*) That's it? Nothing at all?

KATHERINE: (*Working to finish with the gloves, still thoughtfully*) No, no. (*Working her way back out to the hallway*) I'm just trying to . . . I'm trying to understand how a man like you could say all those things without gagging. I suppose it's your legal training, isn't it?

(*They're almost eye to eye now*)

BEN: It isn't very complicated. He was my brother.

KATHERINE: (*Heatedly*) Yes, that's always been the answer, hasn't it?

BEN: Kath, let's not have a fight.

KATHERINE: (*Still very heatedly*) No, let's not. (*He strides away from her to the stairs, grabs his hat, and waits at the top of the stairs, not wanting this to go any further. She starts to remove her gloves*) Come, sit down.

BEN: Sit? We've got to go to the funeral.

KATHERINE: Yes, but you sit down here. I want to talk for a minute.

BEN: Honey, we're going to be late.

KATHERINE: (*The gloves are off, and she moves between the door and the railing*) Just sit down, Ben. Right there. (*Indicates chair*)

BEN: Honey, we're going to be late.

KATHERINE: (*Quietly firm*) Just sit down, Ben. (*He crosses very reluctantly to the chair and sits*) That's right.

BEN: (*As he sits*) Jesus Christ!

KATHERINE: I don't think he's going to be much help. (*She*

turns and walks away toward the head of the stairs) He probably has his hands full deciding what kind of angel to make out of Sigsby. (*Now she's where he stood, and she faces him*) I see what you mean about the hall.

BEN: What?

KATHERINE: It's a better place for a eulogy.

BEN: (*Springs up and moves to her, center*) Katherine, we're going to be late. We have to pick up Fred and Pam and the kids.

KATHERINE: (*Stopping him*) As long as it's just us here in our own upstairs hall, with Sigsby's grave there (*Indicates*) and Preacher Gordon there and Dot and Marlene there . . . I'll give my own little eulogy. (*Seeing that she won't be swayed, Ben resignedly sits once more*) Sigsby Gracie was a no-good son-of-a-bitch. Excuse me, Preacher, but it's the truth. I think he was probably a thief, too, but I can't prove it. All in all that shouldn't make much difference. This town is full of thieves and sons-of-bitches, excuse me again, Preacher, but I think that you're probably one of them too. The problem is, my problem is, that I'm married to a decent man. Not the only one by any means. He isn't special, just decent. I can't be blamed for this. How was I to know. He was a lawyer, and I was raised to believe that all lawyers were crooked. He even had a sort of devilish look about him back then, but it was only skin deep. I don't mean to say that he's virtuous either. He isn't. He's pompous, conceited, selfish, vain, and silly. But decent.

Which is where we get back to Sigsby. I wouldn't mind if Sigsby had just been a no-good and a shyster. But Sigsby liked to humiliate people. He enjoyed making fools out of them. It's not a big sin. Most people probably didn't notice. But when you're the fool, or the wife of the fool, then you do. And I did. (*She is starting to get very worked up about Sigsby. A brief pause*) I don't know whether it was anything more than his tone of voice, Ben. Really. Isn't that silly. To hate a man for his tone of voice. Well, it *was* more. The tone of voice was a sort of string around your neck. And whenever he pulled, you jumped.

There is one particular story. (*This is going to be tough to say*) It's one of those funny Sigsby stories that everybody loves. It was about ten years ago, I guess. I was waiting for you in your office and fell asleep on the couch. You know how the couch sits in the alcove so you can't see it. Well, I woke up and I heard Sigsby on the phone in his office. The door was open and he was talking to somebody about you running for judge. It was when you were thinking about running. I don't know who he was talking to, but whoever it was must have said he was afraid that you'd get elected, because Sigsby said, I remember the words, he said, "Don't worry about Ben. I got his peter in my pocket." And then he laughed and went on talking. (*She has now been barely able to hold back her tears. There is a brief moment when there is nothing to say*)

BEN: Well . . . he always had a sort of dirty mouth.

KATHERINE: Is that all you can say?

BEN: (*Rises, angry*) Did you look in his pocket to see if my peter was there?

KATHERINE: (*Matching his anger and topping it*) Oh, Ben Gracie, I don't care what he said. I care what you say. I care what you think. I want him gone, you understand? I'll be damned if I'll have him around when he's dead.

BEN: What the hell are you talking about?

KATHERINE: I want him dead now that he's dead. I don't want you keeping him alive. Oh, I don't care what you say this afternoon. Go ahead, lie, invent, imagine. But don't lie to yourself. I've waited a long time to get Sigsby out of this house, and I'm not going to put up with him living on in your fantasies about what a fine person he was. (*A pause. Ben walks away from her, past the chair. She moves to the table*) Now that's all I have to say. Let's go to this funeral. (*She takes a Kleenex from her clutch bag, which is still on the table, and uses it to wipe her tears*)

BEN: (*Rather surprised, after this whole scene*) You're going?

KATHERINE: Of course I'm going. Someone has to keep Dot from falling into the grave.

BEN: Katherine, he was my brother. I'm not going out there and say anything bad about him.

KATHERINE: I'm not asking you to say anything bad. (*Putting gloves on*)

BEN: Yea. I'll ah . . . I'll just . . . Maybe I'll just run through what he did . . . (*Moves to her, pleading*) I'm a loyal person, Katie.

KATHERINE: (*Touched*) Yes you are. (*She kisses him gently*)

BEN: (*Awkwardly*) Hell, let's go.

KATHERINE: (*Putting her hat on*) All right.

BEN: (*Starts to follow her, takes out his cards, stops*) I don't need these damn things. I know what he did. (*He tosses them onto the table and follows Katherine to the head of the stairs. He lifts her gloved hand and kisses it lovingly)*

KATHERINE: We better hurry or we're going to be late.
BEN: Yea . . . Well. Let's go.
(He puts on his hat, which he's held all this time. He takes her arm, and they freeze in position as if to descend the stairs)

(Curtain)

The End